To Dad   From

South Asian Archaeology

South Asian Archaeology

*Papers from the
First International Conference
of South Asian Archaeologists
held in the University of Cambridge*

EDITED BY

Norman Hammond

FOREWORD BY

Sir Mortimer Wheeler

NOYES PRESS
Noyes Building
Park Ridge, New Jersey

Contents

Foreword   *Sir Mortimer Wheeler*   ix

Preface   *Norman Hammond*   xi

1   *F.R. Allchin*   Problems and perspectives in South Asian archaeology   1

2   *G.K. Corvinus*   Excavations at an Acheulean site at Chirki-on-Pravara, India   13

3   *Andrew Goudie*   The environmental background to early man in the dry zone of North-Western India: the geomorphic evidence for climatic change   29

4   *Bridget Allchin*   Blade and burin industries of West Pakistan and Western India   39

5   *I.C. Glover*   Late Stone Age traditions in South-East Asia   51

6   *L.S. Leshnik*   Land use and ecological factors in prehistoric North-West India   67

7   *B.K. Thapar*   New traits of the Indus civilization at Kalibangan: an appraisal   85

8   *Rafaello Biscione*   Dynamics of an early South Asian urbanization: the First Period of Shahr-i Sokhta and its connections with Southern Turkmenia   105

9   *Marcello Piperno*   Micro-drilling at Shahr-i Sokhta: the making and use of the lithic drill-heads   119

10   *Klaus Fischer*   Archaeological field surveys in Afghan Seistan, 1960-70   131

11   *George F. Dales*   Archaeological and radiocarbon chronologies for protohistoric South Asia   157

12   *J.-M. Casal*   Excavations at Pirak, West Pakistan   171

13   *J.F. Enault and J.F. Jarrige*   Chalcolithic pottery from four sites in the Bolan area of Baluchistan, West Pakistan   181

14   *Georgio Stacul*   Inhumation and cremation in North-West Pakistan at the end of the second millenium B.C.   197

15   *Maurizio Taddei*   The Mahisamardini image from Tapa Sardar, Ghazni, Afghanistan   203

16 *David W. MacDowall* The Azes hoard from Shaikhan-Dheri: fresh evidence for the context of Jihonika   215

17 *J.C. Harle*   Late Kusana, early Gupta: a reverse approach   231

18 *David Whitehouse*   Chinese stoneware from Siraf: the earliest finds   241

19 *J.E. van Lohuizen-de Leeuw*   Recent discoveries of the historical period in India   257

20 *David McCutchion* Styles of Bengal temple terracottas: a preliminary analysis   265

21 *Janice Stargardt*   The extent and limitations of Indian influences on the protohistoric civilizations of the Malay peninsula   279

Index   303

To the memory of David McCutchion

List of Contributors

Bridget Allchin, *University of Cambridge*
F.R. Allchin, *University of Cambridge*
Rafaello Biscione, *Istituto per il Medio ed Estremo Oriente, Rome*
J.-M. Casal, *Centre National de la Recherche Scientifique, Paris*
G.K. Corvinus, *University of Tübingen*
George F. Dales, *University of Pennsylvania*
J.F. Enault, *French Archaeological Mission in Pakistan*
Klaus Fischer, *University of Bonn*
I.C. Glover, *University of London Institute of Archaeology*
Andrew Goudie, *University of Oxford*
Norman Hammond, *University of Cambridge*
J.C. Harle, *Ashmolean Museum, Oxford*
J.F. Jarrige, *Centre National de la Recherche Scientifique, Paris*
L.S. Leshnik, *University of Heidelberg*
J.E. van Lohuizen-de Leeuw, *University of Amsterdam*
David W. MacDowall, *Admont, Gravel Path, Berkhampsted, Herts.*
David McCutchion, *University of Sussex*
Marcello Piperno, *Istituto per il Medio ed Estremo Oriente, Rome*
Janice Stargardt, *University of Cambridge*
Georgio Stacul, *University of Trieste*
Maurizio Taddei, *Istituto Universitario Orientale, Naples*
B.K. Thapar, *Archaeological Survey of India*
David Whitehouse, *University of Oxford*

Foreword

SIR MORTIMER WHEELER

Within the last quarter-century it has become a possible and pleasant armchair adventure to reach southern Asia from western Europe in a few hours of easy transit. A week-end suffices the Westerner to impose or receive a lecture in Delhi and, in the process, to meet a sizeable number of his professional colleagues from the other side of the world. Only a century ago it took Sir Alexander Cunningham the nucleus of a lifetime to observe a part of the Indian scene from a bullock-cart at a steady two or three miles an hour. Not that comparisons of that simple kind have a meaning of any great consequence; unless it be that speedy travel is often enough a flight from, as much as to, knowledge. Probably the best mode of archaeological progression ever invented, at least in a European landscape, was by horseback, combining as it did a reasonable pace with a point of vantage sufficient to oversee the hedgerows. That is the modest mean, ignoring the alternative extreme that it is today sufficiently easy to span central Europe at 30,000 feet without so much as noticing a cloud-strewn Mont Blanc, on the principle perhaps that it is a better thing to arrive hopefully than to travel.

In that sense the journeying from many and various parts of the world to Churchill College, Cambridge, was a gentle fatigue well worth while for the numerous students of the East who sped there in July 1971. They came from America, Belgium, France, Germany, Holland, India, Italy, the United Kingdom, and no doubt elsewhere; and both formally and less formally discussed a wide range of topics from third-millennium chronology to Chinese stoneware, and most other things besides. Above all, they freely met one another, both on and off the stage. Looking upon the little crowd, one could not help reflecting that such a gathering would scarcely have been thinkable as recently as a generation ago. Then the archaeology of the East was still primarily a minor preserve of European expatriates, with relatively little interchange. Today, under new political and social conditions, the nations of the East in varying but on the whole appreciable degree and in a modernizing idiom have assumed the academic study of themselves both in the present tense and in the long perspective of archaeology and history. If in the recent conference there was a weakness, it lay in the less than adequate representation of this scholarship actually from the Orient, no doubt due in part to inadequate or inadequately organized means of travel. The remote conference-table at Cambridge would most warmly have welcomed and have profited from a more representative participation under this head.

The arduous preparation and conduct of the conference were largely the devoted achievement of Raymond Allchin, Fellow of Churchill College, and his wife Bridget, Fellow of University College, Cambridge. To both of them all gratitude is due.

Editor's Preface

The papers in this volume have been selected from those presented at the first International Conference of South Asian Archaeologists, held in July 1971 in Cambridge. The conference, and a smaller informal one held in 1970, have been the first public activities of the Association of South Asian Archaeologists in Western Europe; this was founded in 1970 to provide a forum for scholars based in Europe who specialize in the prehistoric and historic archaeology of the Indian sub-continent and its Iranian and Burmese borderlands.

In 1970 it was proposed that a conference be held biennially, and that a journal, entitled *South Asian Archaeology*, be published annually or biennially; in many ways this present volume can be regarded as the first number of that journal, recording as it does the excavation and research which have been undertaken by members of the Association over the past few years. The range both in time and space of the work included here is wide, embracing South Asia from the desert basin of Seistan on the borders of Iran and Afghanistan to the tropical forests of Malaysia and Indonesia, and reaching in time and subject from the analysis of iconography on eighteenth- and nineteenth-century Bengali terracottas to the excavation of a working-floor of the Lower Palaeolithic Acheulean industry of between 50,000 and 500,000 B.C. Many aspects of archaeology in the area are examined, from studies of the ancient climate and economy through investigations of technological innovation to a consideration of the effects of the recalibration of radiocarbon dating on the relationships of prehistoric cultures, and the matrix of time in which we pursue our studies is brought into focus by contrasting contributions, one of which examines the history of interest in Seistan over several centuries while another uses recent press-cuttings to give an up-to-date account of fieldwork in India.

For the rest, the papers here presented speak for themselves: in the first Raymond Allchin outlines the general history of archaeology in South Asia and identifies some of the lacunae in our knowledge which need most urgently to be filled, while the subsequent contributions show how some of these tasks are being attempted.

The Cambridge Conference was graced by the presence of Sir Mortimer Wheeler, who has contributed a Foreword to this volume, and many of those there acknowledge a debt to him, either for his pioneering work in South Asia or for his personal interest, or both. The present wide interest in the archaeology of the area and the standard of scholarship which is being applied there owe much to him, and this volume is in many ways a tribute to him, as an archaeologist and as an inspiration to others.

During the setting of this book, the death occurred in Calcutta of one of its contributors, David McCutchion, at the tragically early age of 41. His paper here is a preliminary statement in advance of a major work on Bengali temple terracottas which he planned to write while at Cambridge later this year. His company at the 1971 Cambridge Conference will be remembered as surely as it will be missed at Amsterdam in 1973, and as a small tribute this volume of papers is dedicated to his memory.

Norman Hammond   October 1972

1

Problems and Perspectives in South Asian Archaeology

F.R. ALLCHIN

We employ the term South Asia in a broadly geographical sense, fairly clearly defined by its relationship to South-West and South-East Asia on either side. In its narrower sense we might say that South Asia consists of the Indian peninsula, or of the Indo-Pakistan sub-continent, but our usage is bound to be influenced by cultural and more particularly archaeological considerations, and as such we believe that a somewhat wider definition is to be sought. We may propose that South Asia includes not only the modern territories of India, Pakistan, Ceylon and Nepal, but also those borderlands to east and west which have from time to time been taken into the Indian culture area or the contact zone beyond. In this sense we may include Afghanistan to the west, Burma to the east, and part of Central Asia to the north. Our definition is thus drawn fairly loosely and widely, but with its central focus firmly upon the Indian sub-continent.

Archaeology in South Asia — an historical sketch

European interest in South Asia in a very real sense begins with the arrival of Vasco da Gama at Calicut in 1489. During the next three centuries travellers, visitors and missionaries began to learn about the ancient civilization of India, began to discover her ancient literature and to record some of her ancient monuments. This process of discovery was peculiarly European, and coincided with an almost complete ignorance and indifference on the part of the peoples of South Asia themselves. This indifference arose no doubt as a concomitant of the peculiar absence of interest in history in any European sense of the word, and it provides one clue to the preponderance of the European contribution to the subject in its early stages. The discoveries were by no means only British, but were made by travellers of several different nationalities. Thus among the early records of monuments we find Danish, French, Dutch and Portuguese, no less than British contributions.

The often stray discoveries or observations of this preliminary stage culminated in the closing years of the eighteenth century in the person of Sir William Jones who during his brief residence in Calcutta founded the Asiatic Society of Bengal, having as its aim the investigation and discovery of man and nature in Asia. Jones brought with him a wonderful perspective and his concern embraced the civilizations of all parts of Asia, not only of India, but of China, Tartary, Arabia and Persia. Similarly his interest included not only architecture and the arts, but science and learning, language and letters, religion and philosophy. The importance of the Jones synthesis was that it provided an ordered scheme or programme within which other contributions and researches which now began to appear might be assessed.

The nineteenth century marks a new stage in the history of South Asian archaeology. It is not unnaturally predominated by the British. Among many names we may mention only a very few. First there was James Prinsep who laid the foundations of Indian epigraphy and numismatics, by his completion of the decipherment of the oldest scripts then known, the inscriptions of Asoka (third century B.C.), and by his collecting and publishing of some of the large numbers of ancient coins which had begun to find their way back to the offices of the Asiatic Society in Calcutta. Prinsep recognized that there were two classes of archaeologists, those whose work was in the 'field' and those whose work was primarily in the 'closet'. Among the field archaeologists the first great name is that of Major General Alexander Cunningham who retired from the army after 28 years service, in 1861, to become the first Director of the Archaeological Survey of India. His years of military service had already demonstrated his great interest in archaeology and produced several important publications, but the succeeding two and a half decades of his second career produced even greater and more important results. In a very real sense it can be said that the British Indian Government's acceptance of responsibility both for research and for the preservation of monuments were the direct result of the energy and enthusiasm of Cunningham. A third great name is that of James Fergusson, a near contemporary of Cunningham, who passed, not without difficulty, from his family's jute factory. to a life-long study of architecture, first of India and latterly of the whole world. Fergusson must still be regarded as the father of the study of Indian architecture, and his claim to have introduced to India the principles of archaeological science which had been universally adopted in Europe was no idle boast. From the nineteenth century we can mention only one other name, that of Bruce Foote the geologist, who alongside his geological duties laid the foundations for Indian prehistoric archaeology. Foote's predominant interest was in the Stone Age and in 1950 it was still true that almost every important Stone Age site in the Indian sub-continent owed its initial discovery to him.

The history of archaeological research in Ceylon followed much the same pattern as on the mainland. There are many early references in European travellers' accounts, but more serious work had to await the nineteenth century. The Ceylon Branch of the Royal Asiatic Society formed an early focus (from 1845), and in 1874 an Archaeological Commissioner was appointed. Since then, with various vicissitudes, the Ceylon Archaeological Department has continued to operate. There has been a similar interest in the collection and publication of inscriptions, and in the study of monumental remains. Prehistory was until recent years largely neglected.

We can see that the pattern which emerged during this century was distinctive, and has continued to influence subsequent work. In South Asia archaeology includes both prehistory and history. Not unnaturally the latter was the first to develop: it has always been regarded as embracing among its branches the history of architecture and of art, epigraphy and palaeography, and numismatics. Although there was some excavation of historical sites and monuments during this century these were comparatively neglected. Prehistory developed in a rather piecemeal way: the first group of monuments to attract attention were the Megalithic graves of the peninsula, and from 1823 onwards numerous graves were excavated and their contents published. Hoards of copper tools from north India began to be found quite early in the nineteenth century, but no attempt was made to relate them to their cultural setting, and they remained enigmatic until recently. The beginnings were made for a proper study of the Stone Age, but after Foote's retirement, little further progress was made. At this time there was very little idea of integrating these various groups of material, or of tracing any coherent evolution of the progress of prehistoric man in any part of South Asia.

The opening of the twentieth century marks the beginning of a new and most important stage in the story. Shortly after Lord Curzon's appointment as Viceroy his interest and enthusiasm were aroused by the wonderful monuments of India, and in two addresses to the Asiatic Society of Bengal he developed his idea of the weighty responsibility the Government shouldered and of how it should be achieved. He saw that in India every aspect of archaeology must at that time be the responsibility of Government, and in this light he reorganized the Archaeological Survey to fit it for the task. The immediate result was the appointment of Sir John Marshall as Director General, and under his direction the Archaeological Survey assumed much of the form that it retains to this day. Marshall in his early years concentrated his main efforts upon the excavation of early historic cities and Buddhist centres in north India. He promoted a new series of Annual Reports of better quality than any so far, and greatly broadened the work of conservation of monuments. An important feature of his tenure of office was the recruitment of a number of Indian officers to the Survey, and the encouragement of archaeological departments in some of the larger princely states. Both these developments paved the way for the subsequent transfer of power to the independent Archaeological Departments of India and Pakistan in 1947. Probably Sir John Marshall will be particularly remembered for his excavations at Mohenjo-daro and at Taxila, which to this day remain monuments to the work of the Archaeological Survey under his direction, and for his publications of the Stupas at Sanchi.

Marshall retired from service in 1928, although he remained in India continuing operations at Taxila and working on the publication of the results of his work on the Indus civilization until 1934. The thirties were a time of uncertainty in India, and the Archaeological Survey shared in the general condition. The outbreak of war in 1939 found the Survey largely without impetus or direction, and Sir Leonard Woolley's critical report of that year made it clear that drastic changes were called for.

Change did indeed come in the person of Sir Mortimer Wheeler, from 1944-8 the last Director General of the undivided Indian Archaeological Survey. During this short term of office Wheeler aimed to revitalize the structure. He set about the selection and training of a new cadre of young officers, the revolutionizing of the Survey's methods of excavation, the production of a new periodical publication of quite new standards, the overhaul of the methods of conservation, and above all the intelligent *planning* of a campaign of research. He also sensed that with the changing times the monopoly so long held by Government must soon give way to wider interest with the development of archaeology in the universities. These radical changes prepared the ground for the far greater changes which resulted from the partition of India and Pakistan and the subsequent period of independence. Independence released a flood of new energy and has seen the continuing development of the

Archaeological Departments in both countries, the growth of university archaeology, particularly in India, and a quite unprecedented amount of new research. Not least we may remark upon the growing number of foreign expeditions who have worked in South Asia, and the useful contribution which such teams can make, both in actual research and in providing a means for local archaeologists to gain first hand experience of other methods.

Our account has so far not specifically mentioned either Afghanistan or Nepal. In the case of the former very little archaeological work was done during the nineteenth century, leaving aside the travels of such adventurers as James Masson in the 1830s. Serious work only began in 1922 with the concession granted to the French Delegation. For some years the French had a virtual monopoly, and it is only recently that other teams have been permitted to work. These have included Italian and West German institutes, and several British and American expeditions have also worked there. More recently the Afghan Department of Archaeology has begun to play an independent role. Of archaeology in Nepal during the nineteenth century little need be said, but here too we welcome the creation in recent years of an already active Department of Archaeology.

Some current problems in South Asian archaeology

In what follows I intend to touch on some of the main subjects in the prehistory and protohistory of South Asia upon which interest is currently focussed, and in particular to attempt to point to their implications in terms of future research. The selection of topics is necessarily arbitrary and makes no pretence at being exhaustive; many details, some of great importance, and many current pieces of research are necessarily not mentioned.

1. Perhaps no part of the subject has been more unevenly studied than the *Palaeolithic or Early Stone Age.* Although interest in this arose almost as early as in Europe, yet the further progress has been strangely erratic. Since the pioneering attempt of De Terra and Paterson (1939) to harness the glacial sequence of the Siwaliks and Kashmir to the chronology of the stone industries of those parts (and even of peninsular India), little fundamental advance has been made, except perhaps for the recognition of the group of industries of the Middle Stone Age, and the establishment of their relationship to the periods of aggradation and erosion on the rivers of peninsular India (B. Allchin, 1959; Sankalia, 1964). Until such time as the Himalayan glacial sequence can be firmly related to that of Europe, and this is as

yet far from accomplished, this aspect remains of only limited value. Clearly a new approach is needed, to find techniques which are as well suited for the conditions of the sub-continent, as those which have been used with such success in Quaternary studies in Europe. It is clear that continuing elaborations of typology will get us nowhere. Recently several attempts at interdisciplinary research have been initiated in Western India. Dr Bridget Allchin in concert with Dr Hegde of Baroda University and latterly with Mr Andrew Goudie of Oxford, has been making an integrated study of the plain of Gujarat and its rivers from the standpoint of geology, geomorphology and prehistory. The results so far have been promising, and provide a clear indication of the place of the shadowy Upper Palaeolithic industries in the climatic and geomorphological sequence. Their papers serve to indicate something of the lines they are following (Allchin and Goudie, 1971; Allchin, Hegde & Goudie, 1971; B. Allchin, this volume; A. Goudie, this volume). At the same time Dr D.P. Agrawal of the Tata Institute of Fundamental Research, Bombay, has been coordinating a number of workers studying the sea-levels and shorelines of the west coast, and this too seems likely to produce useful new understanding. Another exciting development is to be expected with the publication of Professor G.R. Sharma's researches in the central Ganges valley (Indian Archaeology, 1966-7; 1968-9). Another necessary advance will come with the discovery of actual occupation sites, so that information may be gleaned about other aspects of life than those provided by the stone tools alone. The paper by Dr Gudrun Corvinus (this volume) records her discovery of an early Palaeolithic working floor in peninsular India.

2. *The Late Stone Age or Mesolithic.* In recent years attention has been focussed on two aspects of the Late Stone Age: its broad chronology, including therefore the possibility of its continuing existence alongside more advanced cultures in some areas, and on evidence of economy, including such interesting topics as the cultivation of plants and domestication of animals. On the former there is a slowly growing series of radiocarbon dates extending back in one instance, (that of Sarai Nahr Rai) to the eleventh millennium B.C. and continuing through the sixth millennium into comparatively recent times (a note of some relevant dates is at the end of this paper). On the latter there have been several excavations of settlements, including Langhnaj in Gujarat (Sankalia *et al* 1965) Adamgarh in Madhya Pradesh (Joshi, 1968), and Bagor (Indian Archaeology 1967-8), in Southern Rajasthan. To date the only site for which a full study of the animal remains is available in Langhnaj, but there is reason to hope that some of the other sites will produce relatively more and clearer evidence. The excavation of Late Stone

Age settlements is also of interest for the opportunity it provides to study culture contact with neighbouring communities. The presence of objects of copper, and perhaps even in the final stages of iron at some of the sites is clearly of great significance and suggests the sort of contact which may be expected during the latter stages of the Late Stone Age.

3. *The origins of the Indus civilization* (and of Indian civilization). The third thing I wish to point towards relates to the origin of the Indus civilization. We have come a long way since, less than twenty-five years ago, Piggott wrote that the Harappa culture had 'no known beginning, no tentative early phases'. I suppose the most important development of the past decade or so has been the discovery and excavation at Amri (Casal, 1964) Kot Diji (Khan, 1965) and Kalibangan (Thapar, this volume) of a whole new period for which the names pre-Harappan and early Harappan have hitherto been used. As evidence of the comparability of the material culture of this phase at widely separated sites begins to emerge it becomes more and more clear that it represents an important constituent of the subsequent civilization, even though it may not be the only constituent. But this new period has in recent years itself been found to be subsequent at some sites to an even earlier phase of which fragmentary reports only are hitherto available. I refer to the reports of a 'neolithic' level below a pre-Harappan at Sarai Khola near Taxila (Pakistan Archaeology, 1968) and of a similar level at Hathala, north of Dera Ismail Khan, in the Gomal valley, a site currently being explored by a Peshawar University team (Khan, personal communication). If these reports mean what at first sight they appear to, then they raise another question of considerable interest, that of the relationship of these Neolithic cultures to those which we know existed in pre-Harappan times in peninsular India. In this volume Dr Dales and Dr Biscione touch upon the cultural developments and chronology in the eastern parts of the Iranian plateau, and Dr Thapar reports briefly on the excavations carried out by the ASI at Kalibangan.

4. *The understanding of the Indus civilization.* My fourth point can soon be made. The earlier round of excavations of Harappa and Mohenjo-daro left many unanswered problems. Clearly there is a prime need for further excavations at the prime Harappan sites so that some of these may be resolved. The extensive excavations at Kalibangan point the way to a better understanding of such matters as planning and defence, and when they are published will probably also supply much important material on other topics such as religion. It seems to be clear that further work on the materials from the early excavations at Mohenjo-daro and Harappa will be of only very

limited value, and that what is mainly needed is fresh excavation. Another aspect of this matter calls for our attention, that of interpretation. Recently Fairservis (1967) has written a short monograph on the 'origin, character and decline' of the Indus civilization. In this paper he attempted to discuss the 'style' of the culture in terms approaching those used by the American sociologist Robert Redfield; and as if to reiterate the importance of such an attempt S.C. Malik (1968) has written a longer book centred round the description of the 'formative period' of Indian civilization, as he calls the Indus civilization. This book has, to judge by review, already acted as a considerable irritant, but there is none the less a valid point when its author complains that little attempt has been made to understand the Indus civilization at the level of sociological interpretation, and I am sure that a reading of Redfield's works would be a useful preliminary to those about to make the attempt. In making this suggestion I do not wish to imply that we should allow the theoretical aspects of our subject to overshadow the necessary factual basis. Archaeology is nothing if it neglects its 'dirt facts' and often a small new discovery can overthrow volumes of theory. For instance some writers have made much of the absence of the plough in the Indus civilization, but the recent discovery of a ploughed field surface in a pre-Harappan context at Kalibangan can now leave us in no doubt that the plough was already known at that time and therefore may be confidently postulated in the civilization itself. L.S. Leshnik in his paper (Leshnik, this volume) discussing some aspects of the agriculture of the Indus civilization draws attention to the need for further consideration of the significance of irrigation in this context.

5. *The Aryans and related questions.* The problem of the Aryans is still very much with us. Speaking in general terms three areas have witnessed important contributions in recent years. The first of these is in the northwest frontier of Pakistan where the Italian mission and subsequently Peshawar University have discovered a series of graveyards and several important excavations have been done. Dr Stacul has already written (Stacul, 1966; 1970) on the dating and classification of these graves of what has been called the 'Gandhara grave complex', and in his paper in this volume he discusses possible external affinities. A second major area of interest is far away in Maharashtra, where Professor Sankalia is now supplementing the limited excavations of several sites of the 'Jorwe culture' by an extensive excavation at Inamgaon (Indian Archaeology 1968-9; Sankalia 1971). The outcome of this work is likely to be of considerable importance in terms of the light it will throw upon the first Indo-European speaking settlements in this region. The third

region is the Punjab and northern parts of Uttar Pradesh, where a number of small pieces of research serve to highlight its great interest and importance in this connection. First there is the evidence of a group of sites such as Amkheri and Bargaon where pottery with strong Harappan or late Harappan affinities has been found often in a disturbed condition, the disturbance resulting from floods (Indian Archaeology 1963-4). The evidence of massive flooding during the latter centuries of the second millennium perhaps ties up with the old theory of the capture by the Jamuna of the former Sarasvati river. Next there is the proof that has recently emerged of the association of a related red pottery, the so called 'Ochre coloured' pottery with copper objects from one of the hoards of the Gangetic copper hoard series at Lal Qila, Bulandshahr Dt. and Safai Lichchhwai in Etawa Dt. (Indian Archaeology, 1968-9; Thapar, personal communication). Altogether this area is one in which we may hope for great things as and when research advances, but on which we do not include any contributions in our present volume.

6. *The rise of cities in the north of India.* My penultimate area of interest is in the rise of cities in the north of India during the first millennium B.C. It is strange that this important topic should have so far received so little archaeological attention, and that it should still be so much discussed in terms of the perplexing and incomplete historical evidence of the late Vedic period. One need only point to the way in which so many of the capital cities of the sixteen Mahajanapadas are surrounded by great banked fortifications and ditches to appreciate how even these features need to be studied to provide accurate dating evidence, and to enhance our understanding of the creation of these cities. Beyond this the potentials for excavation and study of the settlements of these vital centuries are too obvious to need stressing. How little can archaeology, for example, tell us of the food habits, or of the emergence of the caste system, in North India.

7. *The South Indian Iron Age Grave complex.* My last point need not detain us long. It is getting on for two centuries since the first notice was made of the Megalithic graves of South India. Since then hundreds of graves have been excavated and reports, varying from the fantastic to the meticulous excellence of those of Sir Mortimer Wheeler on the Brahmagiri graves, have appeared. But it comes as a shock to realize that for not one grave, let alone cemetery, do we have any absolute dates. It appears to us to be an urgent problem for research to devise means of obtaining absolute dates so that we may gain a clearer view of the chronology of these graves and of their relationship with the Iron Age of South India.

In conclusion I would remark that in any lively and developing science there are bound to be problems which arise from time to time and assume new importance. Among these I would like to mention briefly two types, those of terminology and of chronology. I hope that the Conference on South Asian Archaeology will serve among other things as a forum for the discussion and resolution of some of the problems of terminology. The term 'late Harappan' for example is still widely used for cultures in parts of India which were never directly within the Harappan culture region, and this usage, it appears to us, is bound to lead to much unnecessary confusion. Another instance is the divergence which has been developing between those of us who speak of 'pre-Harappan' for what lies under the Harappan period at Amri or Kalibangan, and those who prefer 'early Harappan'. I think that with the advance of knowledge both these usages are wearing a little thin and the time has come to consider a new approach. Perhaps the term 'early Indus' suggested by Dr Dales in his paper (this volume) may supply the need. On questions of chronology too there are still wide divergences. In my view the advent of radiocarbon dating has revolutionized our South Asian chronology, adding a long series of reasonable determinations for whole periods which must otherwise have remained undatable. I would like to pay particular tribute to the excellent service provided by the Tata Institute of Fundamental Research. To have so long a series of dates from a single laboratory is bound to lend weight to their results. But there are still some who at best reluctantly accept radiocarbon dates. We must not forget the inherent pitfalls in overconfident acceptance of this, or for that matter any other system of dating. The lesson suggested by the study of the Sequoia tree-rings has still to be assimilated and applied to Indian chronology. In this connection Dr Dales has given us a profoundly important indication of the sort of revaluation which we shall have to expect.

Relevant radiocarbon dates are: *Sarai Nahr Rai.* TF-1104, 10,050 ± 110 (10,345 ± 110); *Bagor.* TF-786, 6,245 ± 200 (6,430 ± 200), TF-1007, 5,620 ± 125 (5,785 ± 130), TF-1009, 4,585 ± 105 (4,715 ± 105), TF-1005 and 1006, 3,945,± 90 (4,060 ± 90), etc.: *Adamgarh.* TF-120, 7,240 ± 125 (7,450 ± 130). Carbon dates are given on the 5568 half-life with reading on the 5730 half-life following in brackets.

REFERENCES

Allchin, B. (1959) The Indian Middle Stone Age. *Bulletin of the Institute of Archaeology*, No. 2, 1-35.

Allchin, B. and Goudie, A. (1971) Dunes, aridity and early man in Gujarat, western India. *Man*, N.S. No. 2, 248-65.

Allchin, B., Goudie, A. and Hegde, K.T.M: (1971) The background to early man in Gujarat: preliminary report of the Cambridge-Baroda expedition, 1970-71 season. *Journal of the M.S. University, Baroda,* (in press).

Casal, J.-M. (1964) *Fouilles d'Amri.* 2 vols.

De Terra, H. and Paterson, T.T. (1939) *Studies on the Ice Age in India and Associated Human Cultures*, Washington.

Fairservis, W.A. (1967) The origin, character and decline of an early civilization. *American Museum Novitates, 2302*, 1-48.

Indian Archaeology — 1961-62 — A review.

Indian Archaeology — 1962-63 — A review.

Indian Archaeology — 1963-64 — A review.

Indian Archaeology — 1964-65 — A review.

Indian Archaeology — 1965-66 — A review.

Indian Archaeology — 1966-67 — A review (cyclostyled ed.).

Indian Archaeology — 1967-68 — A review.

Indian Archaeology — 1968-69 — A review (cyclostyled ed.).

Joshi, R.V. (1968) Late Mesolithic culture in Central India. *La préhistoire: problèmes et tendances.* 245-254.

Khan, F.A. (1965) Excavations at Kot Diji. *Pakistan Archaeology*, No. 2, 11-85.

Malik, S.C. 1968. *Indian Civilization, the Formative Period*, 1-204. Simla.

Pakistan Archaeology (1968) No. 5, 28-40.

Sankalia, H.D. (1964) Middle Stone Age cultures of India and Pakistan. *Science*, No. 146.

Sankalia, H.D. (1971) Central India 3000 years ago. *Illustrated London News*, Vol. 259, No. 6877, 41-3.

Sankalia, H.D. and others, (1965) *Excavations at Langhnaj, 1944-63.* Part 1, Archaeology; Part 2, The Fauna; Part 3, The human remains, Poona.

Stacul, G. (1966) Preliminary report on the pre-Buddhist necropolises in Swat (W. Pakistan). *East and West*, N.S. 16, 37-79.

Stacul, G. (1970) The gray pottery in the Swat valley and the Indo-Iranian connections. *East and West*, N.S. 20, 87-102.

2

Excavations at an Acheulean site at Chirki-on-Pravara in India

G.K. CORVINUS

My research in India concerns a period which is still little known, the Early Stone Age. In wealth of Palaeolithic sites India can compete with Europe and Africa. Many collections of Palaeolithic material exist from various sites, but most of them are surface finds not from stratigraphic contexts. They have given us a broad outline of the Palaeolithic industries, but because of their selective nature the data is likely to be very unsatisfactory. Excavations that are needed to give a clearer picture of the Palaeolithic have been undertaken only recently.

Acheulean sites in India

One of the best known sites since its discovery by the British geologist Bruce Foote is probably the Acheulean site near Madras, where Bannerjee has excavated for many years. Unfortunately no publications are out yet. He has found Acheulean tools in lateritic clays and gravels on several raised marine platforms and his aim is to date the industries by their association with the raised platforms.

There are other Acheulean sites in South India, mostly in the quartzitic areas in the Krishna and Tungabhadra valleys. Pappu worked in the upper Krishna valley and excavated in an artefact-bearing boulder conglomerate at a *nullah* of the Krishna river, where he found handaxes and cleavers, probably in a reworked condition.

Two very promising areas are in the rift valleys of the Narmada and Tapti valleys in Central India. The fluviatile deposits of the Narmada river have yielded much cultural and faunal material, where de Terra and Paterson worked out a cultural succession in 1939. Since then various expeditions by Indian archaeologists have been undertaken and Supekar has carried out an excavation into the basal boulder conglomerate at Mahadeo Piparia. At the same place Khatri found in 1961 what he termed the earliest Stone Age industries in India. He called it 'Mahadevian' or the Oldovan of India. Supekar, however, could show that no definite horizon of such an early industry exists, but that Middle Stone Age tools were found together with Early Stone Age tools (crude handaxes and large, rough flakes) in a reworked condition in the boulder conglomerate.

A fine Acheulean site exists at Gangapur on the upper Godavari near Nasik, where Joshi dug a few trenches in 1965. He found an advanced cleaver industry and dated it to Middle Pleistocene on the basis of *bos namadicus* bones. This site needs further excavation, as I am sure this is a primary site and the tools are in their original context, which is not the case for most of the other Acheulean sites in India.

A very rich Acheulean site is at Lalitpur in Jhansi district in M.P., which was excavated in 1963. It proved to be a factory site but was disturbed by erosion.

The site at Chirki

During a geomorphological survey along the river Pravara, a tributary of the Godavari, I found another Acheulean site at the confluence of a small nullah, the Chirki, with the Pravara (figs 2.1, 2.2). Here I found handaxes, cleavers, large flakes, cores etc. in a number of small erosion gullies in a badland area cut into the alluvial deposits of the Pravara (fig. 2.3). The tools were washed out from this alluvium. The surface of the badlands was covered with many small flake artefacts of a Middle Stone Age industry. While the Acheulean bifaces were mostly made from the local basalt, the Deccan-Trap, and were found in the gullies, the small flake industry was mainly made of siliceous material, i.e. of chalcedony, jasper, and agates and was found everywhere: in the gullies, on the slopes and on the highest surface.

This small industry was termed by Sankalia the 'Nevasian' after the village Nevasa, where he found it first. It is not only found at Chirki, but at many places along the river-valley, mostly in the river-bed itself and in the gravels of the Pravara and the Godavari. This industry is of a rather nondescript nature. At Chirki there are only non-prepared flakes with no retouch, flaked from unprepared cores. Many such irregular, small cores are found on the surface, which do not show any Levallois preparation nor any other distinct preparation. Flakes were removed by a blow on any suitable flat part of the core and mostly a flat scar served as the next platform. The striking-platforms on the flakes are plain and are at a wide angle of

Figure 2.1 India, showing the location of Chirki.

about 100°-120° to the ventral face and show a clear bulb of percussion. The dorsal faces are rough and do not always have scars of former flakes, and the ridges are irregular. No retouch is to be seen on the flakes except an abundant pseudoretouch, originating from natural pressure and abrasion in the gravels. The shape of the flakes is irregular and in only a few cases there are signs of a predetermined shape. This industry looks very rough and might well be of older age than the Middle Stone Age. The question was now whether this small flake industry was a separate industry or whether it belonged to that with Acheulean Bifaces, as a light duty component. The aim of the excavation was to see whether I could find an Acheulean horizon in the deposits and if so, whether it was primary or of a secondary, reworked nature. The work was financed by a grant-in-aid from the

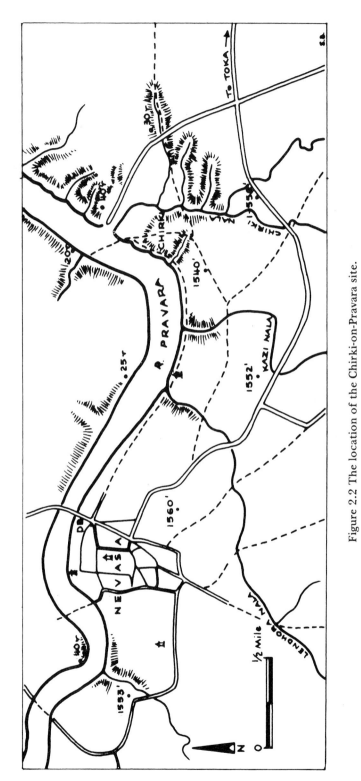

Figure 2.2 The location of the Chirki-on-Pravara site.

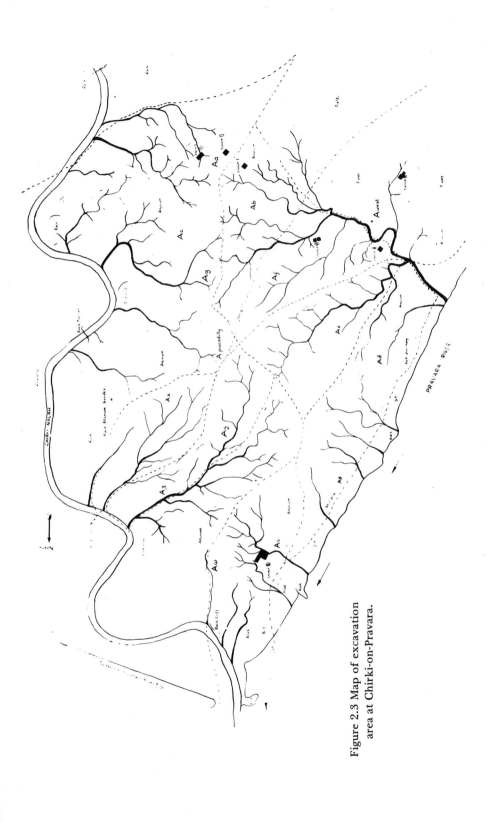

Figure 2.3 Map of excavation
area at Chirki-on-Pravara.

Wenner-Gren Foundation.

The first six trenches did not reveal any artefact-bearing horizon. The trenches were cut into the gravel alluvium which in places was 8 m thick, overlying the basalt bedrock; only one trench reached bedrock. Small flakes of silica were found dispersed throughout the gravel but they were not in any horizon. No bifaces were found.

It was in trench VII at the end of the first season that a very rich Early Stone Age horizon was uncovered underneath the gravel alluvium. The horizon consisted of a colluvial boulder spread of about 20-40 cm thickness, with hundreds of unfinished and finished Acheulean bifaces on top of the rubble horizon and also amongst the boulders. It overlay the basalt bedrock and was covered by the gravel. So the stratigraphy was from the base as follows: bedrock of Deccan Trap basalt; artefacts; the gravel of about 2 m thickness; a mixed reworked, very recent gravelly slopewash with black soil components. 74 m² were exposed in the first season (fig. 2.4).

The erosion gullies, in which I had found the surface tools, had cut the rubble horizon here, in the area of trench VII and had exposed the artefacts and washed them out into the gully bed. The whole badland area where surface tools were found is about one square mile in area, and it was thought possible that at many places underneath the gravel an Acheulean horizon might be present.

The next two seasons, therefore, were used to extend trench VII and to determine the extent of the artefact concentration of trench VII. Six new trenches were opened around VII. Several other trenches were opened in two other areas where there was surface concentration of artefacts; also a grid of sixteen trial trenches was dug to ascertain the extent of the rubble horizon.

The environment

The excavations showed that a patchy rubble horizon exists almost everywhere underneath the alluvial gravel in the whole area of badlands at Chirki. The rubble-boulder horizon was always present where the underlying bedrock formed small, irregular depressions and it was not present where the rock rose somewhat higher.

Wherever I dug down through the sealing gravel to the boulder horizon or to the bedrock, I found the Acheulean artefacts, either on the boulders, if there was a boulder-spread, or on the bedrock where there was not. That means that the extension of man's occupation extended throughout the explored area, but with a definite concentration in the area of trench VII.

The bedrock underneath the Acheulean horizon is firm and

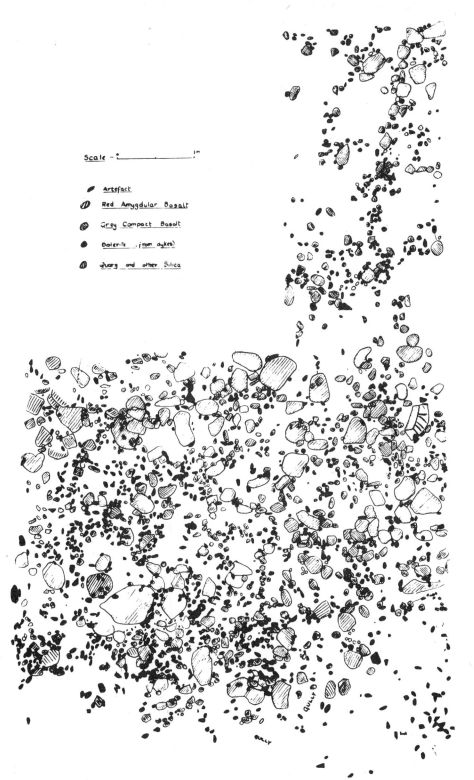

Scale - :_____ 1m

⬮ Artefact

⬭ Red Amygdular Basalt

◍ Grey Compact Basalt

● Dolerite (from dykes)

◑ Quartz and other Silica

Figure 2.4 Map of excavated occupation floor of trench No. VII at Chirki-on-
   Pravara.

unweathered and shows small rills of water action, as fast flowing water in a rapid river forms them on the bare, rocky river bed. The presence of such rill-markings on the bedrock shows that before the Acheulean occupation there must have existed a broad, bare platform of bedrock near a rapid, where the river flowed to a lower level without depositing any material. This can be observed nowadays at several places along the modern river bed, especially downstream of Chirki where there are several nick-points and rapids.

The rock platform became exposed probably as a course of the river changing its course slightly and was then covered irregularly in patches by the rubble of the colluvial boulder deposit. This must have been the time when the first hominids first occupied the area, when the platform was dry and its slight depressions filled with colluvial debris. The blocks and boulders of this debris, of all sizes and all grades of angularity, were used by the Acheulean occupiers to make tools. They used all the materials which were present: three types of local basalt and also the quartz- and chalcedony nodules, which came from secondary-filled veins in the basalt. The best material was a fine-grained dyke-basalt, of which the best preserved tools were made.

The geological sequence, then, must have been as follows: The rock platform underneath the deposits of Chirki was made by the river during a phase of downcutting. The downcutting was accompanied by a slight westward change of the river (fig. 2.5). To the west of Chirki, at the opposite bank of the Pravara, is the thickest alluvium and underneath this thick alluvium of silts and gravels is the ancient, buried valley of the erosional phase. It is about 7 m deeper than the present river bed. This erosional phase must be due to tectonic events during the Pleistocene (probably before the middle Pleistocene) which had lifted up the source area of the Pravara and Godavari in the Western Ghat area. When this uplift came to a stop the river began to fill its cut basin with a succession of silty, sandy and gravelly deposits, thereby sealing also the Acheulean horizon. At the end of this aggradational phase we find microliths on the top and in the black soil. Thus we have the Acheulean tools at the beginning or just before the infilling of the alluvial deposits and the microliths at the end of it. We have no means for any exact dating of the Acheulean horizon other than the explained geological order of events. Unfortunately there are no other deposits below the Acheulean horizon with datable material. The fauna of the alluvial deposits of the aggrading phase in the neighbouring areas is dated by *bos namadicus* and *elephas namadicus* to the Middle Pleistocene. However it seems now that these animals may well have survived into the Upper Pleistocene. The Nevasian flake industry is found

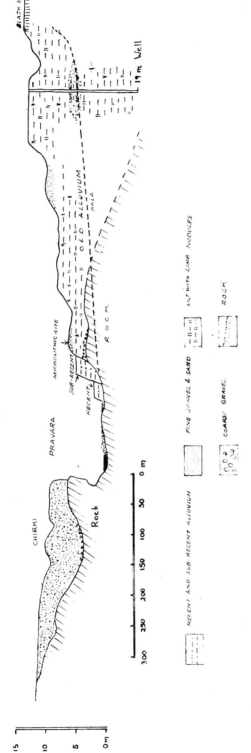

Figure 2.5 Cross section of the Pravara. Valley-Alluvium at Chirki.

plentifully in the river bed, washed out from the alluvial gravels. We have certainly to discard the terms '1st gravel', '2nd gravel', '3rd gravel' etc. as evidence of 3 wet phases: there is no good evidence supporting this theory. There are no unconformities in the succession of deposits, no buried soils, no weathering horizons and there is no such stratigraphy as finding Early Stone Age tools in a first gravel, Middle Stone Age tools in a second gravel and Late Stone Age tools in a third gravel. The gravels are simply the expression of the shifting, meandering and rising river; they are the channel deposits of the river, whereas the silts are floodbank deposits on the inner sides of the meanders. We find Nevasian flakes in all the lenses of channel deposits and almost never in the fine silts. That means they were carried and deposited by the river. If Early Stone Age tools are found at all, they are confined to the lowest deposit in the alluvium, which is often coarse and bouldery. The Chirki Boulder bed is, however, not alluvial, but as I said before, colluvial.

I had said that the Acheulean artefacts in our area belong to the lowest part of the infill and that the Nevasian flakes are found in the gravels of the alluvial deposits, but this is not entirely correct: in the excavations I found a number of these small flakes made from silica *on* and *in* the boulder horizon *with* the Acheulean bifaces. How is it that an evidently younger industry, the Nevasian, is found together with the evidently older Acheulean? There are two possibilities to explain this:

(a) either the Nevasian flake industry is contemporaneous with the Acheulean and constitutes a light industry (in M.D. Leakey's terms). terms).

(b) or it is younger and has been filtered into the open boulder horizon during the sealing by the gravel, at a much later period.

The geological situation points to the first explanation. There is no unconformity between the boulders and the gravel; in fact, the fine gravel forms the matrix of the boulders and must have infiltered the boulder horizon shortly after the Acheulean occupation. The bifaces are too fresh, their edges too sharp: they could not have been exposed for a long period of time before sealing.

The crude technique of the flake industry, too, seems to indicate that it could belong to the same period as the Acheulean. The cores from which the flakes were removed are irregular and unprepared. Similar cores, but made from basalt (i.e. of the material of the bifaces), are abundant among the bifaces. The same is the case with small basalt flakes, which are probably dressing flakes. They, too, do not show any retouch nor any predetermined shape.

It is possible, therefore, that the Nevasian is a component of the Acheulean bifaces and constitutes a light duty industry made of jasper and other siliceous material, accompanying a heavy duty industry made of basalt. A few handaxes of the pick type are made of silicious material as well.

If one compares, however, the Acheulean industry from Chirki with those from other sites, like Latamne in Syria, or Ambrona and Torralba in Spain, one is astonished to see the great difference in the percentage of tools to waste, especially to the small waste. While at most sites the small waste flakes have the higher percentage of the whole assemblage, at Chirki it is quite the opposite. The number of tools is far higher than the waste (1500 finished and unfinished tools, 440 pieces of large waste (larger than 8 cm), 120 small silica flakes and 238 small basalt flakes.

This would be very unusual for an undisturbed workshop. The occupation floor must have been disturbed in its original context. The water of the rising river, which brought the alluvial gravel-sealing, must have washed away most of the smaller components of the factory site, leaving all the larger artefacts and only a small percentage of the smaller ones. Many of the light duty flakes seem to have been washed into the river and got subsequently deposited into the gravels in the down-stream vicinity of Chirki.

Thus the geological observations seems to indicate the following events:

A phase of deep downcutting in a time of uplift of the upstream area at the Western Ghat formed a youthful valley with water rapids and small waterfalls. At the end of this erosional phase came the Acheulean occupation of the valley. Soon afterwards the rising river sealed the floor with fluviate gravels up to 8 m thickness. The river, meandering broadly in its bed, deposited a number of gravel lenses as channel deposits and thick bands of silts and sandy silts as floodbank deposits. At the end of this phase of thick alluviation we find a Late Stone Age industry in the uppermost part of the sediments. After this the river began again to erode, cutting its recent bed into its own, older deposits, thereby cutting and partly exposing the old Acheulean horizon.

1. *The workshop.* I shall now describe briefly the factory site itself and the finds. The assemblage of the Acheulean industry from the excavation consists of over 2400 artefacts:

> 1510 shaped tools
> 95 cores
> 444 large waste
> 238 small basalt flakes
> 120 small silica flakes

The concentration of the tools was greatest in trench VII. It was so thick that sometimes the artefacts were lying not only side by side but also on top of each other. Around one big flat stone, 70 artefacts were lying within arm's length. They were scattered amongst the unworked cobbles of the boulder filled depression on the rock. A number of very large blocks in the northern part of the excavation, at a slightly higher level looked to one of my collaborators, Dr Ansari, like a disturbed stone foundation of some sort. The blocks and boulders of the horizon are very angular and are of all sizes from small gravel to huge blocks of a yard in diameter, indicating that they collected here as colluvial debris.

No ash, and no signs of fire were found, and not many bones. Bones must have been present at the time of occupation, but only a few were preserved and those which were found were extremely brittle: some bovine teeth, a bovine calcareous cast of a horn, a part of a tusk of elephas, a bovine jaw, plus a number of brittle bone splinters.

The stone artefacts do not show any alignment or stream orientation — they lie in all directions indicating that the fluvial action was not so strong as to disturb the floor to a great extent.

A very interesting find was in the last season, the finding of calcareous fossil Pleistocene wood. It was found on the boulder bed, but in a calcareous, sandy part of the alluvial gravel. It is a concentration of several hundred small calcareous pieces of dycot wood and of calcareous casts of branches of wood. Two tree trunks of 1 m and 1.50 m with several branches were also found. The smaller pieces are often rounded and seem to have spindle-like or plano-convex shapes. It has been suggested that they might have been worked or cut by man.

2. *The tool-kit.* The Acheulean artefacts can be grouped best into a core-tool and a large flake tool complex.
The core tool group comprises:

    (1)   handaxes and picks
    (2)   unifacial and bifacial choppers
    (3)   polyhedral tools (polyhedrons, spheroids)
    (4)   cores.

This means

    (*a*)   a handaxe group
    (*b*)   a chopper-polyhedron group
    (*c*)   cores.

The handaxes are made from elongate pebbles or sometimes from split pebbles. They are mostly picks and elongate, pointed handaxes with thick, mostly blunt butts. The points are often well trimmed.

The chopper-polyhedron group is made from spheroidally

weathered basalt nodules, by multidirectional, polyhedral flaking around the whole surface or part of it. The polyhedral flaking is shallow, the ridges and edges on the tool are rather blunt. Polyhedrons are sometimes difficult to distinguish from cores, but by measuring the angles of the edges and the length of flake scars, I hope to find a way of distinguishing true production-cores from non-production cores or polyhedrons. The angles of their edges are blunter, the flake scars smaller than in cores.

Besides the tools and cores there is a group of undistinctive, worked pebbled, unfinished pieces, as well as unworked, large flakes. The flake-tool group consists of:

(1)   handaxes
(2)   cleavers
(3)   various forms of reduced cleavers and intermediate forms with additional lateral cutting edges
(4)   lateral cutting tools
(5)   undistinctive worked flakes
(6)   small light duty flakes made from silica and basalt, and dressing flakes.

All the flakes, except the light duty flakes, are made in a very distinct fashion. Over 90% are side struck.

The most interesting component of the assemblage is certainly the cleaver group, which constitutes a major proportion of the tools. They are made by a very distinctive technique, from large, side-struck flakes, taken from prepared, large cores, always in the same manner.

In one of these trenches were found a number of large cores, on which the use of this technique could be discerned. The core was prepared in such a way that the detached flake was an elongate side-flake with a cleaver edge. This cleaver edge was predetermined, but was not always successful. The cleaver edge was extremely sharp and did not need any further trimming (pl. 2.1a). The cleaver edge was, however, not always kept in its original form, but was often reduced to a smaller size in order to get a reduced chisel-like end or a point or even a pointed handaxe (pl. 2.1c,d). Or it was combined with a lateral cutting edge. The angle of the platform to the ventral face of the flake is about 110°. The platform is almost always on the right side, with the dorsal face upwards. This right side is always the steeper, blunter side of the tool. The platform is usually trimmed after detachment, either partially towards the butt to remove the sharp-angled upper edge of the platform or fully in order to flatten the tool. Thus the right side is almost never a cutting side, but a blunt side. The left side, however, was usually worked uni- or bifacially to produce a flat, sharp lateral edge.

Plate 2.1 (a) Broad Cleaver with straight cleaver edge.

Plate 2.1 (b) Broad Cleaver with oblique cleaver edge.

Plate 2.1 (c) Reduced Cleaver, (dorsal face).

Plate 2.1 (d) Very reduced Cleaver (seen from the vertical face) the original cleaver edge is reduced from both sides leaving just a small edge.

If the maker, however, wanted to have a different tool from a cleaver, he usually concentrated on the cleaver edge to alter the tool. He could reduce the cleaver edge from the left side by lateral flaking so that the cleaver edge merged into the lateral edge, thus producing a lateral cutting tool with a small, chisel-like remnant of the cleaver edge, or reduce the cleaver edge from the right side, making a sharp-angled chisel or point; or he could take a few transversal flakes from the cleaver edge itself, destroying the straight edge and leaving a central point, or he would remove the cleaver edge altogether by transversal and lateral trimming so that the result was a flake handaxe. Thus a great variety of different tools could be made from the same, original cleaver-flake.

The technique shows that Chirki Man had a clear idea of his tool requirements and of the way to produce these tools. Altogether we can distinguish three different techniques of manufacture for the required tool-kit:

(1) the sideflake tool group of cutting tools — the largest group.
(2) the core-tool group of picks, and pointed handaxes.
(3) the pebble-tool complex of choppers, polyhedrons and spheroids.

Thus the tool kit reveals the main activity of Chirki Man at his living site: that of cutting, undoubtedly connected with his food habits.

He must have brought the hunted animal to his camp site, where he used the tools for skinning, dismembering and cutting the animal. The large lateral cutting tools with the merging cleaver edge would be ideal for skinning the carcass. Such activity would not leave distinct usemarks on the edge. The fact is that we do not find any distinct usemarks on the lateral cutting edges nor on the picks and handaxes. But we find a large percentage of cleavers having heavy usemarks at the cleaver edge. That means that the cleavers must have been used for heavier work.

The group of long pointed handaxes and picks is quite a separate group and seems to have nothing to do with the cutting tools. They might not have been used at all for any work which was connected with the carcass.

What purpose the third group of pebble tools had is difficult to say. Apart from a few real choppers most of them are polyhedral stones. Their edges are too blunt and their flake-scars too small for them to be cores.

Acknowledgments

Thanks are due to the Wenner-Gren Foundation, for a grant-in-aid to excavate the site; to the Council of Scientific and Industrial Research in New Delhi and the Deutsche Forschüngsgemeinschaft for scholarships; to Professor Dr Sankalia of Deccan College, Poona, for his guidance and help; and to Professor Dr Müller Beck, Institut für Urgeschichte, Tübingen, for his encouragement.

3

The Environmental background to early man in the dry zone of North-Western India: The geomorphic evidence for climatic change

ANDREW GOUDIE

Introduction

One of the main influences on human economic activity, not least that of primitive societies, is the nature of climate, its fluctuations and changes. Archaeologists and prehistorians dealing with the growth and decline of cultures and civilizations have not been slow to appreciate this fact. In the Indian context, for instance, one thinks of the disputes over the nature and role of climatic changes involved in the rise and fall of the Indus civilization (Raikes and Dyson, 1961; Wheeler, 1968), and the discussions that there have been on the age of the Thar Desert (Ghosh, 1952; Sankalia, 1952).

A major line of evidence that can be used for assessing the nature of past climatic conditions is the geomorphic evidence provided by diagnostic landforms. Landforms of this type have formed a focus for much valuable inter-disciplinary work in Africa (see, for example, Wayland, 1954; Mason, 1967; Partridge and Brink, 1967; Butzer and Hansen, 1968), but in India and Pakistan there has been much less work of this sort, and our background knowledge of the environment of early man in the sub-continent is fragmentary and unsatisfactory. This is in spite of some valuable and well-known pioneer work by Zeuner (1950) and Wainwright (1964) in Gujarat, by de Terra and Paterson (1939) in the Kashmir Valley and western Punjab, and by Rajaguru (1969) and Rajaguru and Hegde (1970) in the Deccan. Other lines of evidence are also likely to be productive, including pollen analysis of the type undertaken by Gurdip Singh (1967, 1970) in eastern Rajasthan, but this paper is restricted to consideration of the value of geomorphic evidence so far used, and the likely situations where it will prove most reliable and usable in the future, with particular reference to the dry zones of India.

The importance of the dry zone

In addition to the fact that the dry or semi-arid zone of India has
been productive from the archaeological point of view, with evidence
from the Lower Palaeolithic through to the Indus Civilization and
later, it is also likely to be one of the most productive parts of India
in terms of the geomorphic evidence for climatic changes, transitional zones between two major morphogenetic processes, as
between the aeolian and the fluvial, or between the glacial and the
non-glacial, being the most likely to show the imprint of a changing
environment. Much less success has so far been achieved in a truly
wet environment, like the heart of a tropical rain forest, or in the
core of a completely dry desert (for example, the Namib of South
West Africa). Some of the best work has been done in semi-arid
zones like the High Plains of the United States, the Kalahari Desert
of Southern Africa, the Sahelian zone of the south Sahara, or the
south east of the Australian desert zone. Large parts of the dry zone
of India (fig. 3.1), especially in Rajasthan and northern Gujarat, are
comparable to the areas mentioned above.

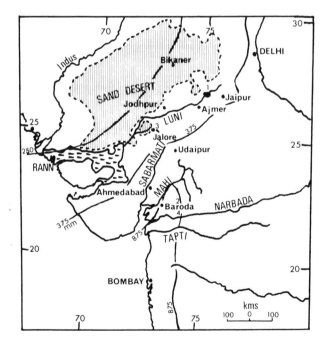

Figure 3.1 Map of the dry zone of North-West India (Isohyets in 1 mm; 1 =
   Sambhar Lake; 2 = Pavagarh Hill; 3 = Jalore sand accumulation; 4 = Visadi
   dune; limits of the sand desert after the Oxford Atlas.

The evidence provided by sand dunes and accumulations

Sand dunes are generally only active in the tropics where precipitation is less than about 150-200 mm *per annum*. Where precipitation is above this figure, vegetation binds the sand (unless human activity is intense as in parts of western Rajasthan today), weathering produces clay and kunkur within the dune (both of which also serve to further reduce the mobility of the sand), and water erosion degrades the flanks of the dunes to angles below that of the repose of sand. Thus, in general, the discovery of sand dunes in areas of high rainfall, indicates a decrease in aridity and an increase in humidity since the dunes were formed.

In India there is now extremely clear evidence for the former much greater extent of the Rajasthan Desert and for the presence of fossil dunes in areas which now have quite considerable rainfall. Verstappen (1970), a Dutch geomorphologist, working in the Jalore area of southern Rajasthan, and making use of both air photographs and field research, encountered large accumulations of fossil sand against inselbergs, and by rather tenuous indirect means dated them as belonging to arid conditions which came to an end about 5000 B.C. The sand was banked up against the hills by the strong south westerly summer monsoon.

Similarly, Gurdip Singh (1970) found fossil dunes overlain by early Holocene lake sediments in the vicinity of Sambhar Lake, eastern Rajasthan, and dated them as being stabilized after 9250 B.P., a date which probably represents the end of the main arid phase more accurately than Verstappen's. Likewise, Allchin and Goudie (1971), working in Central Gujarat, where the rainfall is now 850 mm *per annum*, found numerous dunes and sand accumulations, and, in the absence so far of suitable materials for radiometric dating, attempted some degree of dating through artefacts. Nearly all the dunes visited between Langhnaj in the north and the Orsang River in the south, displayed the diagnostic features of typical fossil dunes, including weathering to depths of over 2 m, extensive kunkur development, marked gullying by water erosion, and a good vegetation cover. They were in addition covered by large numbers of microliths, but such tools were never found within a dune, even though many natural and artificial sections were investigated. This suggests that aridity had largely ceased by the time that Mesolithic man arrived in the area. However, at Visadi, near the village of Bodeli on the Orsang, one dune was encountered which contained an Upper Palaeolithic blade and burin industry of characteristic type (Allchin, this volume). The industry, exposed by agricultural activity, did not seem to be associated with a fossil soil, and this suggests strongly that arid conditions were operative during Upper Palaeolithic times.

These three pieces of independent recent work show clearly that conditions of markedly greater aridity existed in north west India until the early Holocene with precipitation totals probably being more than halved compared to those of the present day. This ties in well with the evidence of other semi-arid areas like the Chad-Hausaland part of northern Nigeria (Grove, 1958), and Australia (Dury, 1967), where similar degrees of climatic change have been noted. Such a marked reduction of rainfall, followed by humid conditions approximating those of the present would almost certainly have had major consequences for human settlement and activity in the zone affected.

Further work still remains to be done on the former spatial extent of the desert and to see if the situation in Central Gujarat applies elsewhere. Also, it would probably be instructive to investigate the so-called 'inundation lakes' found in sand free tracts between the dunes, and to see whether they were associated with deflation dunes called lunettes. The sediments of these crescentic mounds sometimes enable one to establish a sequence of lake drying and filling, according to whether clay pellets (derived from the depression floor and thus indicating dryness) or beach sands (the product of wave activity and therefore wetness) make up the dune. This approach has recently been used successfully for the late Pleistocene in Australia (Bowler, 1970).

The evidence provided by the rivers and their terraces

The river systems of western Rajasthan were formerly both more extensive and more integrated, but are now sand-choked and discontinuous. Their old courses have been established by the geomorphologists at the Central Arid Zone Research Institute, Jodhpur (Ghose, 1964; Ghose, 1965). This applies particularly to the tributaries of the Luni River, such as the Mirti, which is now largely obliterated after Takhatgarh. These tributaries rise within the arid zone or on the flanks of the Aravallis, and therefore any changes in their discharge reflect climatic changes within the desert and semi-desert areas themselves, rather than external influences which have affected dry zone rivers with their sources in the Himalayas. Also, the extent and number of dead river systems suggests that local factors like river capture have not been the prime cause of their state, except in special cases like that of the Saraswati (Wilhelmy, 1969).

The old courses of the Luni tributaries indicate former higher humidity and it would be valuable to examine their alluvial sediments for artefacts and isotopically dateable materials and to establish their temporal relationship to the dunes. This would conceivably show something of the alternation of humid and aeolian conditions, about which all too little is so far known.

Further south, in the plain of Gujarat, there are some major integrated river systems in the form of the Mahi, Sabarmati and Narmada rivers (fig. 3.1), and these possess a terrace assemblage first noted by Allchin and Hegde (1969) and investigated in further detail by Allchin, Hegde and Goudie (1971) (pl. 3.1). The terraces, of which there seem to be two, contain some artefacts, including Lower Palaeolithic tools, and occur at heights of up to 30 m above river level. Terraces of this type have been used extensively in many areas to assess climatic changes, but it is well to appreciate some of the problems involved (Johnson, 1944; Frye and Leonard, 1954; Frye, 1961; and Schumm, 1965). In particular it is worth remembering that different environments will respond differently to climatic change:

(*a*) In an initially arid area like western Rajasthan, precipitation increases would tend to lead to the extension of tributaries through arroyo cutting, and sediment would be flushed out into main valleys during local storms, and because of the loss of water into main channels considerable aggradation of main channels would result.

(*b*) On the other hand, in an initially semi-arid area like Eastern Rajasthan a rather different situation would be likely to arise. An increase of rainfall would increase the strength of the vegetation cover, there would therefore be less runoff, small channels would become obliterated, sediment yields would decrease, but there would be incision of the main channel into alluvial productions of aggradation, thereby giving terraces.

On a broader scale the complexity of the relationship between climate and terraces has been well described by Flint (1957: 218):

Any climate consists of a group of variables such as amount of precipitation, distribution of precipitation throughout the year, mean and seasonal temperature and the like. The response of a stream, in terms of discharge and load, to a change in one or more of the climatic variables will be affected by local topographic texture, steepness of slopes, character of vegetation cover, and other circumstances. Hence a change in only one climatic factor might lead to very different responses in two different streams, and even in two different segments of a single long stream

This is a valuable warning against any over simple interpretation of terrace sequences in climatic terms.

Plate 3.1 (a) *Above:* Terraces on the Mahi river, seen from the road bridge between Godhra and Thasra, north Gujarat.

Plate 3.1 (b) *Below:* Terraces on the Aswin river, a small northern tributary of the Narmada, central Gujarat.

However, the sorting out of the problems involved in the climatic relationships of the Gujarati and Deccan terrace systems is necessary, as it is likely, that climate-induced changes have been the prime cause of the terrace systems. The terraces are almost certainly not eustatic as they occur well inland and the upper and middle courses of many of the rivers are related to local base-levels, including basalt cataracts, rather than to the base level provided by the sea. Also the widespread nature of the terraces and the similarity of their sequences also suggests that local tectonic factors are not the main cause of their development, though they may cause local complications especially in areas of instability like Kathiawar and the Rann of Kutch.

The sediments within the terraces of the Gujarati rivers, which include extremely coarse boulder layers and red fossil soil layers (Hegde, 1964), may enable one to ascertain the climatic sequence with a greater degree of certainty than one would obtain from a study of the morphological evidence alone. Even here, however, great care needs to be exercised in interpreting the significance of beds of coarse boulders. These have often been seen as produced by conditions of great humidity (see, for example, Joshi, 1958), but they could equally result from other conditions. For example, under conditions of lower rainfall erosion could be more intense due to a paucity of vegetation being combined with infrequent storms of high intensity, and this could also lead to the production of coarse aggradational material. Alternatively colder conditions might lead to an intensification of physical weathering by frost and this would supply a larger quantity of coarse material for transport downstream. Similarly, any process which might accentuate the movement of material on slopes, such as increased landslipping resulting from higher rainfall or periglacial conditions, would lead to the supply of coarse debris to the stream channel. In any one situation great care needs to be exercised in the use of terrace and sedimentary evidence.

Acknowledgments

Field work in Rajasthan and Gujarat was made possible through the provision of a Grant-in-aid from the Royal Society, and was greatly facilitated as a result of the generosity of the Director and Geomorphologists of the Central Arid Zone Research Institute. I should like to thank K.T.M. Hegde for his good-humoured company in the Baroda area, and above all Bridget Allchin for introducing me to India and making comments bearing on this paper.

REFERENCES

Allchin, B. and Hegde, K.T.M. (1969) The background of early man in the Narmada Valley, Gujarat: a preliminary report of the 1969 season's field work. *Journal of the M.S. University of Baroda* 12(1), 141-5.

Allchin, B. and Goudie, A. (1971) Dunes, aridity and early man in Gujarat, Western India. *Man*, Vol. 6, No. 2, 248-65.

Allchin, B., Hegde, K.T.M. and Goudie, A. (1971) The background to early man in Gujarat: preliminary report of the Cambridge-Baroda expedition, 1970-71 season. *Journal of the M.S. University, Baroda* (in press).

Bowler, J.M. (1970) Late Quaternary environments: a study of lakes and associated sediments in south-eastern Australia. Ph.D. Dissertation, Australian National University, Canberra.

Butzer, K.W. and Hansen, C.L. (1968) *Desert and River in Nubia.*

De Terra, H. and Paterson, T.T. (1939) *Studies on the Ice Age in India and Associated Human Cultures*, Washington.

Dury, G.H. (1967) Climatic change as a geographic backdrop. *Australian Geographer*, 10, 231-42.

Flint, R.F. (1957) *Glacial and Pleistocene Geology.* New York.

Frye, J.C. (1961) Fluvial deposits and the glacial cycle. *Journal of Geology*, 69, 600-3.

Frye, J.C. and Leonard, A.B. (1954) Alluvial terrace mapping. *American Journal of Science*, 252, 242-51.

Ghose, B. (1964) Geomorphological aspects of the formation of salt basins in the Lower Luni Basin. *Papers from Symposium on problems of Indian Arid Zone, Jodhpur*, 169-78.

Ghose, B. (1965) The genesis of the desert plains in central Luni Basin of western Rajasthan. *Journal Indian Society of Soil Science*, 13(2), 123-6.

Ghosh, A. (1952) The Rajputana desert; its archaeological aspect. *Proceedings Symposium on the Rajputana Desert*, Nat. Inst. Sci. India, Bull. 1, 37-42.

Grove, A.T. (1958) The ancient erg of Hausaland, and similar formations on the south side of the Sahara. *Geographical Journal*, 124(4), 526-33.

Grove, A.T. and Warren, A. (1968) Quaternary landforms and climate on the Ngamiland. *ibid* 135(2), 191-212.

Grove, A.T. and Warren, A. (1968) Quaternary Landforms and climate on the south side of the Sahara. *ibid.*, 134(2), 194-208.

Hegde, K.T.M. (1964) In Wainright (1964).

Johnson, D. (1944) Problems of terrace correlation. *Bulletin Geological Society of America*, 55, 793-818.

Joshi, R.V. (1958) Narmada Pleistocene deposits at Maheshwar. *Journal Palaeontological Society India*, 3,201-4.

Mason, R.J. (1967) The archaeology of the earliest superficial deposits in the Lower Vaal Basin near Holpan, Windserton District. *South African Geographical Journal*, 49, 39-56.

Partridge, T.C. and Brink, A.B.A. (1967) Gravels and terraces of the lower Vaal River Basin. *South African Geographical Journal*, 49, 21-38.

Raikes, R.L. and Dyson, R.H. (1961) The prehistoric climate of Baluchistan and the Indus Valley. *American Anthropologist*, 63, 265-81.

Rajaguru, S.N. (1969) On the late Pleistocene of the Deccan, India. *Quaternaria*, 11, 241-53.

Rajaguru, A.N. and Hegde, K.T.M. (1970) *The Pleistocene Stratigraphy in India.* mimeo.

Saṅkalia, H.D. (1952) The condition of Rajputana in the past as deduced from archaeological evidence. *Proceedings Symposium on the Rajputana Desert.* (Nat. Inst. Sci. India, Bull 1), 43-50.

Schumm, S.A. (1965) Quaternary Paleohydrology, (in H.E. Wright and D.G. Frey, eds.) *The Quaternary of the United States* 265-85.

Singh, G. (1970) The Indus Valley Culture seen in the context of post-glacial climatic and ecological studies in northwest India. *Preprint of the 28th International Congress of Orientalists: Far Eastern Prehistory Association Symposia.*

Singh, G. (1967) A palynological approach towards the problem of some important desert problems in Rajasthan. *Indian Geohydrology*, 3(1), 111-28.

Verstappen, H.Th. (1970) Aeolian geomorphology of the Thar Desert and Palaeoclimates. *Zeitschrift für Geomorphologie Supplementand 10*, 104-120.

Wainwright, G.J. (1964) *The Pleistocene Deposits of the Lower Narmada River and an Early Stone Age Industry from the River Chambal* M.S. University Archaeology and Ancient History Series 7, Baroda.

Wayland, E.J. (1954) Outlines of prehistory and Stone Age climatology in the Bechuanaland Protectorate. *Mem. Acad. R. Sci. colon., Sci. nat. med. 25, 47.*

Wheeler, R.E.M. (1968) *The Indus Civilization* (3rd ed.) Cambridge.

Wilhelmy, H. (1969) Das Urstromtal am Ostrand der Indusbene und das Sarasvati-Problem. *Zeitschrift für Geomorphologie Supplementband*, 8, 76-93.

Zeuner, F.E. (1950) *Stone Age and Pleistocene Chronology in Gujarat.* Deccan College Monograph Series 6, Poona.

4

Blade and burin industries of West Pakistan and Western India

BRIDGET ALLCHIN

The Upper Paleolithic of the Indian sub-continent has for long been something of a will-o'-the-wisp. Its existence was postulated by Burkitt and Cammiade in 1930 on the basis of a single blade from a surface site in South-Eastern India. In 1939 Commander Todd found a blade and burin industry stratified beneath microliths in a section cut in the course of building activities at Khandivli, in the suburbs of Bombay. There were further indications of its presence, a few substantiated by surface finds, but many more of an inferential, or even perhaps a wishful nature during the post war period. During this period the relationship of the hand-axe and chopper-chopping tool industries to one another (Lal, 1956), and the relationship of both to the flake industries and microlithic industries in sequential terms became clear (Allchin, 1959). Right across north India from Gujarat to Bengal the major rivers were found to have cut down into massive accumulations of silt and gravel, which filled their valleys. Sections exposed in this way consistently showed hand axes and other Early Stone Age tools incorporated in gravels which lay on the old land surfaces beneath the silts (Zeuner, 1950; de Terra and Paterson, 1939; Sen and Ghosh, 1963; Mohapatra, 1962). Microlithic sites were found throughout the sub-continent on and immediately below the modern land surface. Within the silts tools representing more developed hand axe industries and a wide range of flake industries were found either in gravel lenses or in an indurated gravel sometimes associated with another old land surface (Joshi, 1962). Conversely it could be said that massive accumulations of silt and gravel were laid down in the valleys of the major rivers of north and central India between the time when hand axes, cleavers and chopping tools were the predominent tools of man, and the microlithic period. It now appears that the period of massive deposition can be narrowed down still further, as the bulk of the accumulation took place before the advent of blade and burin industries.

Advance along lines followed in some other parts of the world has been hampered in South Asia by a dearth of caves and rock shelters in many parts of the sub-continent, and by the absence of undisturbed occupation deposits where cave and rock shelters have been found. For example at Adamgarh hill in the Narbada valley, near Hoshangabad, Early Stone Age (Acheulean) tools and factory debris, and post-Acheulean flake tools were found widely distributed on the slopes of the hill, and in open rock shelters in talus material consisting of fallen rock fragments and lateritic sand and clay derived from the underlying laterite (Joshi, 1964). Stratified above this in the rock shelters was a rich occupation deposit of the Late Stone Age or Mesolithic period (Joshi, 1968).

In 1962 A.H. Dani stumbled upon a remarkable site in the former North West Frontier Province of West Pakistan. This was a large rock shelter, situated about 64 km north of Mardan, near the village of Sanghao, in a narrow mountain valley. The perennial stream which flows down this valley is an affluent of the Swat river, which in turn joins the Indus near Mardan. The rock shelter contains over 3 m of occupation deposit, including quantities of quartz tools and factory debris, animal bones and charcoal (Dani, 1964). Twelve layers were identified, and considered by the excavator to fall into three phases: layers twelve to ten represent the earliest and most prolific phase of the quartz industry; layers nine to five its slightly less prolific continuation; in layers four and three its character changes, microlithic blades appear, and there are signs of disturbance in historic times. Layers two and one are associated with the Buddhist occupation of the cave. Although the excavation was carried out systematically, the greater part of this material was discarded before its importance could be pointed out. Those artifacts which were retained from individual layers are therefore far from representative, but they are classified none the less (Table 4.1). It became clear to me after examining them, and the discarded material on the dumps outside the cave, that prepared cores, flakes struck from them, and byproducts of this process formed a major element of the contents of the deposit in all except the topmost levels (figs. 4.1 to 4.5); an element which had clear affinities both with the Mousterian tradition of western and Central Asia, and with the Indian Middle Stone Age (Allchin & Allchin, 1968). A small hand axe (fig. 4.2, No. 8) in one of the lowest layers, and scrapers and awls from various levels are compatible with both these traditions. In addition there are a significant percentage of blades and burins, the latter forming 4.9% of the tools attained in both the first and second phase. The majority are single blow burins (figs. 4.3 and 4.4) of a

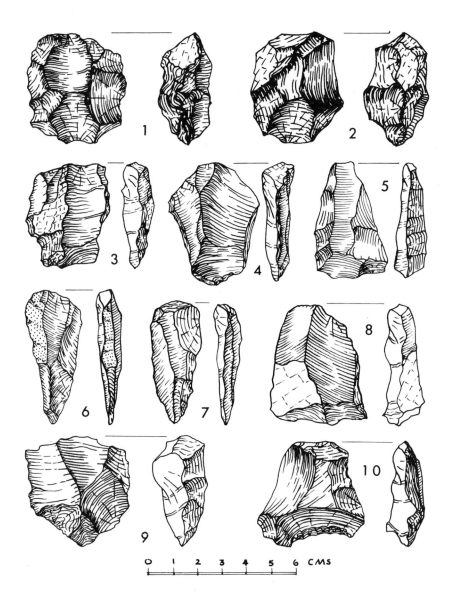

Figure 4.1 Artefacts from Sangao Cave, Layers 12 to 10: Nos 1 & 2, discoidal cores; Nos 3 to 9, flakes of various types struck from prepared cores; No 10, concave or hollow scraper made on the distal end of a similar flake.

distinctive kind, made on rectangular fragments of quartz, in many cases making use of a natural facet of the quartz as a striking platform (fig. 4.2, No. 7). Both Levalloiso-Mousterian cores and flakes, and blades and burins appear to be present throughout the greater part of the deposit. Further, more knowledgeable excavation

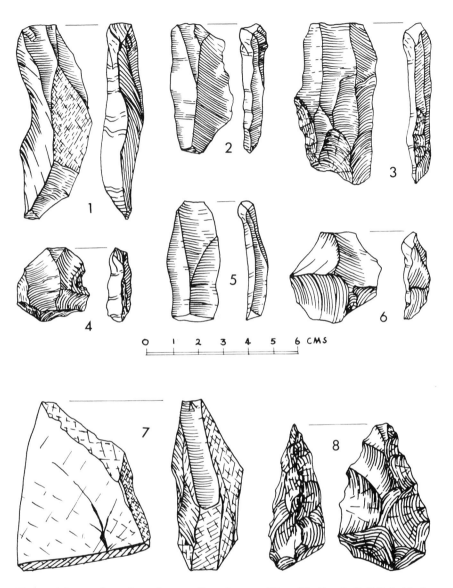

Figure 4.2 Artefacts from Sangao Cave, Layers 12 to 10: Nos 1, 2, 3 & 5, blades
and blade-flakes; No 4, small concave scraper on a flake; No 6, flake struck
from a prepared core; No 7, large burin; No 8, small hand axe.

may show whether we are dealing with a single industrial tradition
embracing several techniques, or a series of related industries. The
use of quartz throughout the occupation deposit is remarkable, as its
very nature renders it a difficult material for tool making. The reason
for the choice is not far to seek, for there is a quartz outcrop within
less than 300 m of the cave. The interest of this site is increased by
subsequent finds in peninsular north and Western India.

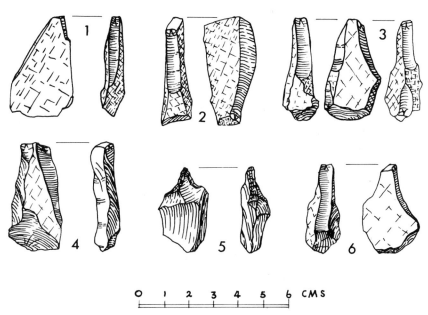

Figure 4.3 Artefacts from Sangao Cave, Layers 12 to 10: Nos 1-4 & 6, burins made from tubular pieces of quartz; No 5, awl or borer made on a flake.

Table 4.1

Sanghao stone industry (artefacts retained from occupation deposit)

	Phase 1		Phase 2		Phase 3	
	(Layers 12 to 10)		(Layers 9 to 5)		(Layers 4 & 3)	
	No.	Type%	No.	Type%	No.	Type %
Flake cores	47	7.26	60	12.44	58	6.94
Flakes	204	31.43	124	25.73	211	25.24
Flakes with secondary working	37	5.72	—	—	1	0.12
Hollow scrapers	6	0.92	2	0.41	3	0.36
Convex scrapers	—	—	2	0.41	—	—
Awls	2	0.31	—	—	6	0.72
Burins	32	4.93	24	4.9	23	2.85
Blade cores	—	—	—	—	2	0.24
Blades	26	4.00	8	1.66	18	2.16
Lunates	—	—	—	—	2	0.24
Fragments	294	45.99	262	54.27	512	61.24
	1	0.16	—	—	—	—
	649		382		846	

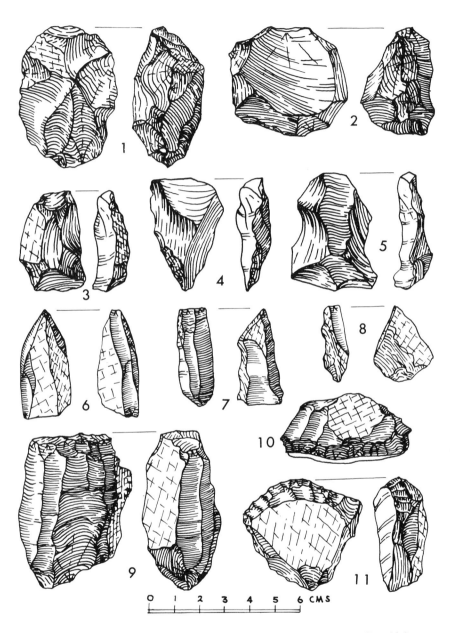

Figure 4.4 Artefacts from Sangao Cave, Layers 9 to 5: No 1, discoidal core; No 2, discoidal core with flake struck off; Nos 305, flakes struck from prepared cores; Nos 6-8, burins; No 9, crude prismatic core; Nos 10 & 11, thick convex scrapers or adze blades.

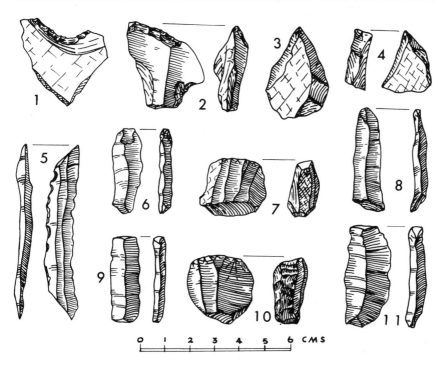

Figure 4.5 Artefacts from Sangao Cave, Layers 4 & 3: No 1, concave or hollow scraper made on a flake; No 2, convex scraper made on a flake; Nos 3 & 4, burins; Nos 5, 6, 8, 9 & 11, blades (No 5 made of chert); Nos 7 & 10, blade cores.

In South-Eastern India, near Renigunta, M.L.K. Murti found a blade and burin industry at a group of factory sites. His description of the industry and excellent illustrations leave no doubt that this is indeed a blade and burin industry. It is made largely of fine grained quartzite, and includes a limited number of scrapers and one awl (Table 4.2), the latter reminiscent of the one from Sanghao (fig. 4.3, No. 5). Such flakes as there are Murti considers to be byproducts of the shaping of blade cores, and there are no prepared cores and flakes of the kind so characteristic of Sanghao. Murti also lists a number of other finds of blade and burin industries in Eastern and Central India, and considers that these represent a series of parallel regional developments from the flake industries of the Middle Stone Age complex towards the microlithic. He indicates instances of blade and burin industries stratified in silts and gravels above Middle Stone Age tools, but below the modern land surface with which the microlithic industries are associated.

In north India, in the region of Allahabad, where the Ganges-Jamuna plains meet the hills of Central India, blade and burin industries have been found at numerous sites by G.R. Sharma and his

Table 4.2

Assemblage of stone artefacts from sites in the Renigunta area, South-East India

	No.	Type %
Blade Cores	19	2.3
Blades	400	48.00
Burins	55	6.6
Baked blades	72	8.7
Points	5	0.6
Scrapers	6	0.72
Awls	2	0.24
Flakes	49	5.9
Core flakes	119	14.3
Chips (Miscellaneous waste material)	105	12.6
	832	

assistants (Sharma, 1970). They have been found at surface factory sites at the foot of the Vindhyan escarpment, in the Son river valley, and elsewhere in the adjacent Central Indian hills, and in sections cut by the river Belan, a southern tributary of the Jamuna. These consistently show two indurated gravels of somewhat different character, the upper sometimes divided from the lower by a deposit of silt, and sometimes resting unconformably upon it. Incorporated in the lower gravel are found Early Stone Age tools — hand axes, cleavers, chopping tools and the byproducts of their manufacture. In the upper gravel are flake tools characteristic of the Middle Stone Age. Above the younger gravel is a second deposit of silt, followed by a third gravel, finer and less heavily cemented than the two former, and then by further silt deposits. The blade and burin industry is found in the third gravel, and in the silts immediately above and below it. The uppermost silts and the modern soil contain microliths and pottery. Percentages of different tool types in the blade and burin industry are not yet available, and for this and many other reasons the forthcoming publication is awaited with great interest. The body of material from stratified alluvial deposits and factory sites is immense, and will provide a much more complete picture than we have for any other region in the sub-continent. In February 1971 Professor Sharma kindly allowed me to see this material, and also the sections in the Belan valley, and I formed the impression that the blade and burin industry closely resembled that described by Murti from Southeast India.

The quartz industry from Visadi dune referred to in the preceding paper (Goudie) has already been described in some detail elsewhere (Allchin and Goudie, 1971). It is a blade and burin industry, with a few scrapers, and a number of flakes some of which are clearly byproducts of the preparation of blade cores (Table 4.3 and figs. 4.6

TABLE 4.3.

Visadi stone industry

	No.	Type %
Macro. cores – blade & blade flake	74	21.76
Core trimming flakes (macro.)	4	1.18
Macro. blades	11	3.24
Scrapers	4	1.18
Burins	21	6.18
Burin spalls	1	0.29
Flakes & blade-flakes	158	46.47
Misc. pieces of raw material	58	17.06
Micro. blade cores	3	0.88
Micro. blades	6	1.76
Total	340	

and 4.7). Visadi is a factory site, and the collection includes an appropriate proportion of cores. They are virtually all blade cores: prepared cores of Levalloiso-Mousterian or Indian Middle Stone Age type are remarkable by their absence, as in the collection from sites in the Renigunta region. Visadi also closely parallels the blade and burin element from Sanghao rock shelter, as illustrations demonstrate more clearly than words. Here again quartz was chosen for tool making as it was available in the adjacent granite hills. The position of the Visadi factory site within a fossil dune, in a place where today the rainfall is much too high to allow the formation of dunes, shows that the industry is contemporary with an arid phase, when conditions were much drier than they are today. Observations in the Allahabad region suggest that there also the blade and burin industry was associated with conditions somewhat different to those of the present day, but precisely what the difference may have been is a

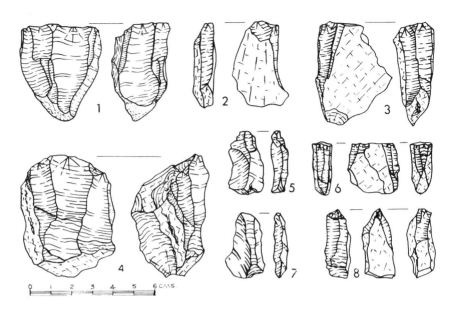

Figure 4.6 Artefacts from Visadi Dune: Nos 1 & 4, cores; Nos 2, 3, 6 & 8, burin; Nos 5 & 7, blades.

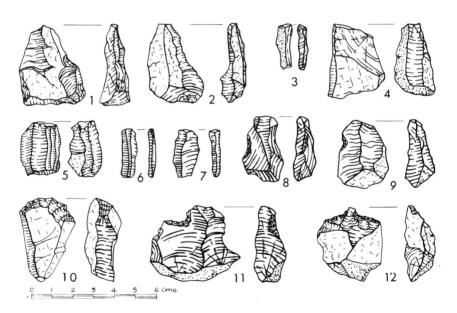

Figure 4.7 Artefacts from Visadi Dune: Nos 1, 2, 8 & 9 flakes; No 3, burin spall; No 4, burin; No 5, microlithic blade core; Nos 6 & 7, microlithic blades; No 10, convex scraper; Nos 11 & 12, hollow scrapers.

matter for further research. As yet we have no indication as to what climatic conditions prevailed north west of the Indus at the time when a blade and burin industry was being made near Sanghao. Not do we know about past climatic conditions in tropical South India. Both these regions may differ considerably from central Gujarat and the United Provinces.

Acknowledgments

Our field work in Gujarat was part of a collaborative project based upon the Centre of South Asian Studies, University of Cambridge, and the Department of Archaeology and Ancient History, M.S. University, Baroda, the support and hospitality of whose head, Professor R.N. Mehta I gratefully acknowledge. I should like to thank Dr K.T.M. Hegde, of Baroda, Mr Andrew Goudie, and Miss Statira Guzder for their collaboration at every stage; Professor G.R. Sharma of Allahabad University for showing me sites and collections from the Allahabad region; Newnham College, Cambridge for awarding me the Phyllis and Eileen Gibbs Travelling Fellowship which made it possible for me to go to India.

Figures 6 and 7 are reproduced here by kind permission of the editor of *Man.*

REFERENCES

Allchin, B. (1959) The Indian Middle Stone Age. *Bulletin of the Institute of Archaeology,* 1-36.
Allchin, B. & R. (1968) *The Birth of Indian Civilization.* London, 71-4.
Allchin, B. & Goudie, A. (1971) Dunes, aridity and early man in Gujarat, Western India. *Man,* Vol. 6, 2, 248-65.
Burkitt, M.C. and Cammiade, L.A. (1930) Fresh light on the Stone Age of Eastern India. *Antiquity,* Vol. 4, 5.
Dani, A.H. (1964) Sanghao Excavation: the first season, 1963. *Ancient Pakistan,* Vol. 1, 1-50.
de Terra, H. and Paterson, T.T. (1939) *Studies on the Ice Age in Indian and Associated Human Cultures.* Washington.
Joshi, R.V. (1962) *Proceedings of the 48th Indian Science Congress,* Part III: Stone Age industries of the Upper Wainganga Basin, Maharashtra State.
Joshi, R.V. (1966) The Acheulean Succession in Central India. *Asian Perspectives,* Vol. 3, 1, 150-63.
Joshi, R.V. (1968) Late Mesolithic Culture in Central India, in *La préhistoire: problèmes et tendances,* 245-54.
Lal, B.B. (1956). Palaeoliths from the Beas and Barganga Valleys, Panjab. *Ancient India,* 12, 58-92.
Mohapatra, G.C. (1962) *The Stone Age Cultures of Orissa.* (Deccan College Research Series), Poona.
Murty, M.L.K. (1968) Blade and burin industries near Renigunta, on the south-east coast of India. *Proceedings of the Prehistoric Society.* N.S. Vol. 34, 83-101.

Sankalia, H.D. (1964) Middle Stone Age culture in India and Pakistan. *Science* Vol. 146, 3642, 1-11.

Sen, D. and Ghosh, A.K. (1963) Lithic culture-complex in the Pleistocene sequence of the Narmada Valley, Central India. *Revista di Scierge Preistoriche*, Vol. 18, 3-23.

Sharma, G.R. (1970) *Indian Archaeology 1968-69, A Review.* 78-83.

Todd, K.R.U. (1939) Palaeolithic industries of Bombay. *Journal of the Royal Anthropological Institute*, Vol. 69.

Zeuner, F.E. (1950) *Stone Age and Pleistocene Chronology in Gujarat.* (Deccan College Monograph Series: 6), Poona.

5
Late Stone Age traditions in South-East Asia

I.C. GLOVER

Relationships between South-East Asia and the Indian subcontinent can be seen at many periods in prehistory, although in neither region is the chronology and context of the archaeological materials sufficiently well-known for a coherent account of the relationships to be written.

It is not possible to draw any single line of division between India and South-East Asia that is good for all periods in prehistory. In some periods the eastern provinces of India (see below) have more in common with Burma, Thailand and Indochina than with Western India. And Burma, so often grouped with India for purposes of academic enquiry, is almost entirely South-East Asian in its prehistoric as in modern culture. Being linked with India is the result of an accident of colonial history.

In the Middle Pleistocene there are obvious parallels between the South-East Asian Chopper, Chopping-tool Complex and the Sohan of North-West India. Despite the occasional occurrence of bifacial handaxes in both areas, two broadly contrasting culture areas can be seen; the one in North-West India, China and South-East Asia, the other in Peninsular India, which is more closely related to Africa and Eurasia.

In the Late Stone Age the typological similarity between the backed microlithic tools of India and Ceylon, and Java, Sulawesi, and Australia, suggests either the widespread diffusion of ideas and techniques, or perhaps, the actual movement of people eastwards out of India.

At a later date, (but still unknown), Assam, Bengal, Bihar and Orissa show such strong links with the South-East Asian Neolithic cultures that, although proper evidence is almost entirely lacking it is possible to think of movement the other way. The growing evidence for quite early, and perhaps independent development of agriculture and settled village life (by at least *c.* 3500 B.C.) in the region bounded by South China, Assam, Bengal, and the mainland of South-East Asia, might provide an incentive to re-examine the status and chronology of the Indian Eastern Neolithic cultures.

In early historic times, of course, South-East Asia came under very strong Indian influence, and it seems likely that active trade existed between the two areas long before Hindu/Buddhist religious and cultural models began to influence the native South-East Asian traditions sometime about the first or second centuries A.D.

This paper, although it deals with a South-East Asian topic, may therefore be seen as relevant to the archaeology of South Asia also.

Dr Bridget Allchin's (1966) valuable survey of the archaeology and ethnography of South-East Asia stressed the continuity and survival there of stone age cultures and it is clear that in some places, communities dependent largely on hunting and gathering still exist (Glover, 1972), although they all obtain iron tools and cloth from village farmers. However, the long survival in isolated regions of simple, pre-agricultural societies has tended to foster the view that agriculture and settled village life was a comparatively late development in South-East Asia, undertaken only under the stimulus of culturally more advanced peoples migrating from the north. But in South-East Asia, as in India, mutually interdependent groups continue to live at very different levels of social and technological development in the same area, but exploiting different environments. This is, I believe, a very ancient pattern, for despite the long survival in some areas of societies living what we might call a 'stone age way of life', there is some evidence, from recent fieldwork to show that there was an independent development of a food producing economy in South-East Asia, based on tree fruits, tubers and other forest plants, at a date roughly comparable to the much better known, 'Neolithic revolution' of Western Asia. Archaeologically, this development can tentatively be identified with a distinctive culture, usually known as the Hoabinhian, and which is widely distributed from Burma to Indo-China and from South China to Malaya and Sumatra.

The Hoabinhian has traditionally been thought to be entirely post-Pleistocene in age, and to represent the material remains of the hunter-gatherer groups who still survive in the equatorial forest zone. Both these characterizations are wrong to some extent, I believe, and I will return to this question later.

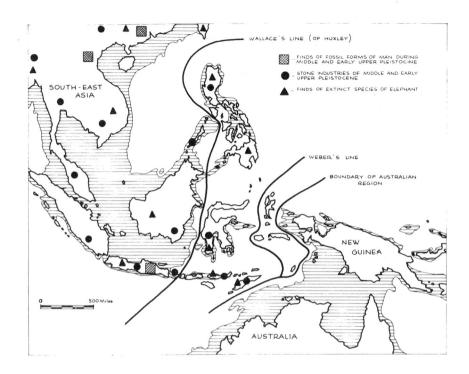

Figure 5.1 Find-spots of fossil forms of man, extinct species of elephant and stone industries of the Middle and Early Upper Pleistocene in South-East Asia.

The Middle and Upper Pleistocene in South-East Asia (Fig. 5.1).

To understand the development of the Late Stone Age traditions, a brief summary of the evidence for man in South-East Asia in the Middle and Upper Pleistocene is necessary. One of the main problems here, inevitably, is chronology. Very little palaeoclimatic work has been done in South-East Asia and the dating of the Pleistocene has depended very much on correlating the faunal successions from Java and Indo-China with those of China and India, which then can be related in a rough sort of way with the principal phases of Pleistocene glaciations (Movius, 1944; Boriskovsky, 1970: 2).

In South-East Asia, deposits which first contain the true one-toed horse (*Equus*), an elephant (*Archidiskodon*), and an advanced bovine (*Leptobos*), are attributed to the Lower Pleistocene or Villafranchian and are correlated with the pre-Gunz and Gunz phases of Alpine glaciation. Few archaeological, and no hominid materials, are known of this age from South-East Asia and the fauna contains no living species (Hooijer, 1961-2: 485). The Middle Pleistocene contains up to a third of living species including *Elephas namadicus* and various

Stegodons. In Java the Djetis and Trinil faunas, which also contain *Homo erectus* and perhaps an Australopithecine, are both placed in the Middle Pleistocene, which is correlated roughly with the Great, or Mindel-Riss, Interglacial (Hooijer, 1961-2: 486). Radiometric dating of the Trinil fauna from Java is in progress and soon it may be possible to relate the Javanese to the African sequences without relying on faunal correlations alone. Rather doubtfully associated with the Trinil fauna (van Heekeren, 1957: 32-3) in a number of stream terraces in south Java are assemblages of core and flake tools which have been frequently described by von Koenigswald (1936), Movius (1944), van Heekeren (1957) and others as the Patjitanian industry. Characteristic of this tradition are the unifacially flaked core choppers, proto hand-axes, scrapers, and bifacial chopping tools. Acheulean-like bifacial hand axes are very rare in South-East Asia; nevertheless Boriskovsky (1968) has argued that Movius' characterization of the chopper-chopping tool complex is misleading, and that there is no essential difference between the Middle Pleistocene traditions of Eastern Asia and Africa and Eurasia.

It is only in the Upper Pleistocene that regional differences in stone tool traditions can be recognized within South-East Asia although reliable dating earlier than about 40,000 years ago is still lacking. The Upper Pleistocene fauna is almost entirely modern, that is composed of still living species, except for *Stegodon*, which seems to have survived longer in Java and the Lesser Sunda Islands than elsewhere (Hooijer, 1961-2: 486; 1970), and occasional other surviving forms in isolated islands. At Niah Caves, Sarawak, only one extinct animal, a giant ant eater (*Manis palaeojavanica*), was found in deposits from the last 50,000 years or so (Hooijer, 1961-2: 486), and at Tabon Cave, on Palawan island in the Philippines, again only one extinct species, a deer, is known in the past 20,000 years (Fox, 1970: 38-9). In Java, of course, the famous Solo Man is thought to be of Upper Pleistocene age and also the stone, bone and antler tools from the Ngandong terraces of the Solo River. Recently, however, some doubt has been thrown on the derivation of both the Solo Man skulls and the tools (T. Jacob, personal communication), and we shall have to wait for further work on this material. More certainly of Upper Pleistocene age are the flake assemblages from the Notopuro Beds in the Sangiran dome, and Kendeng Hills of Central Java. These implements are made of chalcedony, chert and jasper and include side and end scrapers, borers, points and occasional blades. The tools are made on thick flakes with plain striking platforms and generally obtuse striking angles. Some flakes are long and narrow, but there is no evidence of the manufacture of true blades, or Levallois flakes, from prepared cores. This material has been called the Sangiran industry by van Heekeren (1957: 43-5) and he himself has recorded very similar artefacts from Tjabengè in the Soppeng district of South Sulawesi (ibid., 47-54), associated with an Upper Pleistocene fauna, derived not from Java, but from South China via the Philippines.

Further south, in Flores in the Lesser Sunda Islands, Father Verhoeven has described collections of tools found near Mengeruda, both from on the surface and *in situ* with *Stegodon* fossils, which show characteristics of both the Patjitanian (i.e. Javanese Middle Pleistocene) and Sangiran industries; that is to say heavy core tools, unifacially flaked from one end, and large, flat scrapers usually made from volcanic rocks or quartzite, as well as smaller, more blade-like chert flakes and scrapers (Maringer and Verhoeven, 1970).

Figure 5.2 Sites of the Hoabinhian and Flake traditions in South-East Asia.

Late Upper Pleistocene industries at Niah and Tabon

Two dated sequences of cave deposits are known from island South-East Asia — from Niah and Tabon caves, where, as I mentioned, C14 dates back to *c.* 40,000 B.P. and 30,000 B.P. respectively are available (Harrisson, 1967: 95; Fox, 1970: 18). The Pleistocene levels at Niah seem to be poor in artefacts; and, apart from the morphologically modern *Homo Sapiens* skull, contain no more than a few, unretouched flakes, of which one has been described by Harrisson (1959: 3), misleadingly, I think, as a 'mid-Sohan' quartzite flake. This flake is dated to about 40,000 B.P. (*ibid.*), and is thus the oldest C14 dated artefact from Southern Asia. Small unretouched quartzite flakes continue into later times at Niah, and somewhere between 15,000 to 10,000 B.C. (Golson, 1972; Harrisson, 1967: 95) edge-ground axes appear in the sequence. There, together with similar finds from New Guinea (J.P. White, 1971), various parts of Australia (C. White, 1971: 148-53) and Indochina (Mansuy, 1925: 32) confirm the opinion once put forward by Tweedie (1965: 3) that edge-ground tools are an ancient and independent technological development in South-East Asia, and are not necessarily an indication of a settled, agricultural way of life.

Late Pleistocene flake traditions are better known from Tabon cave, Palawan, where Fox (1970) has recovered a good sequence of artefacts and bones from about 40,000-9000 B.P. Fox has analysed the material in terms of five sequential flake assemblages (ibid., 24-37) which show very little change over time, and are very difficult to characterize in any positive way. Flakes are generally large, 80 per cent of one sample being more than 5 cm long, and made of a coarse brown chert, from pebbles whose cortex often remains on the flake. Although some flakes were obviously used, less than one per cent have any secondary modification and these, according to Fox, defy easy classification into types based on morphology or the positioning of retouch. Illustrations suggest that these tools can best be described as flat, multi-edge scrapers; with a single implement having concave, convex and straight working edges, and occasionally small prepared notches. Tabon and Niah both show a long continuity of a very simple, even primitive flake tool tradition in the Late Pleistocene, with the absence of specialized forms and core tools. This tradition, although poorly known as yet, is quite different from the perhaps earlier, but still Upper Pleistocene, Sangiran and Tjabengè industries of Java, Celebes and Flores; and nothing comparable to either is so far known from the mainland of South-East Asia.

Hoabinhian traditions on the mainland

On the mainland the more commonly accepted view has been that varieties of the chopper-chopping tool complex, such as the Late Anyathian of Burma (Movius, 1943: 378-87) continued into Late,

Hoabinhian pebble chopper

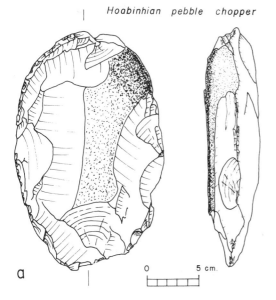

a

0   5 cm.

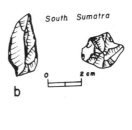

South   Sumatra

0   2 cm

b

MAINLAND   SOUTHEAST   ASIA

*On the mainland and in north Sumatra
unifacially or bifacially flaked river
pebbles, usually of volcanic rocks, are
the most common artefacts in sites
dating from c. 12,000 - 5,000 years
ago. Flake tools are rare and are
seldom retouched.*

*Contemporary sites in the islands contain
finely retouched flake tools made from
obsidian in south Sumatra, west Java,
and the Philippines, and chert in east
and central Java, Sulawesi, and the
Lesser Sunda Islands.*

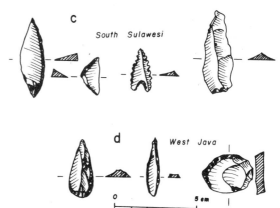

c   South   Sulawesi

d   West   Java

0   5 cm

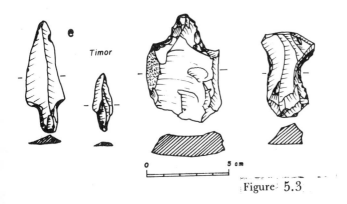

e
Timor

0   5 cm

f

East   Java

Figure 5.3

and even post-Pleistocene times, giving rise to the flaked pebble tradition of the Hoabinhian (fig. 5.3a). On the other hand, Professor Boriskovsky (1969: 93-4) believes that the lack of a recognizable Upper Palaeolithic flake tradition in Indochina, Thailand, Malaya and Burma is probably due to lack of research. Boriskovsky cites the recent identification of blade and burin industries in India (Murty, 1968) as a parallel case. Bridget Allchin (this volume) discusses the present knowledge of this tradition.

Certainly, there is no archaeological material on the mainland of South-East Asia which can be dated with any certainty to between say 30,000-12,000 years ago, and which would provide a parallel sequence to Niah and Tabon. The earliest dated site is Spirit Cave, Thailand, recently excavated by Chet Gorman (1969, 1971) from the University of Hawaii. There, a rich sequence of artefacts, bone and vegetable remains has been recovered, dating from between about 12,000 B.P. and 7500 B.P. Gorman divides the material into two cultural levels: the lower of which, Level I includes layers 2a-5 and contains typical Hoabinhian material — unifacially flaked quartzite river pebbles, ochre-covered grinding stones and a few utilized flakes of quartzite, which Gorman (1971: 312) identifies not as exploitative tools, for hunting, collecting or preparing foods, but as wood and bamboo working implements for fashioning such items as spears, bows and arrows, digging sticks and so on.

A detailed analysis of the faunal remains from Spirit Cave is not yet available, but it includes bovines, various deer, pigs, tortoise, reptiles, birds, rodents and freshwater shellfish, crustacea and fishes. Intermittent, but not necessarily seasonal occupation, is suggested by the growth patterns of land snails and the presence of freshwater bivalves which are difficult to collect in the rainy season.

The botanical remains from Spirit Cave, Level I are extraordinarily interesting, since they include species of *Prunus* beans, peas, *Areca*, bottle-gourd, waterchestnut, pepper vine, various nuts and cucumbers, of which the beans and peas, according to the botanists at the Bishop Museum, Hawaii, show morphological changes from the wild species which suggest that they were in the process of domestication (Gorman, 1971: 316).

Cultural Level II at Spirit Cave, which is dated to 8750-7500 B.P., contains pottery, slate knives and quadrangular adzes, which are the hallmark of the South-East Asian Neolithic cultures. These dates seem to be rather early compared with the traditional date of about 4000-4500 B.P. (Tweedie, 1965: 5), but they cannot be rejected on that account. At Laang Spean in Cambodia (Mourer, 1970), for instance, late Hoabinhian tools accompanied by more elaborate pottery than that found in Spirit Cave have been dated to over

6200 B.P. (ibid., 146). In Thailand, lowland village settlement seems to have developed by at least 3500 B.C. (Gorman, 1971: 303) and by 2500 B.C. pottery and domesticated animals had reached eastern Timor in the Lesser Sunda Islands (Glover, 1971).

The Hoabinhian culture has traditionally been thought to be entirely Recent in age, because of the lack of any associated fauna. But in South-East Asia, sites such as Niah and Tabon, 30,000 years old, contain almost exclusively modern species of animals, and there seems no reason to think that the end of the Pleistocene glaciation in temperate latitudes had any drastic effect on life in the humid tropics. The world-wide temperature change of about 5°C. would, of course, have altered the altitudinal zones a little, and large areas of the continental shelves (fig. 5.1) were drowned between 19,000 and 12,000 B.P. (Jennings, 1971), but the impact seems to have been insufficient to necessitate a complete reorientation of cultures such as occurred in more extreme latitudes. The dates from Spirit Cave, and the yet unpublished Ongba Cave, west central Thailand (Gorman, 1971: 303), put the Hoabinhian back to the very end of the Pleistocene; and though the Hoabinhian artefacts are difficult to order typologically, it seems that Spirit Cave does not represent the very beginning of this tradition.

Regional and temporal variations of the Hoabinhian culture must occur but they are difficult to interpret from the published evidence (Mathews, 1964; Gorman, 1971). The area covered was vast: from Burma to Indochina, from Yunnan, Szechwan and Kwangtung (Chang, 1963: 47) to Malaya and Sumatra, the latter being the only part of island South-East Asia where the distinctive Hoabinhian assemblages have been found (van Heekeren, 1957: 70-5). Sumatra contains an interesting situation because in the north and northeast many coastal shell middens have produced undoubted Hoabinhian materials, whereas caves and open sites from central and south Sumatra have revealed a quite different industrial tradition based on flaked obsidian (fig. 5.3*b*) which, though yet little known, appears to be similar to material from Java, Sulawesi and the islands east (Heekeren, 1957: 106; van der Hoop, 1940: 200-4).

Terminal Pleistocene and recent sites in Island South-East Asia

In Sulawesi, in 1902-3, the Sarasin brothers (1905) excavated four caves near Maros, and found (although they did not realize their significance) geometric and other backed microliths in a rich assemblage (fig. 5.3*c*) which became known as the Toalian, after a supposed surviving hunter-gathering group in the area. In the 1930s van Stein Callenfels, van Heekeren, Willems, and others continued research in South Sulawesi though little of their work saw detailed publication. However, van Heekeren (1957: 86-102) was able to reconstruct a consistent pattern of association between pottery, certain classes of stone and bone tools, and faunal and molluscan food remains. At one site, Panganreang Tudea, he proposed a three part sequence with blades and flake scrapers in the lowest level, succeeded by more evolved blades with unifacial points and geometric microliths, then hollow-based points with denticulate edges, and pottery on the surface.

In 1969 a joint A.N.U. — Indonesian team investigated more Toalian deposits in Sulawesi (Mulvaney and Soejono, 1970) and obtained a clearer idea of the artefact sequences, as well as getting some C14 dates (Mulvaney, 1971: 144). There are important differences between sites which will not be discussed here, but at one cave, Ulu Leang, we obtained something like van Heekeren's Panganreang Tudea sequence, with scrapers, followed by bone points and long, asymmetric backed blades, then, in the top 30 cm or so, hollow-based denticulate points which we call Maros points, together with pottery and bone points. A date of about 5800 B.P. was obtained just before the appearance of pottery and Maros points.

In the Philippines, caves on Palawan and elsewhere, showed that the flake tradition, known at Tabon in the Upper Pleistocene, continued on well into the Recent period (Fox, 1970: 48) with an increasing proportion of pieces with secondary working, and a gradual reduction in size (ibid.). However, nothing like the carefully worked backed blades or hollow-based points of Sulawesi are yet known from the Philippines.

In the Lesser Sunda Islands, a flake tradition is known from Flores, but I will illustrate it from my own work in Portuguese Timor (Glover, 1971). There, from a number of limestone caves, I have been able to build up a sequence of artefact and food remains dating from 15,000 B.P. Early finds are rare, but there appears to be no major break in stone working traditions from the Late Pleistocene to about 2000 B.P., when flaked stone seems to have been largely abandoned as a tool-making material. Tool types (fig. 5.3e) are principally, varieties of scraper of which concave side scrapers with steeply worked edges are most common. From about 4500-5000 years ago, pottery and some domesticated animals appear in the sequence, and also some more specialized tool types, such as tanged points. However, neither backed blades nor Maros points are found in Timor, and here, as in Flores, and in the Philippines, and, for that matter, further east in New Guinea (J.P. White, 1967: 435, 450) there seems to have been a long development from the Late

Pleistocene until mid-Recent times, of an isolated flake tradition, into which new elements were added with the arrival of domesticated animals and pottery and agriculture, but which survived essentially unbroken until the arrival of metal tools.

In Java similar developments can be seen in some seventeen caves from the centre and east of the island, and from open sites near Boger and Bandung (van Heekeren, 1957; Bandi, 1951), although well documented and dated excavations are entirely lacking. The artefact types in Java are different again; hollow based bifacial points of various siliceous stones from Central and East Java (fig. 5.3*f*) backed blades, geometric microliths and unifacial points of obsidian (fig. 5-3*d*) in West Java.

Mainland and island South-East Asia compared

On the mainland, there is a picture of, if not backwardness (remembering those early, partly domesticated plants) but at least of technological conservatism in stone working traditions; for Hoabinhian flaked pebble tools survived as the dominant stone implements until the development of agricultural village settlements.

In the islands, various flake and blade industries, descendents of local Upper Palaeolithic traditions, developed in relative isolation. From about 3000 B.C. new elements such as pottery, more specialized tool forms, domesticated and imported animals appear in the deposits, signalling perhaps either immigration or the wide diffusion of new cultural orientations. Some of the new stone tool types such as the Maros points of Celebes, the hollow-base points of East Java, or the tanged points of Timor, have no immediate ancestors in South-East Asia, and they are perhaps local developments. The suite of backed blades and geometric microliths, known so far only from West Java and Celebes, can be matched in many areas of the Indian subcontinent; in the east, from Bengal, south to Ceylon, and we must at least consider the possibility that they were derived from India. In Australia, similar backed tools appear before 3000 B.C. (Mulvaney, 1968: 126; Moore, 1970: 42) and are distributed around the coasts from the northwest to the southwest. And in some early sites of this tradition in Australia bones of a domesticated dog, the dingo, have been found, an animal which was previously unknown both in Australia and in Island South-East Asia (see Golson, 1971, for a discussion of the implications of this).

In order to bring these problems into better focus much more fieldwork is necessary in Eastern India, South-East Asia and Australia. The chronology of the Indian microlithic industries is not at all well known. Burma, Sumatra and even Java are archaeologically almost unknown, with no well-excavated, published and dated material available. Where it is possible to synthesize the available evidence, as I have tried to, and show a broad pattern of contrast between mainland and islands in the Late Pleistocene and early Recent periods, further research will certainly alter and confuse the relatively simple picture outlined here. It is difficult, at the moment, to give a satisfactory explanation of the contrast between mainland and islands other than to regard them as regional culture provinces. A simple environmental explanation, that the Hoabinhian was an adaptation to the equatorial zone where there is heavy, year round rainfall, and the flake traditions were confined to the monsoon lands with more seasonal variation in rainfall, is not tenable. For in Thailand, Burma, Indochina and South China, we find Hoabinhian traditions in a region of strongly seasonal climate. And earlier, I characterized the difference as one between mainland and island; but this is not always true. The divergent traditions can first be recognized in the Upper Pleistocene, at a time of probable low sea-levels, when Sumatra, Java, Borneo, and Palawan were linked to the Asiatic landmass (fig. 5.1). And yet at a later date, when Sumatra was certainly an island, the northern part of the island was included within the Hoabinhian culture province.

This is no place to discuss, in detail, the shortcomings of the existing frameworks for understanding South-East Asian prehistory. There have been, in the past few years, several attempts (e.g. Solheim, 1967, 1969; Bierling, 1969; Chang, 1970; Gorman, 1971; Higham, 1972) to show how the data from modern excavations is incompatible with the models proposed by Heine Geldern (1932) and other diffusionists influenced by the Vienna School of Anthropology (e.g. Colani, 1927; Beyer, 1949; van Stein Callenfels, 1938; van Heekeren, 1957; and Christie, 1961). The new data is not yet adequate for the formulation of a broadly useful model which can relate the environmental variables of this complex region over many thousands of years with the scattered facts from archaeology. This paper attempts only to stress one of the many outstanding problems of South-East Asian archaeology that can be seen in the contrasting but contemporary traditions which can be recognized on the mainland and in the islands during the Late Stone Age.

REFERENCES

Allchin, B. (1966) *The Stone-tipped Arrow — Late Stone Age Hunters of the Tropical Old World.* London.

Bandi, H.-G. (1951) Die Obsidianindustrie der Umgebung von Bandung in Westjava. *Südseestudien: Gedenkschrift zur Erinnerung an Felix Speiser,* pp. 127-61 Museum für Völkerkünde, Basel.

Beyer, H.O. (1949) Outline review of Philippine archaeology by islands and provinces. *Philippine Journal of Science,* 77 (3 and 4) 1947, 205-374 (pub. 1949).

Bierling, J. (1969) Migration towards Melanesia: a re-valuation. B.A. (Hons.) Thesis, Department of Anthropology, University of Sydney, November 1969 (unpublished).

Boriskovsky, P.I. (1968) Basic problems in the archaeology of Vietnam. *Asian Perspectives* 9, 83-5.

Boriskovsky, P.I. (1969) Vietnam in primeval times: part 3 (translated from *Pervobytnoe proshloe V'etnama,* Nauka, Moscow, 1966). *Soviet Archaeology and Anthropology,* 8 (1), 70-95.

Boriskovsky, P.I. (1970) The new problems of the Palaeolithic and Mesolithic of the Indo-Chinese Peninsula. Paper presented to the 28th International Congress of Orientalists, Canberra, January 1971, and published by Nauka, Central Department of Oriental Literature, Moscow 1970

Chang, K.C. (1963) *The Archaeology of Ancient China.* New Haven.

Chang, K.C. (1970) The beginnings of agriculture in the Far East. *Antiquity,* 44, 175-85.

Christie, A. (1961) The sea-locked lands, in *The Dawn of Civilization,* Piggott, S. (ed.), London, 277-300.

Colani, M. (1927) L'Age de la pierre dans la province de Hoa-Binh (Tonkin). *Mémoires dü Service Géologique de l'Indochine,* Hanoi 14 (1).

Fox, R. (1970) *The Tabon Caves — Archaeological Explorations and Excavations on Palawan Island, Philippines.* Manila, National Museum Monograph 1.

Glover, I.C. (1971) Prehistoric research in Timor, in *Aboriginal Man and Environment in Australia,* Mulvaney, D.J. and Golson, J. (eds), Canberra, 158-81.

Glover, I.C. (1972) Settlements and mobility among the hunter-gatherers of south-east Asia, in *Man, Settlement and Urbanism,* Ucko, P., Tringham, R. and Dimbleby, G. (eds), London, 157-64.

Golson, J. (1971) The dog in Australian and Asian prehistory. Paper delivered to Far Eastern Prehistory Association Symposium, 28th International Congress of Orientalists, January 1971, Canberra (unpublished).

Golson, J. (1972) Both sides of the Wallace Line: New Guinea, Australia, Island Melanesia and Asian Prehistory, in *Early Chinese Art and its Possible Influence in the Pacific Basin,* Barnard, N. (ed.), New York, 533-95.

Gorman, C. (1969) Hoabinhian: a pebble-tool complex with early plant association in South-East Asia. *Science* 163, 671-3.

Gorman, C. (1971) The Hoabinhian and after: subsistence patterns in South-East Asia during the late Pleistocene and early Recent periods. *World Archaeology,* 2 (3), 300-20.

Harrisson, T. (1959) New archaeological and ethnological results from Niah Caves, Sarawak. *Man* 59, 1-8.

Harrisson, T. (1967) Niah Caves: progress report to 1967. *Sarawak Museum Journal,* 15, 95-6.

Heekeren, H.R. van (1957) *The Stone Age of Indonesia.* s'-Gravenhage, M. Nijhoff.

Heine Geldern, R. (1932) Urheimat und früheste Wanderungen der Austronesier. *Anthropos,* 27, 543-619.

Higham, C.F.W. (1972) Initial model formulation in *Terra Incognita*, in *Models in Archaeology*, Clarke, D.L. (ed.), London (forthcoming).

Hooijer, D.A. (1961-2) Palaeontology of hominid deposits in Asia. *Pleistocene Dating and Man, Advancement of Science*, 18, 485-9.

Hooijer, D.A. (1970) Pleistocene South-East Asiatic pygmy Stegodonts. *Nature*, 225 (5231), 474-5.

Hoop, A.N.J. Th. á Th. van der (1940) A prehistoric site near Lake Kerinchi, Sumatra, in *Proceedings 3rd Congress of Prehistorians of the Far East, Singapore 1938*, Chasen, F.N. and Tweedie, M.W.F. (eds), Singapore, 200-4.

Jennings, J. (1971) Sea level changes and land links, in *Aboriginal Man and Environment in Australia*, Mulvaney, D.J. and Golson, J. (eds), Canberra, 1-13.

Koenigswald, G.H.R. von (1936) Early Palaeolithic stone implements from Java. *Bulletin of the Raffles Museum, Singapore* (Ser. B), 1, 52-60.

Mansuy, H. (1925) Contribution à l'étude de la préhistoire de l'Indochine V: Nouvelles découvertes dans les cavernes du massif calcaire de Bac-Son (Tonkin). *Mémoire du Service Géologique de l'Indochine*, 12 (1), Hanoi.

Maringer, I. and Verhoeven, Th. (1970) Die Steinartefakte aus der Stegodon-Fossilschicht von Mengeruda auf Flores, Indonesien. *Anthropos*, 65, 229-47.

Maringer, I. and Verhoeven, Th. (1970) Die Oberflächenfunde aus dem Fossilgebiet von Mengeruda und Olabula auf Flores, Indonesien. *Anthropos*, 65, 530-46.

Maringer, I. and Verhoeven, Th. (1970) Note on some stone artifacts in the National Archaeological Institute of Indonesia at Djakarta, collected from the Stegodon-fossil bed at Boaleza in Flores. *Anthropos*, 65, 638-9.

Mathews, I. (1964) The Hoabinhian in South-East Asia and elsewhere. Ph.D. Thesis, Australian National University, Canberra (unpublished).

Moore, D.R. (1970) Results of an archaeological survey of the Hunter River Valley, N.S.W. Part 1: The Bondaian Industry of the Upper Hunter and Goulburn River Valleys. *Records of the Australian Museum*, 28, (2), 25-64.

Mourer, T. and Mourer, C. (1970) The Prehistoric industry of Laang Spean, province of Battambang, Cambodia. *Archaeology and Physical Anthropology in Oceania*, 5 (2), 128-46.

Movius, H.L. Jr. (1943) The Stone Age of Burma. *Research on Early Man in Burma* Part II, *Transactions of the American Philosophical Society* (n.s.), 32 (3): 341-94.

Movius, H.J. Jr. (1944) Early Man and Pleistocene stratigraphy in Southern and Eastern Asia. *Papers of the Peabody Museum*, 19, (3).

Mulvaney, D.J. (1971) Archaeology in Sulawesi, Indonesia. *Antiquity*, 45, 144.

Mulvaney, D.J. and Soejono, R.P. (1970) Archaeology in Sulawesi, Indonesia. *Antiquity*, 45, 26-33.

Murty, M.L.K. (1968) Blade and burin industries near Renigunta on the south-east coast of India. *Proc. Prehistoric Society* (n.s.) 34, 83-101.

Stein Callenfels, P.V. van (1936) The Melanesoid civilizations of Eastern Asia. *Bulletin of the Raffles Museum, Singapore* (Ser. B) 1, 45-51.

Sarasin, P. and F. (1905) *Versuch einen Anthropologie der Insel Celebes: Die Toala-Höhlen von Lamontjong*. Wiesbaden.

Solheim, W.G. (1967) South-East Asia and the West. *Science*, 157, 896-902.

Solheim, W.G. (1969) Reworking South-East Asian prehistory. *Paideuma*, 15, 125-39.

Tweedie, M.W.F. (1965) *Prehistoric Malaya* (3rd. ed.), Singapore.

White, C. (1971) Man and environment in Arnhem Land, in *Aboriginal Man and Environment in Australia*, Mulvaney, D.J. and Golson, J. (eds), Canberra, 141-57.

White, J.P. (1967) Taim bilong bipo. Ph.D. Thesis, Australian National University (unpublished).

White, J.P. (1972) New Guinea: the first phase in Oceanic settlement, in *Studies in Oceanic Culture History*, 2. *Pacific Anthropological Records*, 12, Green, R. and Kelly, M. (eds), Hawaii, 45-52.

6

Land Use and ecological factors in prehistoric North-West India

L.S. LESHNIK

By the early centuries of the second millennium B.C., the patterns of land use today obtaining in North-Western India had already been established. What is remarkable about them is at once their diversity and their efficient adaption to the several ecological zones. The two major exploitative modes are nomadic pastoralism and sedentary agriculture, and again within these groups, important variants are present. In the Indus Valley, there are settlements of the well-known Harappa culture, an archaic State whose economic foundations rested upon a base of hydraulic farming. To the west of the Indus system, in the now uninviting, arid uplands of Baluchistan, and eastward, beyond the Rajasthan desert in peninsular India, there existed numerous small farming communities. These were largely self-sufficient and independent of the neighbouring urban civilization. The available evidence suggests that these small farming communities were culturally as different from one another as the exploitative techniques upon which they depended.

In Baluchistan, the scanty rainfall alone was scarcely sufficient to support any but the hardiest weeds, not to speak of field crops. Most of the rivers which mark the map of Baluchistan are hardly worthy of the name, for they flow only during brief periods when they carry the waters of the melting snows, and they are nowhere suited for direct irrigational use. Instead a kind of basin-terracing system was employed, which captured large deposits of moist, fertile silt washed down the streams in spring, and providing an excellent, nutritious soil for sowing grain crops. Sometimes, massive boulder walls (*garbar bunds*) were thrown across the mouth of a gorge, to retain the waters themselves. It was in the nature of this system that only spring crops, mainly wheat could be sown. Such sowing however, often must have been late, arising from the necessity of awaiting a sufficiently deep deposition of silt, with the consequence that productivity was low.

The rainfall in peninsular India, about 20-25 inches yearly and unfavourably distributed, was also in itself inadequate for reliable crop production. The rivers of the Malwa and Deccan plateaus rise not on spring snow water, but in the hot season, when the monsoon rains swell them. But because so much aggradation of their beds has taken place, they too are useless for irrigation in palaeo-technic farming systems, that is, farming systems which depend upon mechanical energy rather that that provided by combustible fuels (i.e. neo-technic). What made settled agriculture possible in these regions was the presence of a particularly moisture-retentive soil that admirably suited the conditions of early farming.

In addition to these three farming systems, there existed in the Valley of Kashmir small and seemingly very isolated communities that depended for the most part upon hunting, but perhaps some cultivation as well, as suggested by underground storage pits. This so-called Kashmir Neolithic with certain Central Asian affinities is as yet very little known. Contemporary with these grain producing societies were nomadic cattle, sheep and goat herders who traversed the uplands of Baluchistan and the unarable regions of the Indus Valley. Similar, though perhaps more primitive, pastoralists likewise left traces of their presence — typically in the form of microlithis — in peninsular India (Leshnik, 1968*a*: 309ff.). Considering that animal herders everywhere live in symbiotic relationship with agriculturalists, it is to be expected that the remains of their encampments should be found scattered among settled communities as is the case in the peninsula. At the periphery of the cultivated and grazing areas, at least in Rajasthan and Central India, there lived societies not yet converted to food production. Such hunters and gatherers, also represented by microlithic tools, have their cultural descendants in such peoples as the modern Bhil.

Of these societies, two assume a particular significance. The inherent interest of the Indus civilization needs no emphasis. It is not only the earliest 'Hochkultur', 'high culture' in South Asia, but beyond that its study has and will continue to contribute much to our understanding of the rise of civilization in general. The more humble peninsular communities have by contrast commanded much less attention and so far as regional cultural history is concerned, this is unfortunate. Unlike the spectacular Indus civilization, there is a demonstrable temporal continuity of the early agricultural settlements, so that one can discern a gradual evolution from a society of primitive cultivators to one of rural participants in the classical civilization of India. Both of these societies were agrarian, and any understanding that we hope to gain about them will be very patchy in the absence of knowledge of their farming systems. Indeed, it is just this area where our picture of the Indus civilization is most incomplete. Nearly half a century ago, it was determined that the Harappans made use of wheat, barley, sesame, cotton and (wild?) dates, and had domestic sheep, goats, cattle, fowl and perhaps pigs. More recently, rice has been found at one or two late Indus settlements in Gujarat but otherwise there is no direct evidence for the character of the Indus farming system (Wheeler 1968: 84f.). We can however attempt to reconstruct this system at least in its outlines, since it, like all agricultural systems, must have been the result of interactions between: environmental, operational and social-economic factors. Other lines of evidence have fortunately provided a good deal of information about this last, while the relevant environmental factors have on the whole remained constant with such changes as have occured being identifiable so that their effects upon the system can be considered. For information regarding the operation factors, we shall have recourse to two models.

The one derives from ancient Mesopotamia, and is particularly well suited to our study since there are many important similarities between the Indus area and its western neighbour. Moreover, just these problems which arise in the study of Indus agriculture have been considered for Mesopotamia so ably by R. Adams and others in recent years (Adams 1965, 1966, 1967). The city of Mohenjo-daro of course was not just a copy of Ur — there are equally important differences — but none the less there is much to be learned from the latter. The Mesopotamian case however rests upon a far better class of evidence than can ever be hoped for in the Indus Valley. Essentially, it consists of:

1. *Textual evidence.* The cuneiform tablets are a mine of information that has not yet begun to be exhausted. By contrast, the inscriptions of the Indus civilization are not only undeciphered but so brief that their information value can only be very limited. If temple or other lengthy administrative accounts of agricultural operations ever existed as in Mesopotamia, Indus examples are likely to have been written on palm leaves and are now lost forever.

2. *Pictorial evidence.* The kind of information about daily life shown occasionally on cylinder seals is lacking in the Indus Valley. Evidently the Indus seal-cutters were concerned only with ritual scenes centering upon certain animals. There is for example nothing to compare with a cylinder seal which unambiguously depicts a plough with an attached seed-drill. However, a design scratched on a potsherd from Mohenjo-daro probably depicts a *shaduf* or beam-lift, used to raise water, and there are several terracotta models of bullock carts. Both are still in use today in India, and were, moreover, part of

the ancient Mesopotamian scene as well.

3. *Topographical evidence.*   In Mesopotamia, ancient canals and settlements along them have been identified, making possible the close analysis of settlement and land use patterns for various periods (Adams, 1965). The present Indus hydrography hardly holds out much promise in this regard, for traces of ancient irrigation canals, still partially visible in the last century are now wholly erased. The sole exception seems to be in the South Punjab where Sir Aurel Stein observed a linear alignment of Harappan settlements along the course of a canal traversing Bahawalpur and Bikaner districts (Field, 1959: 177).

The Indus river is notoriously vagrant. 'Nothing, indeed, can be more misleading in connection with such a river . . . than to base arguments for particular identifications on the hydrographical circumstances of the present day; for it may be regarded as almost absolutely certain that hardly any channel now carrying water was in existence in . . . distant times . . .' (Haig, 1887: 19). As a result, villages shifted many times and this vastly complicates the study of settlement patterns (Fairservis, 1961: 15ff.), especially in the absence of a really tight ceramic sequence.

Because the Mesopotamian agricultural system is better known than that of the Indus civilization, it serves as a useful model. But it can provide no more than a broad back-drop, illustrating the relation of agriculture to other aspects of culture in an archaic oriental State. A closer approximation of Indus land-use patterns and agriculture can be gained by examining the practices current in Sind and the Punjab until the early decades of this century (Aitken, 1907; Fagan, 1900; Punjab Government, 1884; Smith, 1919). At that time, the completion of large scale irrigation works by the British Government, and the accompanying advent of neo-technic cultivation methods marked an irreversible departure from the traditional farming system. The essential continuity over six millennia of agricultural practices in Mesopotamia has been demonstrated (Adams, 1965) and India, where rural conservativism is legendary, presents a parallel example.

The major limiting parameter of any kind of cultivation, namely the climate, can be held constant for the Indus Valley. Until quite recently, most authors writing about the Harappan civilization have assumed just the contrary, arguing for a formerly wetter climatic regime. A careful re-examination of all the evidence by Raikes and Dyson (1961) and others (Bryson and Baerreis, 1967) has however shown such an assumption to be unnecessary and indeed improbable. Hence, the cultivator's main concern of obtaining sufficient moisture at the proper time for his crops in this semi-arid region remains unchanged. Millennia of uninterrupted cultivation and grazing together with deforestation particularly in the Upper Punjab and in Western Sind have resulted in depleted fertility and the creation of new waste lands and open, sandy patches. Harappa itself provides a startling illustration of this. The very area which once provided for an urban population of perhaps 25,000 persons is now hopelessly sterile over an expanse of 1000 acres. Although such modifications of the soil's potential have certainly increased the difficulty of farming, they are not likely to have altered the system itself. On the contrary, the 'present' (i.e. before 1900 and to be understood in this sense henceforth) practices, are not well adapted to these modified conditions, but reflect instead the usages of an older tradition. Apparently, soil conservation and rejuvenation were only minimally attended to by the cultivators of the last century. True, crop rotation, usually with a wheat-cotton-wheat alternation was routinely done, and pulses were often inter-cropped with wheat. But manuring was rare, fallowing neglected and anti-erosion measures hardly known. And while the cultivator devoted much attention to securing water for his fields, he was much less concerned with adequate drainage (Aitken, 1907: 240). Consequently, alkaline deposits in the root zone of the plants reduced fertility or in extreme cases, as near Harappa, rendered the soil altogether sterile (Wace and Phillips, 1935: 122).

So far as the actual implements of cultivation are concerned, those employed today can all reasonably be assigned an antiquity stretching back to Harappan times. For tillage, the plough and harrow are used, a seed-drill sometimes facilitates sowing, weeding is done with a hoe, harvesting with a sickle, threshing requires only a team of bullocks to stamp out the grains, and winnowing is done with the aid of a wooden stool and a plaited basket. The central implement in this simple inventory is of course the plough, and the question of its presence in the Harappan civilization has raised some doubts. Fortunately, the splendid discovery of a field near Kalibangan marked unambiguously by furrows, and of pre-Harappan date has definitely decided the matter. (Thapar, this volume, 89). Such evidence lends strong support to the view of Haudricourt and Delamarre (1955: 85) that '... une même civilisation agricole s'étendait vraisemblement dans toute la zone iranienne, Inde occidentale compris . . . avant l'arrivée des Aryens.' Following this line of reasoning still further, we would also postulate the Harappan use of the seed-drill. (The plough with seed-drill attached, shown on the Akkadian cylinder seal (Handricourt and Delamarre, 1955: 62) could easily pass as an illustration of the present-day Punjabi implements.)
Neither the external climatic conditions nor the implements of

agriculture have changed significantly over the last four thousand years. Nor, seemingly, have agricultural practices in regard to soil conservation. Yet there is one post-Harappan innovation which must have modified the homeostasis of the older system in an important way. Perhaps sometime towards the beginning of this era, a new grain crop, *jowar (sorghum vulgare)* was introduced into India. Hitherto the important grains had everywhere been wheat and barley and both of them are spring, or *rabi* crops. *Jowar,* a hardy plant which can be grown on lesser soils than wheat, tolerates heat well, and is modest in its moisture requirement, is instead an autumnal *(kharif)* crop. Its introduction meant a shift of emphasis in the farming pattern from *rabi* to *kharif* cultivation. But beyond that, this shift involved a transfer from *extensive* to *intensive* agriculture. The presence of an easily grown *kharif* grain crop enabled the farmer to take two harvests yearly, rather than a single one, with a resultant increase in production per unit of land. This, however, was certainly a post-Harappan development and must be discounted when using present-day practices as a model.

Like its simpler neighbours, the settlement sites of the Indus civilization are all located in a semi-arid climatic region. There is no dispute about the idea that Harappan agriculture was dependent upon artificial irrigation, but there is a difference of scholarly opinion about the nature of this arrangement, particularly whether it was perennial or seasonal. In part these differences are merely semantic since not all writers on the subject hold the same notion as to what exactly constitutes perennial irrigation. Those authorities whose concern is with irrigation systems in general, and for whom the Harappan is only one example, suppose irrigation to have been perennial (Drower, 1958: Forbes, 1965: 12). This conclusion seems to rest primarily on a positive assessment of the organizational potential of the Harappan State. On the other hand, authors with special knowledge of the Indus Valley are agreed in the view that Harappan irrigation was seasonal, but little attention has been given to the detailed techniques involved (Fairservis, 1967: 24f.; Johnson, 1971: 5; Lambrick, 1964: 75; Possehl, 1967: 32; Raikes and Dyson, 1961: 247f.; Spate, 1967: 468f.).

The two types of irrigation commonly practised in the Indus Valley are (*a*) wells, and (*b*) gravity flow (inundation and perennial canals). Far from being mutually exclusive these types must be considered as being largely complementary. Their relative importance is however not equal, for inundation irrigation dominates and this is frequently supplemented by the use of wells. (In 1893, some one million acres in the Indus system were being irrigated in this fashion [Buckley, 1893: 10].) Artificial canals (both seasonal and perennial) from which water is taken by means of the *shaduf* and Persian wheel are next in importance, while a third method, (*c*) storage irrigation, is rare. A strict distinction between perennial and inundation canals is not possible, since some water courses may indeed flow all the year, but their discharge becomes so small at the dry season as to be practically negligible. Those few canals of the Indus system which are perennial in this sense are cut to an extra depth and can receive water even when the main river is low, but their real purpose is to increase the discharge during the inundation (Buckley, 1893: 8).

The present agricultural systems of Sind and the Punjab, both dependent upon irrigation, are in most respects quite comparable while differing in some ways as a function of topography. Prior to the great irrigation projects, it is possible to recognize four major land-use zones in both districts (Aitken, 1907: Punjab Government, 1884; Fairservis, 1967) (fig. 6.1):

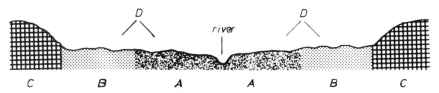

Figure 6.1 Land-use of zones of the Punjab.

A. Cultivated areas, parallel and close to the rivers (*bet* land), and

B. Cultivated areas farther away from the rivers. These are low-lying areas, collectively called *kadir.*

C. Uplands used chiefly for grazing and the cultivation of some rain-fed crops. In the Punjab, this Zone is called *bhangar.*

D. Depressions and marshes.

The land of Zone A clearly benefits most directly from seasonal floods and the rich deposits of alluvial soil they bring. This is the most valuable land and is therefore given over mainly to the favoured crop, wheat. In regard to the *bet* land in Sind, H.T. Lambrick, whose long residence in Sind entitles him to speak authoritatively on its ecology, has expressed the opinion that the Harappans avoided the riverine tracts (1964: 75). They were, he supposes, unable to cope with the flood waters, and therefore laid out their fields in Zone B, with the river area remaining a forested strip. Yet this assumption seems unnecessary, for not only would the most fertile tracts thus be lost to cultivation, (see Marshall, 1931: 1) but further, the techniques of *sailaba* (inundation) irrigation practised today are no more complex than those which would certainly have been available to the

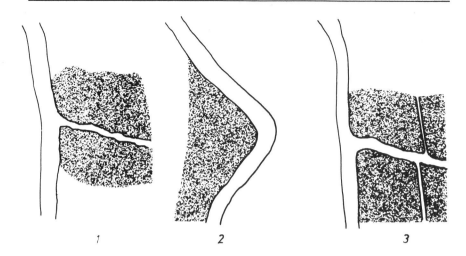

1   2   3

Figure 6.2 Zones of flow irrigation.

Harappans (Fagan, 1900, 123f. Wace and Phillips 1935, 7f.). They depend upon the judicious positioning of the fields with two locations being particularly advantageous in Zone A (fig. 6.2). The first (*budh*) would be along the numerous inlets and creeks which lead off the main rivers (fig. 6.2, 1). The dry beds lying above the cold weather level of the main river are filled during the floods (which reach a high level in mid-August-September). When the rivers fall (subsidence begins towards the end of October, and a low-water level is reached in January) these short arms are transformed into lakes, sometimes with the aid of weirs at the take-off. But before that, they frequently spill over and flood the adjacent, low-lying land. Thereafter, the remaining water is used for irrigation through lifting devices. Land that lies at the apex of a sharp bend in the river (*dhak*) requires even less attention. If the level of the adjacent ground is suitable, the high river jumps its banks and spills for many miles down-stream (fig. 6.2, 2).

Next, there is the *sailaba* technique applied to the inland Zone B of the Punjab. This is an extension of the *budh* system, using natural channels but with artificial courses (*chhar*) leading off from them (fig. 6.2, 3). Where possible, the water surface is kept above ground level for at least a few miles beyond the head, although the alignment of the canals is influenced more by the needs of the individual villages than topography. Hence their courses are tortuous, like the river itself (Buckley, 1893: 21). On these canals, too, lifts are used to bring the water onto the fields. The devices now employed are the *shaduf* and Persian wheel, but only the former can be dated to the Harappan period. (Leshnik, 1968*b*: 917). The canals in Sind are generally wider than those of the Punjab and also differ from them in being aligned obliquely with the river, to take advantage of the fall of the plains. These courses are entirely seasonal and carry almost no water in the winter months. But during the flood season the low river banks are easily topped by the swollen waters, making the use of lifting machines less common than in the Punjab.

In Zones A in Sind and the Punjab and in Zone B of the Punjab, wells are additionally used to irrigate fields but there are zonal differences in their function and construction. The wells of the riverine tracts serve mainly in time of drought, for even though the floods may fail, the water table in the vicinity of the river often remains high enough to be readily accessible. When well irrigation becomes necessary here, the area of land under cultivation is considerably reduced, but production is still possible. In this Zone, the wells are hardly more than hollows scooped out of the earth and seldom lined. Their location makes damage by flooding virtually certain and it would be uneconomic to invest in more permanent constructions. The water is raised by the *shaduf* and after one or two years of use, the walls are allowed to collapse. Where wells are used in the outer area, Zone B, they are more often the single source of irrigational water in contrast to the supplemental character of the wells along the river. Being farther distant, the wells of Zone B are deeper. These wells are intended to be permanent, and are frequently lined with bricks. Water is raised by the *mhote*, in which bullocks (usually a pair) draw a bucket from the well while walking down a ramp. The principle is simple but its application by the Harappans must remain conjecture.

The use of wells in the outer area results in a kind of infield-outfield system. Land directly adjoining the well is the best watered and best cared for and is sown with wheat. Beyond the limit where water can easily be brought, there is a tendency to use the land for lesser crops. Often two crops are taken on the well-irrigated (*kada*) lands, and then the *kharif* crops are placed as close to the well as possible in order to economize on both labour and water in the summer. The amount of energy required to work *kada* land is greater than that in Zone A for the bullocks are needed to draw water at just the time when they should be ploughing and the limited availability of such traction power restricts the cultivable land area (Wace and Phillips, 1935: 125). Moreover, these wells are affected by the level of the flood waters too, many of them operating only when the water-table is sufficiently high. In years of drought, they and the canals may remain dry, resulting in an endemic instability for this zone.

Zone C in the Punjab comprises the uplands which separate the flood plains of two rivers. This *bhangar* land, in itself not infertile, is difficult to cultivate since it receives no flood water and the sub-surface water is at a depth of some sixty feet or more. None the less, on some tracts, rain-fed (*barani*) barley is raised, but the amount is minimal. Primarily, the grass-covered *bhangar* land provides excellent grazing for the herds of nomadic pastoralists. Additional areas of pasture can be found in unarable parts of the irrigated areas although these are less often used by specialist herders than by the agriculturalists for their own animals (which are used for work rather than food purposes). This is especially so in Zone A where the uncultivated patches carry a thick growth of rich grass. On sandy areas along the river a reed plant used for preparing ropes and baskets grows (Punjab Government, 1884: 18), and in both Zones A and B in the Punjab, undrained marshes are to be found, though here they lack the economic significance they have in Sind. Finally, it should be emphasized that the areas here called Zones A, B and D are defined in relation to the each other and the position of the river. When the river shifts, the Zones may be altered.

Very few of the *kharif* crops are grown in Zone A since this land is under water during most of the summer growing season (cf. Table 6.1). Even rice, in any case not a very popular crop with the Punjabis, is not generally sown in this Zone along the river, since it would then make the land unfit for wheat. *Bajra*, the other major *rabi* crop is sown on the less fertile tracts of Zone A, while the *kharif* cotton crop is confined to the adequately drained outer areas. Harappan cotton too, must have been grown on such areas, and in no way competed with grains for land. As Table 6.1 also shows, the *rabi* grain crops are sometimes sown with a drill instead of broadcast (in order to deposit them in the deeper, moisture-retentive layers), and this may well date back to Harappan times (the annual agricultural cycle is shown in Table 6.2). In Sind, Zone C land disappears after the five northern rivers merge into the single stream of the Indus. But good grazing here is afforded in the nearby Western Hills, which substitute for the *bhangar* lands. A special feature of Sind are the large marsh areas, Zone D. These low-lying regions often retain much water after the river floods subside and they provide suitable conditions for the cultivation of rice. Lake Manchhar is one such area, which in a good year extends over some 200 square miles, but then may shrink to less than a tenth of this size in time of drought (Smith, 1919: 71, 14). In Harappan times, the wild life and fish resources of such swamps may have been exploited, but there is thus far no evidence that rice or any other *kharif* grain crop was actually cultivated in the Indus Valley (Fairservis, 1967).

Not the least among the many puzzles thrown up by the Indus civilization concerns its temporal continuity. The half millennium or

Table 6.1

CROP	LAND CLASS				MANURED?	SOWN		
	CANAL IRRIGATION	WELL IRRIGATION	FLOOD IRRIGATION (SAILABA)	RAIN IRRIGATION (BARANI)		BROADCAST	DRILL	TRANSPLANT
KHARIF:								
RICE	X	–	X	–	never	X	X	X
SESAMUM	X	–	–	–	never	X	–	
COTTON	X	X	–	–	sometimes	X	–	
RABI:								
WHEAT	–	X	X	rare	sometimes	X	X	
BARLEY	–	X	X	rare	sometimes	X	X	
PULSES	–	–	X	–	never	X	–	

Source: Punjab Government 1884, 106

Table 6.2

RIVER CONDITION	CROP SEASON	MONTHS	PLOUGHING	SOWN	HARVEST
LOW		MID-MARCH MID-APRIL	–	–	BARLEY, PULSES, VEGETABLES
RISE		MID-APRIL MID-MAY	X*	COTTON, RICE, MELONS	WHEAT, GOURDS, PULSES
		MID-MAY MID-JUNE	X	COTTON, RICE (BROADCAST)	GOURDS, ROWAN
	KHARIF	MID-JUNE MID-JULY	X	RICE (BROADCAST) SORGHUM, BAJRA	–
		MID-JULY MID-AUGUST	WHEAT, BARLEY	MAIZE, RICE, (BROADCAST), SORGHUM, SESAMUM, MILLET	
HIGH		MID-AUGUST MID-SEPTEMBER	WHEAT, BARLEY	PULSES	ROWAN
		MID-SEPTEMBER MID-OCTOBER	X	VEGETABLES, PULSES,	COTTON, RICE, MAIZE
		MID-OCTOBER MID-NOVEMBER	X	WHEAT, BARLEY, VEGETABLES	RICE, COTTON, MILLET, MAIZE, SORGHUM, PULSES
SUBSI-DENCE	RABI	MID-NOVEMBER MID-DECEMBER	X	WHEAT, BARLEY	SORGHUM, PULSES, COTTON
		MID-DECEMBER MID-JANUARY	COTTON	–	COTTON
LOWEST		MID-JANUARY MID-FEBRUARY	COTTON	–	ROOTS (TURNIPS)
LOW		MID-FEBRUARY MID-MARCH	–	MELONS, VEGETABLES	ROOTS

*represents ploughing for crop shown after

Source: Punjab Government 1889, 88

more in which Harappa existed represents a surprising stability which stands out in contrast to the vagrancy of the rivers, whose torrential waters can overnight destroy fields and cut new channels. (There are only three fixed points of the Indus itself, at Sukh, Jhirk and Kotri.) Such shifts can have a great, if transitory effect on agriculture as well as settlement patterns. It has for example been recorded that *sailaba* cultivation increased nearly twofold (from 82,412 to 156,585 acres) between 1856 and 1874, as a result of a westward movement of the Sutlej, and a similarly eventful shift of the Ravi is noted for 1851 (Punjab Government, 1884: 96). But heavy flooding is only one aspect of this unreliable river regime. The other is drought, though it is the less frequent occurence. In Sind and the Eastern Punjab, nearly one in four years has an abnormal quantity of water in the rivers (e.g. the number of flood and drought years between 1875 and 1950 was respectively 11 and 8 (Raghavan, 1961: 6)). The common practice of raising extensive embankments of earth along the river banks affords the cultivator some protection from excessive flooding, but the amount of labour involved is great. It is clear that the Harappans also attempted to control the rivers in this fashion, for we have the evidence of brick built flood walls at several urban sites. Droughts, a too early subsidence or a late rise of the river, even transient vagrancies on the other hand can to some extent be countered by reliance upon wells and this would tend to give particular importance to Zone A lands. Only they could be depended upon to some extent for continued productivity when the river waters are low. With such simple measures it becomes possible to somewhat stabilize the conditions of agriculture, and in the case of the cities, to secure a lengthy period of continued settlement at the same site. Extensive silt deposits at various levels of the urban areas however show that the control of floods was at best only partially successful. This ultimate helplessness in the face of natural forces deprived the Harappans of all the benefits of a system of perennial irrigation, despite their advanced engineering skill and undoubted organizational ability. Perennial irrigation is dependent upon a series of permanent headworks which regulate the flow of water. But as the British discovered for themselves, the construction of locks, sluice-gates and weirs in the Indus system is economically not feasible. One canal which they built moved three times in twelve years, and needed new connections each time at 'enormous cost' (Wace and Phillips, 1935: 266). And then, what the quantity of water would not allow, the velocity would not tolerate, for even strong weirs in established channels are subject to frequent breaching.

The Harappans were therefore restricted to practising seasonal irrigation, with all its attendant risks. It also seems possible to conclude that Harappan agriculture was *intensive* in some aspects, and *extensive* in others. To the extent that double-cropping, manuring, fallowing and other principles of conservation were not normal concerns, unit productivity of land would have been low. The food necessary to maintain a large urban and rural population was necessarily raised over large areas,* with little attention to efficient land management. This is entirely possible in circumstances where there is no special pressure on land, as might be inferred from Lambrick's estimate of 10 persons per square mile in Harappan Sind (1964: 62). The limitation on the area cultivated is then determined by such factors as the size of the co-operating social unit, the availability of water and of animal power. On the other hand, those tracts which are cultivated with the aid of wells, the *kada* lands, represent productive techniques which are more nearly intensive. (For Mesopotamia, a transition from extensive to intensive agriculture is accompanied by increasing social stratification (Adams, 1966: 35ff.) but it seems premature to attempt any similar reconstruction for the Harappan civilization.)

The urban character of the Harappan settlements, and more particularly the large granaries found at several sites, point to a surplus production of food grains. But we are altogether ignorant of the political demands and legal obligations which convinced the peasant of the need to work for others. Probably the effective sanctions were ultimately vested in members of a theocracy. The major co-operative tasks in this system of agriculture were only two: the throwing up of embankments, and the clearance of silt from the canals such as there were. If it is correct that Zone A (i.e. the area of direct flooding) was the more important, and that in any case the canals were short, as Fairservis suggests (1967: 28), then both of these tasks required only a village level of organization. This in turn implies that the Harappan State was more directly involved with the collection and perhaps distribution of surplus grain than with its production. In the absence of *kharif* cropping and mixed farming, the Harappan agricultural system required seasonal spurts of activity. During the hot months, the cultivator was relieved of working on the fields and it is possible that he then provided corvée labour for the completion of large building tasks such as flood walls etc. in the cities, as did his Mesopotamian counterpart.

---

* Fairservis (1961: 17) has arrived at the same conclusion, but for somewhat different reasons. He emphasizes the modern necessity of adequate drainage provisions in Sind and projects this backward to Harappan times. But I have it on the authority of Sir Joseph Hutchinson that only with the seepage caused by modern canalization did this become a problem in the area.

On the eastern side of the Aravalli Mountains, beyond the Rajasthan desert, the agricultural system of the so-called Neolithic-Chalcolithic communities of Malwa and the Deccan was quite different. None of the peninsular rivers lend themselves for irrigational use in palaeo-technic systems. Their beds are considerably lower than the surrounding fields, and the increment of water they receive at the time of the monsoon rains is not sufficient to make them top their banks. Yet except for certain coastal strips, the peninsula is a semi-arid region where the rainfall is seldom in excess of 25 inches annually and the little moisture that falls is unfavourably distributed. Agriculture here is entirely dependent upon dry-farming techniques. In addition to containing rich nutrients this soil has the excellent capacity to absorb and retain great amounts of water. It can be used, even abused continuously over long periods without its productivity being seriously affected, and is therefore eminently suitable for exploitation by primitive agricultural techniques (Raghavan, 1961: 36). It is no mere chance distribution when one finds all the early farming communities of the peninsula located in the Black Cotton Soil areas. Wheat and barley, here also the main crops of the period are cultivated in the winter months after the ground has been saturated by the monsoon rains. Evidence of rice, a *kharif* crop has indeed been found at one site, in Central India (Sankalia, 1962: 75) but it is altogether improbable that this grain could ever have had any real importance in the peninsula, given the scarcity of water. (Today, the small amount of rice that is grown in the region is sown broadcast in basins set in seasonal streams by a few industrious families. Such cultivation is done on an irregular basis and this could hardly have been otherwise in former times.)

There is some evidence for the presence of domestic cattle, pigs, sheep and goats but as with the Harappans, animal husbandry was more peripheral than integral to the farming system, as the paucity of skeletal remains shows. There are, moreover, no indications that animal power was used for traction, and while this lack of information still leaves open the possibility that bullock carts were used, there are reasons to suppose that the plough was *not*. The best of these reasons is that it was not really necessary. In the summer time, when the Black Cotton Soil looses its moisture, it shrinks greatly, to produce deep, gaping cracks admitting sunshine and air in abundance. Sufficient aeration is achieved without artificial intervention, and this phenomenon has given rise to the very appropriate aphorism that 'the Black Cotton Soil ploughs itself'. Then too, the small size and low density of the settlements (about 200 inhabitants at a site such as Navda Toli) (Sankalia, 1962: 73) argues for a low level of productivity such as would be achieved by quite simple techniques of cultivation.

In contrast with the Harappan peasant, who was a member of a larger, stratified society, and had among other things, the obligation to produce a surplus, the Black Cotton Soil cultivator belonged to a simpler folk society. In such a society, the goal, and probably limit of agricultural production was the satisfaction of communal needs, which were themselves moderate. We are dealing here, it would appear, with subsistence-level agriculture. Certainly, there was a degree of inter-change among the various peninsular settlements, but this was not hierarchically ordered. Each community remained essentially independent, with a homogenous population and only a slight division of labour. (House-plans suggest that the actual co-habiting units were nuclear families, but the possibility of larger groupings of hutments into compounds needs to be examined.) At this level of society, the organizing principle is kinship rather than class, as at Harappa.

Sometime in the middle of the Harappan period in the Indus Valley there was a population expansion to the south. Why this should have happened is not fully explained, but the region in which the new settlements were founded was a quite deliberate choice. The area of Cutch has only recently turned into the undrained, saline waste it is today. In the time of Alexander the Great, and earlier, it was still an inland sea, fed by a branch of the Indus River. Thus the extension of settlement into the Kathiawar Peninsula represents a natural seeking out of familiar environmental conditions just as earlier there had been an expansion from Sind into the Punjab. The Harappan in fact, expanded to the limits of its ecological zone, as already noticed by Fairservis (1967). There exist in Kathiawar considerable tracts of Black Cotton Soil as well, and on them were settlements of the peninsular communities. In this region, and so far. as can now be seen, only here, the two neighbouring cultures came into direct physical contact. Both found the particular kind of environment to which their agricultural systems were adapted. True, the Harappans could no longer rely upon flow irrigation, since the Kathiawar Rivers ill-lend themselves to such use. But an alternative of storage irrigation remained open to them, and as the evidence from Lothal indicates, this was availed of. At Harappan Lothal we have an excellently preserved very large basin, which was supplied with water by a channel taking-off from a nearby river. *Shadufs* brought the stored water into small irrigational channels which led onto the fields, where at least in some places, wells were also located (Leshnik, 1968*b*).

The sites of the Indus Valley come to an enigmatic end; that is, they fade out of the picture without leaving any readily recognizable mark on the successor cultures. In Kathiawar, the Harappan decline takes on a different form, as it involves a mingling with the simpler farming cultures, a process which could only have come about with the break-up of the Harappan social form. In their expansion, important as it was, environment did not represent the sole limiting parameter. Harappan socio-economic organization was predicated upon the production of a grain-surplus, and their agricultural system was geared to this end. Yet a surplus could not be produced east of the Aravalli Range with the available farming techniques and therefore this area was not settled, and hardly influenced by the Harappans. There has always been a cultural watershed roughly demarcated by the Rajasthan desert: This was the eastern limit of the ancient Iranian *koine*, Alexander the Great proceeded no farther than the Indus River and still today the north-western borderlands of India belong more to the Islamic West than to Hindu India. The reasons for this are complex, and partly grounded in the necessarily different exploitative techniques peculiar to each side of this cultural divide. An analogy from ancient China seems to fit the circumstances of the Harappan period here quite nicely. Morton Fried has argued (1962) that the Chinese did not extend their settlements into the more primitive South because of differing cultural standards, and particularly because of the less efficient social organization they found there. The ancient Chinese polity was not a military State, as Harappa also was not, and conquest for its own sake was not an aim. In both cases, the agricultural system of the neighbouring peoples was based upon subsistence level production which could not satisfy the needs of the great States, therefore making an expansion in their direction pointless. Only when the Harappan decline was well advanced, as at the Kathiawar site of Rangpur, is a merging of the two cultures evident. Significantly enough, the character of the resultant hybrid culture appears closer to the small farming communities than to the Indus 'high culture'. Very soon, most of the typical Harappan elements, e.g. town planning, public buildings and structures, seals and writing disappear, and there is a retrogression to simple village life.

REFERENCES

Adams, R.McC. (1965) *Land behind Baghdad: A History of Settlement on the Diyala Plains.* Chicago.
Adams, R.McC. (1966) *The Evolution of Urban Society.* Chicago.
Adams, R.McC. (1971) Historic patterns of Mesopotamian irrigation agriculture, in *Papers for Special congress Seminars: A. Irrigation Civilizations, XXVIII* Congress of Orientalists, Canberra (mimeographed), 1-9.

Aitken, E.H. (compiler) (1907) *Gazetteer of the Province of Sind, Karachi.* Government of India Press.

Bryson, R.A. and Baerreis, D.A. (1967) Possibilities of major climatic modification and their implications: Northwest India, a case for study. in *Bull. of the American Meteorological Society*, Vol. 48, No. 3, March, 136-42.

Buckley, R.B. (1893) *Irrigation Works in India and Egypt*, London.

Drower, M.S. (1958) Water-supply, irrigation and agriculture, in *A History of Technology*, Vol. I, Singer, C., Holmyard, E.J. and Hall, A.R. (eds), Oxford, 520-7.

Fagan, P.J. (1900) *Gazetteer of the Montgomery Distric 1898-99* (revised ed.) Lahore, Civil and Military Gazette Press.

Fairservis, W.A., Jr. (1961) The Harappan Civilization — New Evidence and More Theory, in *American Museum Novitates No. 2055*, New York.

Fairservis, W.A., Jr. (1967) The origin, character, and decline of an early civilization, in *American Museum Novitates No. 2302*, New York.

Field, H. (1959) *An Anthropological Reconnaissance in West Pakistan, 1955.* Papers of the Peabody Museum of Archaeology and Ethnology, Vol. LII, Cambridge, Mass.

Forbes, R.J. (1965) *Studies in Ancient Technology*, Vol. II. Leiden.

Fried, M. (1962) Land tenure, geography and ecology in the contact of cultures, in *Readings in Cultural Geography, Wagner, P.L. and Mikesell, M.W. (eds)*, Chicago, 302-17.

Haig, M.R. (1887) *The Indus Delta Country, A Memoir.* London.

Haudricourt, A.G. and Delamarre, M.J.-B. (1955) *L'homme et la charrue à travers le monde* (5th ed.), Paris.

Johnson, B.L.C. (1971) Irrigation in West Pakistan, in *Papers for Special cCongress Seminars: A. Irrigation Civilizations*, XXVIII International Congress of Orientalists, Canberra.

Lambrick, H.T. (1964) *Sind. A General Introduction.* History of Sind Series, Vol. I, Hyderabad (Sind) Sindhi Adabi Board.

Leshnik, L.S. (1968a) Prehistoric Exploration in North Gujerat and parts of Rajasthan. *East and West*, n.s. Vol. 18, Nos. 3-4, 295-310.

Leshnik, L.S. (1968b) The Harappan 'port' at Lothal: another view. *American Anthropologist*, Vol. 70, No. 5, 911-22.

Marshall, J. (1931) *Mohenjo-daro and the Indus Civilization*, London.

Possehl, G.L. (1967) The Mohenjo-daro Floods: A Reply. *American Anthropologist*, Vol. 69, No. 1, 32-40.

Punjab Government (1884) *Gazetteer of the Montgomery District, 1883-84.* Lahore, Civil and Military Gazette Press.

Raghavan, D. (ed.) (1961) *Handbook of Agriculture.* New Delhi, Indian Council for Agricultural Research.

Raikes, R.L. and Dyson, R.H. (1961) The prehistoric climate of Baluchistan and the Indus Valley. *American Anthropologist*, Vol. 63, 265-81.

Sankalia, H.D. (1962) India, in *Courses Toward Urban Life*, Braidwood, R.J. and Wiley, G.R. (eds), Chicago, 60-83.

Smith, J.W. (1919) *Gazetteer of the Province of Sind B* Vol. IV, Larkana District, Bombay Government of India Press.

Spate, O.H.K. (1964) *India and Pakistan. A General and Regional Geography*, London.

Wace, F.B. and Phillips, F.C. (1935) *Punjab District Gazetteer*, Vol XVIII. A. Montgomery District (revised ed.) 1933 Part A. Lahore, Government Printing Press.

Wheeler, R.E.M. (1968) *The Indus Civilization* (3rd ed.) Cambridge.

7

New traits of the Indus civilization at Kalibangan: an appraisal

B.K. THAPAR, Archaeological Survey of India

It is nearly half a century since the remains of the Indus civilization were first brought to light, and India took its place of pride, along with Egypt and Mesopotamia, as a centre for the emergence of civilization in the ancient world. During this period, many sites belonging to this civilization have been excavated — and some of them on a large scale — with the result that *when* and *where* have now been broadly determined. And it may be averred that sizeable evidence is now available to know what Henri Frankfort would call the *form* of this civilization (Frankfort, 1961). This stage of knowledge, often giving an impression of jejuneness, is indeed not a very complacent one, for the *dynamics* of this civilization still remain to be fully ascertained. Viewed from this aspect, the recent assertion that the Indus civilization is the Cinderella of the ancient world (Bibby, 1970) seems to be meaningful.

While it is widely accepted that there is sufficient coherence in the various manifestations and in the *cultural style* of this civilization throughout its area of distribution, it is equally true that each of the excavated sites shows some features not present at the others. What do such phenomena imply? Do they exhibit certain characteristics, either of the technical or of the social order, which may help us to understand the dynamics of this civilization? The investigation is worth while, and the present paper attempts to review the evidence obtained from Kalibangan, situated some 310 km north-west of Delhi on the left bank of the now-dry bed of the river Ghaggar. The excavation (Lal and Thapar, 1967) at this site, extending to nine seasons of field-work during 1961-9, brought to light a sequence of two periods of occupation, of which the upper one belonged to the Indus civilization and the lower to the antecedent phase. In the present inquiry, evidence relating to four aspects of this civilization will be discussed, viz. (1) ancestry or origins; (2) settlement pattern; (3) ritualism; and (4) burial practices.

Ancestry or origins

Before discussing the origins of the civilization, I would like to enlarge a little on the nomenclature. Excavations at Amri (Casal, 1961), Harappa (Wheeler, 1947), Kot Diji (Khan, 1964) and Kalibangan have indicated the existence, at each site, of the remains of a settlement of a distinctive culture, lying stratified below that of the Indus civilization (Harappa Culture). The former deposit has been variously designated as proto-Harappan, early Harappan and pre-Harappan. While the use of the first two terms as a culture-label would give an impression of a recognizable state in a sequence of development of the Harappa Culture (from adolescence to maturity), the term pre-Harappan emphasizes the stratigraphic priority and would imply an earlier or even an alien or a variant culture.

Apart from the question of interpretation, there are two other factors which are relevant to the issue: (1) the occupation of the Indus civilization at each of the above sites seems to have started quite suddenly; and (2) the ceramic industries of the preceding deposit at these sites are not homogeneous, but show instead regionalization, indicative perhaps of different 'culture areas'. In the light of the above considerations, the use of any of the three terms, proto-Harappan, early Harappan or pre-Harappan, as a blanket term for a deposit immediately preceding that of the Harappan is obviously unsatisfactory, especially at the present stage of our research when (1) the excavation at each of these sites has been vertical and (2) the evidence from recent field-work, carried out by the University of Peshawar, in the Gomal Valley in Dera Ismail Khan District of West Pakistan still remains to be properly analysed. Under the circumstances, it would be appropriate to use site-names, with the period shown in roman figures. This system of nomenclature may be useful at least for a time. Thus, for Kalibangan, the earlier of the two occupation periods is termed as Kalibangan I.

Now to the evidence of material remains. The settlement of Period I was situated on the bend of the river beyond the active flood-plain, and was a parallelogram, some 250 m from north to south and 180 m from east to west. It was found to have been fortified from the very beginning of the occupation. The fortification wall was made of mud bricks (30 x 20 x 10 cm), and in its extant position showed two structural phases. In the earlier phase, the width at the base was about 1.9 m, while in the latter, it measured 3-4 m, the extra thickness having been added on the inner side. Both the outside and inside faces of the wall must have been plastered originally with mud-patches, which were found preserved at some places.

Within the walled area, the houses were built of mud bricks of the same size as those used in the fortification wall, the masonry being English bonding, with alternate courses of headers and stretchers. The use of baked bricks was attested by a drain. In the limited area of the excavation (largely on the slope of the mound), it was not possible to obtain complete plans of houses. Nevertheless, it could be inferred that a house consisted of three to four rooms with a courtyard. From the width of the walls (some of them only the length of a single brick), it would appear that the houses were single-storeyed. The other noteworthy features of these houses were the presence of (1) ovens, both of underground and overground variety resembling the present-day *tandoors* commonly used in the region, and (2) cylindrical pits, lined with lime plaster, possibly for storing drinking water.

This occupation continued through five structural phases, rising to a height of some 1.60 m, when it was brought to a close by a catastrophe (perhaps seismic), as evidenced by the occurrence of displaced (faulted?) deposits and subsided walls (pl. 7.1) in different parts of the excavated area. Thereafter the site seems to have been abandoned, though only temporarily and a thin layer of sand, largely infertile, accumulated over the ruins.

The distinctive culture trait of this period was, however, the pottery (Thapar, 1969). Six different fabrics, labelled A, B, C, D, E and F, were recognized in the assemblage (Indian Archaeology, 1962-3). Of these, Fabrics E and F, distinguished essentially by surface-colour (E for buff and F for grey) did not show marked individualities, either in shape or in painted designs, their main features being shared by other fabrics. Furthermore, in frequency, they were somewhat uncommon. Of the remaining, Fabric A was the most characteristic one, and also the most commonly used. Care-lessly potted, it was drab-red to pinkish in surface-colour and painted over in light black combined at times with white. The designs were painted in free style and included thick horizontal bands covering the neck and the rim, moustach-like bifold scroll, criss-cross, wavy lines and symmetrically joined semi-circles. The range of shapes comprised vases and bowls showing ring and occasionally pedestal bases. Fabric B was marked by a roughened or rusticated surface, often bearing painted designs, flowers as well as animals and birds. It is of interest to note that among the animal designs, the bull was also painted, a feature not found on the Indus pottery. Only one shape, viz. a globular jar, was represented in this fabric. In surface treatment this fabric simulated the Wet wares of Quetta and north Baluchistan.

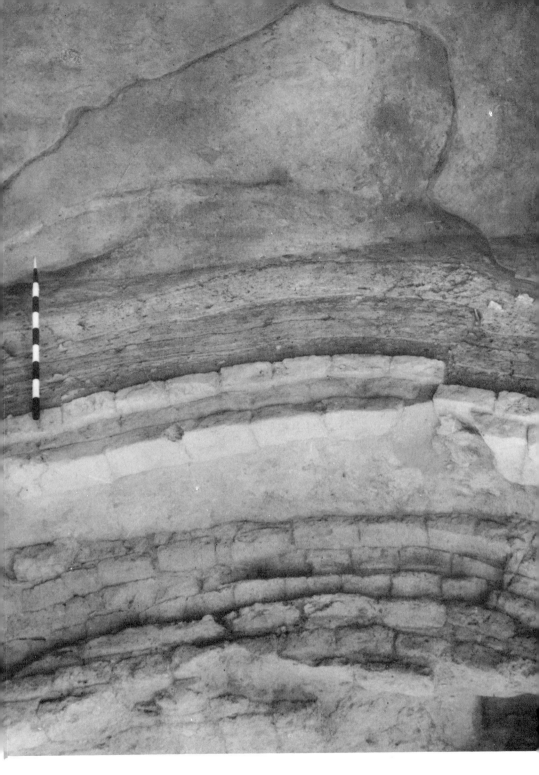

Plate 7.1 Kalibangan-1. (XE2 qd. 2) Fall of the pre-Harappan walls.

Fabric C was characterized by a fine-textured paste and slipped surface in shades of red and purple-red, the latter recalling the pottery of the pre-defence deposits at Harappa. The painted designs, which were in black, included the carefully-ruled horizontal bands, loops, criss-cross, also fish-scales. The shapes represented in this fabric included: bulbous jar, dish-on-stand and straight-sided bowl. It is significant that one of typical Indus shape and also a design were represented in this fabric. Fabric D was distinguished by vessels with sturdy section. A characteristic shape, however, was the basin or trough with a heavy ring base, decorated on the inner side with sharply incised lines forming various patterns and on the outside with rows of cord impression. The shape and the design is closely paralleled at Amri in Period IIB.

Among the other objects in use during the period, the more noteworthy were: small-sized blades of chalcedony and agate, occasionally serrated and backed; beads, variously of steatite (disk-shaped), shell, carnelian, terracotta and copper; bangles of shell, terracotta (both of rectangular and round section) and copper; fragmentary terracotta bulls; toy cart-wheels; querns with mullers; bone points, and copper celts including a curious axe.

The economy of these people must have relied largely on agriculture. Although no cereals were found in the course of excavating, the discovery of a ploughed field (pl. 7.2), situated to the south-east of the settlement outside the town-wall, is highly significant. The field showed a grid of furrows, with one set, more closely spaced, running east-west, and the other, widely spaced, running north-south. Curiously enough, this pattern bears a remarkable resemblenace to modern ploughing in the neighbourhood, where two types of cereal (pulse in one direction and mustard in the other) are grown in the same field, the combination depending upon the size and growth of the plants. No remains of either a plough or a ploughshare or a coulter have, however, been obtained from the escavation, but the existence of a field showing tolerably well-preserved furrows provides concrete evidence for the use of the plough. The material of which the ploughshare or coulter was made and its shape still remain to be known. Since cultivation during that period seems to have depended on flood-irrigation, supplemented by seasonal precipitation, it is reasonable to infer that only the winter crop, viz. the *rabi*, was grown, the sowing being done in the autumn after the river-flood, resulting from the tropical monsoon, had subsided.

The above evidence has a bearing on the origin of the Indus civilization. It has been seen that some of the elements of the culture represented by Period I anticipated the Indus civilization: (1) in

Plate 7.2 Kalibangan-2 Furrows of the cultivated field on the southern side of mound, with section. Pre-Harappan period.

pottery, fish-scale, *pipal*-leaf and external cord-impressions as decorative patterns, and dish-on-stand, ring-stand, ovoid jar with accentuated flange round the neck, and lid as forms; and (2) among other objects, the use of terracotta bulls, terracotta toy cart-wheels, bangles of copper, shell and terracotta, steatite disk beads, querns and copper celts. We must add to this list the concept of fortified town-planning and the knowledge of the English bond in masonry. However, beneath all these traits that are common to both these assemblages there lies a basic difference in the range of ceramics, the size and material of blades, the size of the bricks, the orientation of the houses, and above all in the scale of urbanization and other essentials of civic life including literacy (there being no evidence for the use of seals, with or without script, during Period I). And it is this difference which is the more striking. Nevertheless, we cannot conceive of the Indus civilization as a wholly isolated and independent growth. In order to ascertain its incipient stages, we have to review, besides Kalibangan, the evidence from (a) Amri, Harappa and Kot Diji where a preceding culture below the Harappan has been revealed, and (b) Sarai Khola (Khan, 1968), near Taxila in the Haro

Valley, where a culture of comparable affiliation has been found stratified above a Neolithic deposit. Of these the excavation at Harappa has been very restricted with the result that apart from pottery no other associated objects were found. A detailed analysis of the evidence here would involve considerable discussion and I shall not attempt it. Let me simply indicate that (1) the ceramic range of each site was essentially different from the others, there being three distinct traditions, viz. Amri, Kot Diji and Kalibangan with very little interchange among them; (2) hesitant infiltration of Harappan influence in the form of overall scale patterns on pottery appeared towards the upper half of the deposits at Amri and Kot Diji; (3) new forms, which include dish-on-stand, appeared in the later levels at Sarai Khola; (4) among objects of Harappan context, terracotta cakes were found at Amri and Kot Diji, toy cart-wheels at Sarai Khola and Kalibangan, terracotta bangles at Amri, Kot Diji, Sarai Khola and Kalibangan, terracotta bulls at Amri, Kot Diji, Sarai Khola and Kalibangan, querns and grinders at Amri, Kot Diji, Sarai Khola and Kalibangan, shell bangles at Amri, Sarai Khola and Kalibangan, and copper bangles at Kot Diji and Kalibangan; (5) small-sized blades were known at Amri, Kot Diji, Sarai Khola and Kalibangan and leaf-shaped arrow-heads in stone at Kot Diji and Sarai Khola; (6) the settlements at Kot Diji and Kalibangan were fortified, and there is a possibility of the existence of a rampart at Amri in Period II B; and (7) the size of the mud bricks in use during the period was 30 x 20 x 10 cm (ratio 3:2:1) at Kalibangan and about 38 x 19 x 9 cm (ratio 4:2:1) at Kot Diji.

Now the obvious question arises: did the Indus civilization evolve out of these cultures (Ghosh, 1965)? The answer, I am afraid, is not an unqualified yes. Although these cultures displayed a significant pattern of a fairly uniformly developed level of material culture, affording possibilities of synoecism, the role of the *idea* and stimulus-diffusion (Daniel, 1968; Wheeler, 1968) from Mesopotamia, notably in such traits as the system of writing and monumental architecture and the importance of the *genius loci* cannot be underrated. Thus the native development of village-town complexes (Fairservis, 1967), as represented by these cultures, was spurred on by the diffusion of the *idea* of civilization from Mesopotamia. The problem still remains: *where* did the *form* of the civilization develop? Both at Kalibangan and at Kot Diji the evidence is conclusive that the settlement of the Indus civilization started with a fully mature expression, following an abandonment of the site by the settlers of the preceding culture. At Harappa, the position is almost similar, and at Amri, where there is no break in occupation between the two settlements, the intrusive nature of the Indus civilization is evident. The *form* of the civilization, therefore, does not seem to have developed locally at any of these sites. Could we visualize that the *form* was established piecemeal? It may also be noted that at Kalibangan the pottery of the preceding culture continued in use (though less and less) nearly half-way through the occupation of the Indus civilization, suggesting a manifest co-existence of two ceramic traditions for some time. These village-town cultures show a widespread diffusion in the Indus and the Ghaggar Valleys and seem to constitute a sub-stratum of the Indus civilization. In this context one could as well label the former Early Indus cultures. Further field-work and area excavations in the region would furnish the much-wanted evidence for the gaps in our knowledge of the growth of the Indus civilization. Besides, the as yet unexcavated deposits, lying below the sub-soil water at Mohenjo-daro, also hold out an alluring possibility of containing the antecedent or incipient stages of the Indus civilization; some of the pottery excavated from the lower levels of this site would support this supposition (Mackay, 1938; Alcock, 1952).

The recent explorations in Districts Karnal, Rohtak and Hissair, supplemented by a small-scale excavation at Mithatala, conducted by Shri Suraj Bham of the University of Kurukshetra, have extended the reach of this culture further east along the Chautang and other affluents of the Ghaggar. The material is still under study but a preliminary examination shows that the ceramic range resembles that of Kalibangan Period I (personal communication).

Settlement pattern

The main features of the settlement of the Indus civilization (Period II) were: (1) the 'citadel' in the west, represented by a smaller mound (KLB-1); and (2) the 'lower city' towards the east, represented by a much more extensive mound (KLB-2). The general layout of this city (pl. 7.3) was thus comparable with that of Mohenjo-daro and Harappa. The citadel was situated on the top of the preceding occupation which was already a mound some 1.60 m in height. The lower city was laid out on the natural plain towards the east, leaving a gap.

The citadel complex is roughly a parallelogram, some 240 m from north to south and 120 m from east to west, and consists of two almost equal but separately patterned parts (rhomboids in plan). Both parts were surrounded by a fortification-wall, ranging from 3-7 m in width and reinforced at frequent intervals with rectangular salients or bastions. The fortifications were built throughout of mud

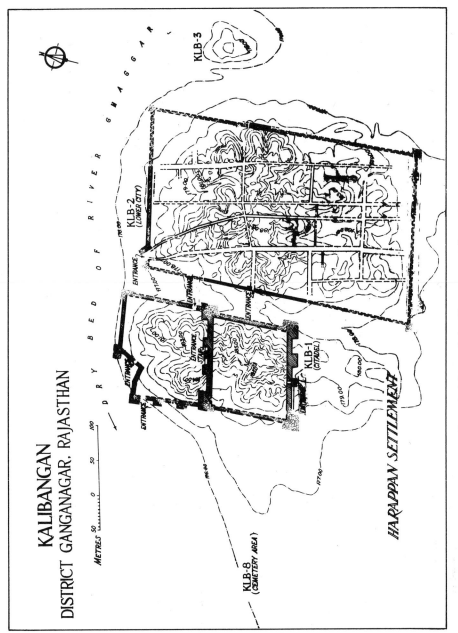

Plate 7.3 Plan of the Harappan settlement.

Plate 7.4 Kalibangan-1 General view showing rampart (defence) walls facing South and West looking North-East.

bricks; two sizes of brick, viz. 40 x 20 x 10 cm and 30 x 15 x 7½ cm (ratio 4:2:1), representing two principal structural phases, were used in the construction, the larger bricks in the earlier phase and the smaller ones in the latter. On the north and west, the fortifications overlie those of the preceding period, while on the east and south, including the central partition, these were built on the ruins of the earlier occupation. Both the outer and the inner faces of the wall were originally plastered with mud, traces of which were visible at many places.

The southern half of the citadel was more heavily fortified not only with corner-bastions but also with salients (pl. 7.4) along the wall on the north and south. The enclosed area contained some four to six massive platforms of mud and mud bricks, each separate from the others and intended perhaps for a specific purpose. Of these, sizable portions of four, including the complete outline of one (about 50 x 25 m), have so far been exposed. The size of each of the platforms varied as did the width of the passages separating them. At no point were these platforms joined to the fortifications. Access to the working-floor of the platforms was by means of steps which rose

Plate 7.5 Kalibangan-1 Animal bones in a cistern.

from the passage. At one place the passage fronting the steps was found to be paved. Through the passages also ran baked-brick drains, a series of which, conforming to the structural phases of the platforms, was brought to light. As in the fortifications, the smaller-sized bricks (30 x 15 x 7½ cm) were used in the later structural phases of the platforms, and the larger-sizes (40 x 20 x 10 cm) in the earlier. Of the buildings which stood upon these platforms, no intelligible plans are available, having been obscured by depredations of brick-robbers. Nevertheless, the available remains do indicate that some of these might have been used for religious or ritual purposes. On one of the platforms (with the known complete outline), besides a well and a fire altar, a rectangular pit (1.25 x 1 m) lined with baked bricks (pl. 7.5), containing bones of a bovine and antlers, representing perhaps a sacrifice, was found. On another seven rectangular 'fire altars' were discovered aligned beside a well (pl. 7.6). More will be said of the features of these curious 'fire altars' below (see p. 101).

The entrances to this part of the 'citadel' were located on the south and north. The south entrance, by virtue of its being a baked

Plate 7.6 Kalibangan-1 Burnt brick wall, ovens, storage jar looking East.

brick structure, seems to have suffered heavily from modern despoliation with the result that its structural details are poorly preserved. Nevertheless, enough remains to indicate that the entrance (some 2.60 m in width) consisted of steps fronting the fortification-wall and flanked by oblong salients. The entrance from the northern side was through a mud-brick stairway which, running along the outer face of the fortification-wall between the two centrally located salients, led up to the height at which there was access across the fortifications. In this entrance complex two structural phases were recognized again, of which the earlier consisted of steps (mud-brick size: 40 x 20 x 10 cm showing a tread of 40 cm and a riser of 10 cm), and the later perhaps a ramp screened by a 1.50 m wide wall of mud bricks (size 30 x 15 x 7½ cm).

In case I have given the impression that during the Harappan occupation of this site the small-sized bricks (30 x 15 x 7½ cm) were introduced only in the later phases, let me say that these bricks were used right from the beginning of the occupation for domestic structures. It was only in the fortifications and the massive platforms that the large bricks (40 x 20 x 10 cm) were employed in the earlier

Plate 7.7 Kalibangan-1 Excavated remains of houses.

phases and smaller ones later on. It is significant, however, that the
ratio of dimensions of both these sets remains 4:2:1.

From the location of the entrances, it is reasonable to argue that
the southern entrance may have been meant for the general public
from the lower city and the northern entrance for the residents of
the northern half of the citadel. The structural features of these,
however, preclude the possibility of any vehicular traffic within the
enclosed area which was possibly considered sacred.

The northern half of the 'citadel' contained residential buildings,
perhaps of the elite (pl. 7.7). These were surrounded by a fortification-wall, along which remains of salients and bastions were
found on the north and west. There were three entrances to this part
of the citadel, each controlled by a bastion. None of these entrances,
however, were found to be of the ramp or stairway type. Inside the
eastern entrance was a brick-on-edge pavement, joined to the
partition fortification-wall. Full details of the street-planning of this
part have not so far been discovered. One of the north-south
thoroughfares was excavated over a length of over 40 m. Starting
from the easterly of the two salients of the partition forti-

fication-wall, it ran obliquely in the direction of the entrance on the north.

The lower city is also a parallelogram, some 235 m from east to west and 360(?) m from north to south, and lies to the east of the citadel beyond the broad space (roughly 40 m in width). It was found to be enclosed by a fortification-wall built of mud bricks (size 40 x 20 x 10 cm), the width of the wall ranging between 3.50 and 9 m. Within the city was a gridiron plan of streets running north to south and east to west, dividing the area into blocks. The existence of four arterial streets running north to south, and three running east to west, has been proved by excavation, and it is surmised that the northern portion of the city may contain more east-west streets. There were also quite a few east-west lanes which were staggered in plan and served perhaps as delivery or entrance-lane for certain house-blocks. The width of the streets ranged from 1.80 to 7.20 m and often corresponded to multiples of 1.80 m. To avoid damage from busy vehicular traffic, wooden fender-posts were provided at some of the street-corners. The only structural encroachment into the street was the existence of rectangular platforms (of uncertain use) immediately outside some houses. The streets, except in the late phase, were unmetalled. No evidence of regular street-drains has so far been encountered: house-drains which were either of wood, or of baked brick, were discharged into storage-jars buried in the street. The existence of two entrances to the fortified area, one on the north (pl. 7.8) and the other on the west, was established by excavation. While the western one, which was supervised by a guard, opened into the third east-west street (counting from south upwards), the northern one communicated with all the north-south streets, notably the first and the second (counting from the left) which converge at this point. From the location it could be inferred that the western entrance was used by the city-dwellers for communicating with the citadel, and the northern for commercial traffic.

A look at the city-plan would show that the alignment of the streets is at variance with that of the fortification-wall. The precise reasons for this apparent deviation still remain to be duly explained, but it could be argued that the alignment of the fortifications was conditioned by the layout of the preceding occupation. The streets were laid out by the Harappans according to their own planning which may have been modified as occupation proceeded. In the northern half of the citadel also there was a street which ran obliquely to the fortification-wall. Excavation, however, has proved that the city-wall and the streets were planned at one and the same time, viz. from the very beginning of the occupation. It was observed

Plate 7.8 Two streets and mud brick structures of houses together with the defence wall, on the North side of the mound, looking South-East.

that the house-walls near the fortification-wall faithfully followed the alignment of the latter and those nearer the streets that of the streets themselves.

From the very beginning of the occupation the houses were built of mud bricks (30 x 15 x 7½ cm), the use of baked bricks (of the same size, and also wedge-shaped) being confined mostly to drains, wells, sills and bathing platforms. In the typical chess-board plan of the city each house faced two, if not three, streets, and consisted of a courtyard with six to seven rooms aligned on two or three sides. Entrance to the house was either through the courtyard or through a corridor running between sets of rooms. Some of the courtyards contained a well, evidently used by two or three families. The finds obtained from the occupation of this period were all characteristic of the Indus civilization and need not be listed here. Among these, however, five objects deserve special mention: (1) a cylinder seal; (2) a terracotta cake, incised on the obverse with a horned human figure, and on the reverse with a human figure pulling an obscure object; (3) a terracotta human figurine; (4) a terracotta bull showing the dynamic mood of the animal; and (5) a graduated scale.

Chemical analysis (personal communication from Dr B.B. Lal, the Archaeological Chemist in India) of the nineteen metal objects show that copper, containing small amounts of lead, iron and tin as impurities, was used for making various types of artefacts. The small amounts of tin in three or four specimens do not appear to be intentional additions, for the proportion of tin is not high enough to produce bronze. Similarly, there is no evidence for the employment of brass at Kalibangan.

Before proceeding with the next stage of our investigation, it would be worth while to compare the above evidence with that obtaining at other extensively excavated Indus sites showing similar layout, viz. Mohenjo-daro and Harappa.

Citadel. Both at Mohenjo-daro and at Harappa the citadel is found to be fortified, at the latter site on a more massive scale. The buildings within the citadel were found to be raised upon an artificial platform of mud and mud bricks which is shown to be contemporary (coeval) with the fortification-wall. At Kalibangan the situation is different: the southern half of the citadel contained some four to six individual platforms were found to be contemporary with the fortifications, at no point were they found to be integral or one-build with it, being separated from the latter by a passage. Besides, no bipartite plan of the citadel (as at Kalibangan) has been brought to light either at Mohenjo-daro or Harappa. Perhaps future excavators at these sites could keep this in mind. For example, does the apparent division of the citadel-mound at Mohenjo-daro conceal a bipartite plan or is it purely superficial and a result of the Indus floods?

Lower City. At Kalibangan, the lower city is found to be fortified, while at Harappa, no such evidence has been discovered. At Mohenjo-daro, in 1964-5 Dr G.F. Dales (1965) found in the HR area 'a massive construction' which he suspected to be a fortification-wall. The work, however, could not be continued thereafter. Pending further excavations, these structures are thought to be a series of revetments of the eastern side of the channel. It would be premature, therefore, to conjecture that the lower city was fortified. Both at Kalibangan and at Harappa, the gap between the citadel and the lower city represented open land. At Mohenjo-daro, on the other hand, there are indications that a canal or a branch of the Indus may have flowed through the gap. If this were the case, there must have been bridges for communication between the citadel and the lower city, the evidence for which is sadly lacking at the present stage. Another striking feature of the street-plan of Kalibangan is the absence of street-drains in the lower city and the northern half of the citadel (residential annexe), in marked contrast to their presence at Mohenjo-daro (in the lower city). At the former site, street-drains, both open and covered, were found at various levels only in the southern half of the citadel, where these, and with the wells found on the platforms, seem to be related to some elaborate ritual with ceremonial ablutions which called for a good flow of water.

Ritualism

Our information on the complex problem of the Indus religion is based largely on seals, terracotta female figurines, with elaborate head-dresses, a few stone images, and aniconic objects and phalli, all commonly known at Mohenjo-daro and Harappa. It is surprising that at Kalibangan, except for the seals, none of the above categories of objects have been found, and that even among the seals none depict a deity. What does this mean? Was the religion of the Indus people at Kalibangan different from that of the people of Mohenjo-daro and Harappa? At present, there is no satisfactory answer to these questions. The available evidence at Kalibangan is as follows:

No cult objects have so far been identified among the excavated finds. Mention has already been made of the existence of a 'row of fire altars' on top of one of the platforms in the citadel. Similar fire altars have also been found individually in many houses in the lower city. Apart from these, an exclusive structure, containing a group of five such fire altars, was found to the east of the lower city outside the fortification-wall (pl. 7.9). No other structure existed on this little mound. The absence of normal occupation-debris suggests therefore that the structure was intended for some religious purposes.

The recurrent features of these altars were as follows: a shallow pit, oval or rectangular on plan, was dug out; fire was made and put out *in situ* as shown by the presence of fragments of charcoal in the lower part of the pit; a cylindrical, occasionally faceted or rectangular, block or clay (sun-dried, occasionally pre-fired) was fixed in the centre; flat triangular or circular terracotta cakes were placed around the block, perhaps as symbolic offerings.

It would appear, therefore, that the ritual connected with these fire altars played a dominant role in the religious life of the Harappans at Kalibangan. The importance of water in connection with these rituals has already been mentioned, viz. the almost extravagant provision of wells and drainage in the citadel area. No such fire altars have so far been reported from Mohenjo-daro or Harappa. The observance of this ritual, therefore, seems to be peculiar to the region of Kalibangan. The religion of the Indus civilization would thus be an amalgam of various regional beliefs and practices.

Plate 7.9 Kalibangan-3 Close view showing several altars surrounded by a mud brick wall, looking North.

Burial practices

The cemetery of the Harappan period is located to the west-south-west of the citadel on the present active flood-plain of the river; formerly, however, it must have been beyond the reach of the annual floods. Excavation revealed three types of burials: (1) extended inhumation in a rectangular or oval grave; (2) pot burial in a circular pit; and (3) pottery deposit in a rectangular or oval grave. The last two methods were not associated with any skeletal remains.

Of the first variety, the recurrent features were as follows: on the floor of an oblong pit, the dead body was laid in an extended position with the head towards the north; grave goods consisting of pots, personal ornaments, including toilet objects were arranged around the body (essentially the upper portion); the pit was then filled with the same earth. Three of the graves call for special mention. In one of them the body was lying prone with its head towards the south, quite contrary to normal interment. The other grave (40 x 20 x 10 cm) was lined with mud bricks covered with approximately 2 cm of thick plaster. The floor, however, was not

Plate 7.10 Kalibangan Grave No. 32 KLB-8 (Cemetery) long grave with steps together with the full skeleton and pottery of the lower grave. (Burials I & II).

paved. The third grave was notable for the evidence it showed of two types of burial (pl. 7.10), one superimposed on the other. The lower interment, consisting of pottery, was without any skeletal remains while the upper one contained the normal extended human body with pottery and one bead, both of gold and carnelian, around the neck. The grave in this case was quite large and had steps, on the eastern side, down to the grave-floor.

Of the second variety, the grave pit was oval or circular and contained as well as an urn other pots, including platters and dishes-on-stand. Besides pottery, some of the pits also contained beads, shell bangles, and steatite objects.

Of the third variety, the grave-pit was rectangular or oval with the longer axis oriented north-south, as in those of the first variety, but was marked by the absence of any skeletal remains. The grave-goods consisted of pottery and occasionally of personal ornaments like shell bangles and beads. The striking feature of these graves was the filling which showed two stages: after the funerary deposit (consisting largely of pottery), the pit seems to have been left unfilled resulting in the accumulation of bands of fine sand and clay;

at a later stage, the remaining part of the pit was filled in by human agency with cloddy earth. It may be recalled that bands of sand and clay were also noticed in the grave showing a succession of two interments see p. 103).

The occurrence of these three varieties of burial has posed problems of a sociological nature. Meanwhile, it may be affirmed that the grave-goods obtained from each of these types is characteristically Indus. In their mode of occurrence they show a pattern, the significance of which cannot yet be appraised but is worth noting. Graves of the first and second type occur in separate (reasonably defined) areas, the latter lying to the north of the former. Graves of the third variety are found, largely in the area of the first, but occasionally in that of the second.

While at Mohenjo-daro no regular cemetery has so far been located, all the excavated graves (of the mature Harappan period — Cemetery R-37) belong to only one type, viz. the extended inhumation in rectangular or oval graves which is closely similar to the graves of the first variety at Kalibangan. The graves of the second and third variety at Kalibangan seem to have been recorded, as orderly burials, for the first time in a Harappan assemblage.

REFERENCES

Bibby, G. (1970) *Looking for Dilmun*, London.
Alcock, L. (1952) Exploring Pakistan's past, the first year's work. *Pakistan Quarterly* 2, No. 1.
Casal, J.-M. (1961) *Fouilles d' Amri*. 2 vols. Paris.
Dales, G.F., Jr. (1965) New investigations at Mohenjo-daro. *Archaeology*, 18, No. 2.
Daniel, G. (1968) *The First Civilizations, the Archaeology of their Origins*, London.
Fairservis, W.A., Jr. (1967) The origin, character and decline of an early civilization. *American Museum Novitates*, No. 2302, New York.
Frankfort, H. (1951) *The Birth of Civilization in the Near East* (2nd impression), London.
Ghosh, A. (1965) The Indus civilization: its origins, authors, extent and chronology, in *Indian Prehistory*, Misra, V.N., and Mate, M.S. (eds), Poona, 113-56.
Indian Archaeology 1962-63 — A Review. Cf also issues of 1960-1 to 1961-9.
Khan, F.A. (1965) Excavations at Kot Diji. *Pakistan Archaeology*, No. 2.
Khan, F.A. (1968) Sarai Khola. *Pakistan Archaeology*, No. 5, 28-47.
Lal, B.B. and Thapar, B.K. (1967) Excavations at Kalibangan: new light on the Indus Civilization. *Cultural Forum*, No. 34, New Delhi, 79-88.
Mackay, E.J.H. (1938) *Further Excavations at Mohenjo-daro*. 2 vols.
Thapar, B.K. (1969) The pre-Harappan pottery of Kalibangan, an appraisal of its inter-relationship. *Potteries in Ancient India*, Patna.
Thapar, B.K. (1967) Cf also. Lal above.
Wheeler, R.E.M. (1947) Harappa 1946: the defences and Cemetery R-37. *Ancient India* No. 3, 59-130.
Wheeler, R.E.M. (1960) Archaeology and the transmission of ideas, in *Alms for Oblivion*, Wheeler, R.E.M., London, 1966.
Wheeler, R.E.M. (1968) *The Indus Civilization* (3rd ed.), Cambridge.

8

Dynamics of an early South Asian urbanization: First Period of Shahr-i Sokhta and its connections with Southern Turkmenia

RAFFAELE BISCIONE, Istituto per il Medio ed Estremo Oriente, Rome.

One of the most conspicuous pottery styles of the Indo-Iranian borderland is the so-called Quetta ware, first identified by Professor Piggott in that valley in 1946 (Piggott, 1947). This type of pottery, as is generally known, was also found in the Helmand and Arghandab valleys, in the layers of periods Mundigak III and Shahr-i Sokhta I, and in Southern Turkmenia, in the period Namazga III, all datable to around 3000 B.C.

The origin of this pottery style posed a difficult problem to scholars, because it shows few connections or none at all with the previous traditions of the Indo-Iranian borderland. Soviet excavations in Southern Turkmenia, however, have produced much more evidence to solve this question.

There (fig. 8.1), in the narrow fertile strip north of the Kopetdagh range and in the ancient oases watered by the river Tedžen (the lower course of the river Hari-rud), the so-called Quetta ware appeared in the period Namazga III, Late Chalcolithic, and it has been possible to reconstruct the whole process which led to its formation. Indeed, Soviet scholars, chiefly Professor Masson, Dr Sarianidi and Dr Hlopin, succeeded in showing the continuity of the pottery tradition throughout the Chalcolithic period (Masson, 1962: 28-9; Sarianidi, 1965: 28-9; Hlopin, 1963: 22; Hlopin, 1969: 49-50). They have clearly demonstrated that Quetta ware was the logical continuation of the ceramic styles of periods Namazga I and II, Early and Middle Chalcolithic (Sarianidi, 1965, ibid.). We must therefore conclude that the birthplace of Quetta ware was Southern Turkmenia, and its spreading over so wide an area was a later phenomenon (Masson, 1961a: 213; Masson, 1964: 437-9; Sarianidi, 1965: 50) (fig. 8.2).

In the period Namazga III, Southern Turkmenia was divided into two cultural provinces, the western one, in the area at the foot of

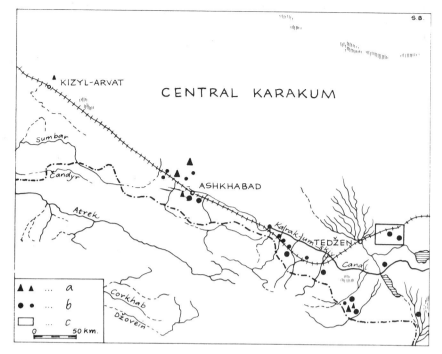

Figure 8.1 Map of Southern Turkmenia. a. Bronze Age sites; b. Chalcolithic sites; c. sites of Geoksjurian group (after *Lisicyn*).

Kopet-dagh, and the eastern zone, in the silty plain of the river Tedžen. In the latter area almost all painted pottery is Quetta ware. Probably the road followed by Turkmen influences in their expansion south-eastward was the upper course of the river Hari-rud to the Hindu-kush, and then to the confluence of the rivers Helmand and Arghandab, where Mundigak lies.

In the period Mundigak III, Quetta ware appeared there (Casal, 1961: I, 99, 119-24; II, figs. 44, 45, 60, 87, 95, 117, 124, 125, 128, 129, 131), and this was probably the centre from which Turkmen influences reached the Helmand delta, where Quetta ware was found in the layers of Period I at Shahr-i Sokhta. (Tosi, 1969: 324-5; figs. 37-8).

The Quetta valley was probably reached by a delayed wave, because in the period Damb Sadaat I, which has connections with Shahr-i Sokhta I, there was no trace of Quetta ware (Tosi, 1969: 325 and 381). It appeared in Damb Sadaat II, and some of the motifs were identical to those of Namazga IV, Early Bronze Age. (Fairservis, 1956: figs. 414-15; Masson, 1964: 437-9; Sarianidi, 1965: 50.)

The connections which linked Southern Turkmenia and the Indo-Iranian borderland have been emphasized first by Piggott and then by Masson (Piggott, 1947: 141-2; Masson, 1957: 159). Casal, exposing parallels in finds and the chronology of Mundigak and other contemporary cultures, stressed the importance of connections with Southern Turkmenia and tried to draw a table of chronological

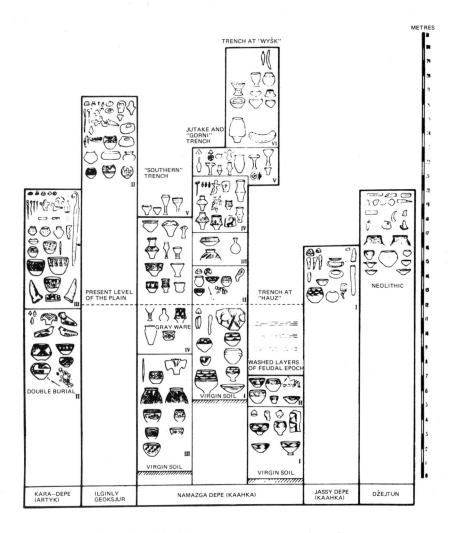

Figure 8.2 The Namazga sequence at various sites.

connections (Casal, 1961: 99-101, 103, 104). Unfortunately his
statements, based on the publication of the first years of Soviet
research, have proved incorrect. He compared the period
Mundigak III with the period Namazga II A and the contemporary
Anau II, on the basis of two sherds of Quetta ware found at Anau,
and six polychrome sherds of Quetta type from Kara-tepe, a big
village of the Chalcolithic Age, and on the basis of polychromy. But
the two sherds from Anau were simply the first specimens of the
Quetta style, the six sherds from Kara-tepe are in later Soviet works
considered as belonging to the period Namazga III. The prevalence
of polychromy is in Namazga I, but is quite common also in
Namazga III. The prevalence of Quetta ware in this last period has
led Soviet scholars to establish more fitting parallels between the

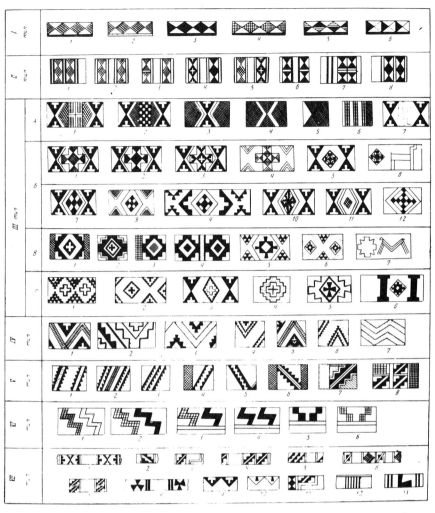

Figure 8.3 Typology of painted decorations of Namazga III pottery from Geoksjur (after *Sarianidi*).

period Namazga III, which is not represented at Anau, and the period Mundigak III.

Tosi, in his second preliminary report on Shahr-i Sokhta, accepted the Soviet point of view that Turkmen influences extended over such a wide area (Tosi, 1969: 381).

It may be useful to make a short résumé of the pottery of Namazga III. As I have already said, Southern Turkmenia at that period consisted of two cultural provinces. The western one lay at the foot of the Kopet-dagh, watered by the small rivers flowing from the mountains. The main centre was the village of Karatepe, which was abandoned before the end of the period, and covered an area of *c*. 15 hectares. According to Masson (Masson, 1961*b*: 355-62) the painted pottery was buff or red, with brown or polychrome decoration.

Figure 8.4 Namazga III pottery from Geoksjur (after *Sarianidi*).

Most of the pottery was buff with brown zoomorphic or geometric decoration. The animals reproduced were stags, snow leopards, cows (only a small percentage) and birds, probably eagles and ducks. The leopards are almost unrecognizable, and were due, in Masson's opinion, to southern influences, from Hissar and Sialk, while the stags had deep root in local tradition. Often these animals alternated with solid stepped triangles or concentric circles, motifs which can be found in Quetta ware.

The geometric decoration was the most widespread, and was composed of linear elements, lozenges and triangles. Another group of geometric pottery showed eastern influences, and was based on solid lozenges, crosses, and stepped triangles which are typical of

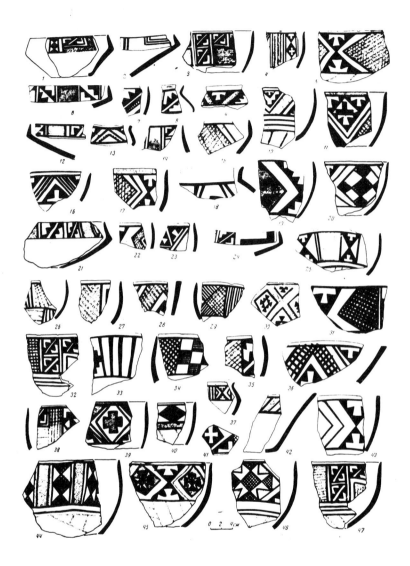

Figure 8.5 Namazga III pottery from Geoksjur (after *Sarianidi*).

Quetta ware.

Red ware was rare, and had only geometric decorations. The polychrome ware was also rare, and was either imported from the eastern area or made locally in the villages in close imitation.

The eastern area, as I have said, is a silty plain watered by the river Tedžen. Most of the villages lay in its ancient inner delta, which irrigated their fields with the help of canals. The main centre was the village of Geoksjur, which had an area of about 12 hectares and was surrounded by a rather wide network of irrigation canals (Lisicyna, 1969: 282).

The most widespread and most typical ware was buff in colour and had a buff slip, with polychrome painted decorations in black and red. The motifs are for the most part geometric. Compositions of stepped lozenges, crosses inscribed in lozenges, stepped triangles, chequered panels, chains of solid triangles, and solid crosses containing lozenges are very common throughout the whole period (figs. 8.3, 8.4, 8.5).

A small percentage of the pottery is grey, in this case also indicating southern affinities (Sarianidi, 1965: 20-3).

The delta of the river Tedžen was shifting north-westward and the villages were abandoned before the end of the period Namazga III. Some time later the district became a dry and desert area, as it is today.

South-west of the delta the villages continued to develop, as the area was not affected by the shifting of the river-bed. Pottery decoration evolved and became simpler and more linear, but still resembled Quetta ware, until eventually it gave birth to the highly stylized patterns of the period Namazga IV.

For these reasons, Soviet scholars have proposed dates later than the ones suggested by Casal, and they are supported by a number of radio-carbon determinations through the whole Namazga sequence. According to Sarianidi's communication in the Second Seminar in Iranian Archeology (Shiraz, September 1970), charcoal collected at Kara-tepe in levels belonging to the period Namazga III gave the result 2750 B.C. ± 220 years, and other charcoal from Geoksjur gave 2760 B.C. ± 100 years. The dating of the late Namazga IV period is concentrated at the end of the third millennium (2120, 2146, 2190 B.C. ± 100 years), and it was therefore held as quite probable that Namazga III was included between 3100-2600 B.C.

The period Mundigak III, (at least the beginning of it), should be dated somewhat later, and Damb Sadaat III later still, after 2600 B.C. Further evidence such as compartmented seals and clay figurines support this point of view (figs. 8.6, 8-7) (Masson, 1964: fig. 82; Sarianidi, 1965: 50 and figs. 24-5).

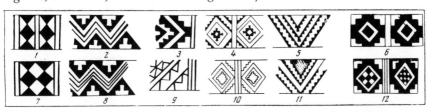

Figure 8.6 Comparison of pottery with painted decoration of periods Namazga III (1-6) and Mundigak III (7-12) (after *Sarianidi*).

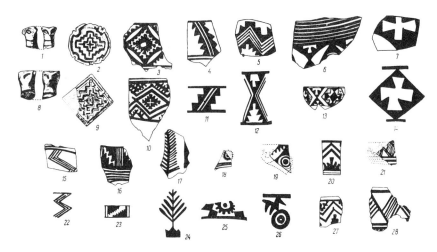

Figure 8.7 Comparisons of painted pottery decoration, seals and figurines of periods Damb Sadaat II (Nos 1-7, 15-21) and Namazga III (Nos 8-14, 22-28) (after *Masson*).

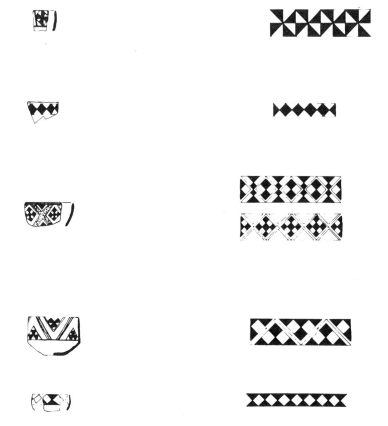

Figure 8.8 Comparison of painted pottery decoration of periods Namazga III (left) and Shahr-i Sokhta (right).

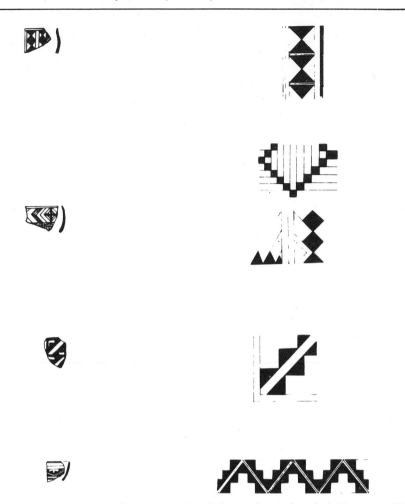

Figure 8.9 Comparison of pottery painted decorations of periods Namazga III (left) and Shahr-i Sokhta I (right).

The connections between Shahr-i Sokhta's Period I and Namazga III, especially in the eastern area, are quite marked. Unfortunately the pottery finds of the period Shahr-i Sokhta I are mostly represented by sherds, and it is rather difficult to reconstruct the decorative motifs. Moreover, the amount of sherds from Period I is quite small if compared with the incredible number from the later periods. However, even from this relatively disappointing situation it has been possible to draw a first sketch.

In his second preliminary report, Tosi stressed the similarities between the two areas and the sherds of the 1969 expedition have confirmed and furthered his theory. Out of 80 significant pottery motifs gathered, about 40 can definitely be classified as Quetta ware.

Complete similarity of motifs is obviously rare, and is found in only 6.5% of the patterns, but many of the most typical decorations

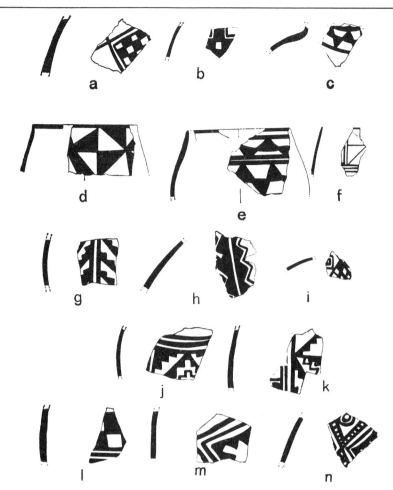

Figure 8.10 Shahr-i Sokhta. Buff Ware from Period I (after *Tosi*).

of Southern Turkmenia have also been found in Sistan. A greater number of these, about 20%, are very similar, sometimes almost identical. More than a quarter of the sherds of Shahr-i Sokhta's Period I can therefore be safely put beside the Turkmen ones. (figs. 8.8, 8.9).

The number of similarities is still greater if we examine some of the patterns which do have not an exact Turkmen counterpart, but consist of some of the most typical Geoksjurian elements, such as the stepped lozenge, the cross, and the chequered panels combined in a way not found in Southern Turkmenia, but very much in keeping with its style (fig. 8.10, pls. 8.1, 8.2, 8.3).

A good many sherds, not included in the above-mentioned calculation because they did not allow a clear reconstruction of the motifs, none the less show similarities with the sherds of the Tedžen delta, underlining the relationship which connected these two areas.

Plate 8.1 Shahr-i Sokhta. Buff Ware from Period I.

Plate 8.2 Shahr-i Sokhta. Buff Ware from Period I.

Plate 8.3 Shahr-i Sokhta. Buff Ware from Period I.

Until now I have spoken only about connections with Southern Turkmenia because Mundigak, which was probably the centre from which Turkmen influences reached the Helmand delta, is not so rich in Quetta ware as Shahr-i Sokhta itself, and its pottery of this style is rather poor and simplified in its patterns. The Quetta valley, as I already said, was not yet affected by Turkmen influences.

The differences between Shahr-i Sokhta and Mundigak suggest the possibility of a closer connection between the Helmand delta and Geoksjur oasis via Khorassan, probably after a first wave had come from Mundigak. Unfortunately this part of Iran has not yet been excavated by archaeologists, and the connection is still hypothetical. Vases with a painted decoration in the style of Namazga IV found in Khorassan, however, give a possible clue about the use of this road, at least in periods later than Namazga III (Frankfort, 1924: pl. VII, 2; Masson, 1964: 447; Vanden Berghe, 1959: pl. 15a).

Tosi, in his second preliminary report, also cited Kechi Beg ware as a fitting counterpart of the pottery of the period Shahr-i Sokhta I (Tosi, 1969: 325 and 381), but he rightly stressed the importance of Turkmen similarities. The sherds of the 1969 expedition have confirmed his statement. The fragments which can be linked to Kechi Beg ware are only a small part of the finds, 15% of the significant sherds. The figure is even lower if we compare the small number of fragments with the much larger number of Quetta-type sherds. As a matter of fact, the decorations of Kechi Beg type were simpler and were repeated several times in the inner surface of bowls, so that it was easy to reconstruct the patterns. The number of significant sherds belonging to the Kechi Beg type is therefore proportionally greater than the ones of Quetta type. An exact calculation has not been made, because it is difficult to tell how many sherds belong to the same vase, but a rough estimation gives the number of fragments belonging to the Kechi Beg type as a third of the number of Quetta type sherds.

As we have seen, Southern Turkmenia in the Chalcolithic period might have been termed a 'secondary centre' of civilization. It was the farthest point reached by Mesopotamian influences, and later it was also the farthest point reached by the trade of the Indus civilization. In Namazga V, Harappan beads, figurines and vases, or their local imitations, were found together with objects imported from Mesopotamia and buildings imitating ziggurats (Masson, 1970: 6-9, 21-2).

Southern Turkmenia was the northern outpost of urban society until the first half of the second millennium, but the Namazga culture, although strong and vital in Namazga III period, seems to have exhausted itself with the expansion into the Indo-Iranian borderland.

In later periods, in fact, it did not continue to show the characteristics I have described. The evolution which led the Namazga culture to the proto-urban stage went on, but the capacity for expansion was much reduced. Its influence was no longer felt by the advanced societies of the Indo-Iranian borderland, but only in the north-east, by the more backward culture of Čust in Ferghana.

The evolution of the Namazga culture later stopped abruptly. In the second part of the Namazga V period there was a decline and impoverishment in all fields. From the middle to the end of the second millennium, in the Namazga VI period, the process of deterioration continued (Masson, 1968: 186-7). The Namazga culture survived, but the process of urbanization was interrupted, and it was not until well into the first millennium that the city appeared north of the Kopet-dagh.

REFERENCES

Casal, J.-M. (1961) *Fouilles de Mundigak*. Paris.
Fairservis, W.A., Jr. (1956) *Excavations in the Quetta Valley, West Pakistan*. New York.
Frankfort, H. (1924) *Studies in Early Pottery of the Near East*. London.
Hlopin, I.N. (1963) *Eneolit Juznyh Oblastej Srednej Azii: Pamjatniki Rannego Eneolita Juznoj Turkmenii*. Moscow-Leningrad.
Hlopin, I.N. (1969) *Pamjatniki Razvitogo Eneolita Jugo-Vostocnoj Turkmenii*. Leningrad.
Lisitsina, G.N. (1969) The earliest irrigation in Turkmenia. *Antiquity*, XLIII, 279-87.
Masson, V.M. (1957) Dzejtun i Kara-depe. *Sovetskaja Arheologija*, 1.
Masson, V.M. (1961a) The first farmers in Turkmenia. *Antiquity*, XXXV, 203-13.
Masson, V.M. (1961b) Kara-depe u Artyka: *Trudy JuTAKE*, X, Ašhabad.
Masson, V.M. (1968) The urban revolution in Southern Turkmenia. *Antiquity*, XLII, 178-87.
Masson, V.M. (1970) *Raskopki na Altyn-depe v 1969 g.*; *Materialy JuTAKE*. Ashabad.
Piggott, S. (1947) A new prehistoric ceramic from Baluchistan. *Ancient India*, 3.
Sarianidi, V.I. (1965) *Pamjatniki Pozdnego Eneolita Jugo-Vostočnoj* Turkmenii. Moscow.
Tosi, M. (1969) Excavations at Shahr-i Sokhta: preliminary report on the second campaign, September-December 1968. *East and West*, XIX, 283-386.
Vanden Berghe, L. (1959) *Archéologie de l'Iran ancien*. Leiden.

9
Micro-drilling at Shahr-i Sokhta; the making and use of the lithic drill-heads

MARCELLO PIPERNO

Among the many lithic tools collected at Shahr-i Sokhta in the last few years by the Italian Archaeological Mission in Iran (Tosi, 1968; 1969), there is a particular range of objects classified as 'drill-heads'. The study of their characteristics is useful in explaining not only the technique of micro-drilling used in the hole-boring of beads and other objects, but also the kind of connection which existed during the third millennium B.C. between Shahr-i Sokhta and the contemporary Indus civilizations.

Such tools, in fact, similar in shape and size to drill-heads of Shahr-i Sokhta, have been found fairly frequently at Chanhu-daro, and the problems of how they were made and used have been discussed by Mackay (1936). The conclusions he reached are reported in the publication of Chanhu-daro excavations (Mackay, 1943).

A re-examination of these tools seems necessary on account of the questions left unresolved by Mackay and in the light of discoveries made at Shahr-i Sokhta which would seem to indicate, as we shall see later on, that they were connected not only with the perforation of beads, but also with the preparation of numerous stone seals with geometric designs, characteristic of this site and of other sites of the Indo-Iranian borderland, which have been defined as 'compartmented seals' by Piggot (1946).

So far we have found about 40 drill-heads, the majority of them collected on the surface of the mound. All the specimens which have been found *in situ* come from the buildings attributed to the Second and Third Periods of the cultural sequence established by Tosi (1968) and datable between 2700 and 2300 B.C.

Only in a few areas has excavation been deep enough to bring First Period remains to light, and so it is not at present possible to verify that these tools were in use from the beginning of the settlement.

As for the Fourth Period, until now almost only identifiable in the remains of the 'Burnt Building', the absence of these drills can perhaps be explained as due to the character of the building, which was a place where the perforation of beads and the fabrication of stone-seals may not have been carried out.

However, it is necessary to bear in mind that in this period the stamp seals of steatite seem to have been replaced by clay seals, while beads are virtually absent. It is not impossible that the working of beads was connected with the trade in hard stones like lapis lazuli, cornelian and turquoise, which is well documented during the Second and Third Periods, but which appears to be much reduced during the Fourth. Therefore, these tools will be examined here, on the whole, as coming from the 2nd and 3rd Periods.

Some of the unused tools, and others which have been scarcely used, permit reconstruction of their original form before the heads were reduced to the cylindrical shape seen in the majority of samples.

Typologically they can be defined as backed tools made with a very regular abrupt retouch, often over the whole surface length of the piece, giving it a rod-like shape sectionally almost square and of a thickness which varied from 2 to 4 mm (fig. 9.1 a and b). The material from which these tools have been made is often a sort of granite, sometimes basalt and, in a few specimens, flint. Some of the implements were later worked to narrow the working part and leave the butt-end protruding laterally (fig. 9.1. c and d).

The length of the useful part of the drill-heads probably varies according to the type of work each was designed for. We may assume that tools like the one reproduced in fig. 9.1e were employed in the longer drilling required for beads, while the instruments similar to the one shown in fig. 9.1f were specially used to make stone seals where the drill needed to incise the motif did not cut deeper than 2 or 3 mm.

In fig. 9.2, some of the drills are shown with the working surface worn completely smooth and with a perfectly cylindrical shape, though there are still traces of flaking on the handle part of the retouched surface designed to hold the head firm in the rod of the drill.

Mackay (1936: 6), thinking that the cylindrical form found in many of the tools had been given to the drill heads before they were put into use, states that 'all these drills . . . were made by roughly flaking the stone into a rod-like shape, and then grinding them in much the same way as the beads.'

Because of the relatively high number of tools found at Shahr-i Sokhta, we can by examining them reconstruct phase by phase the

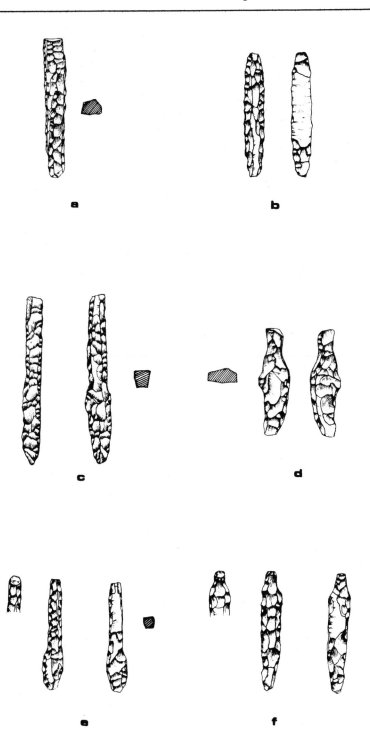

Figure 9.1 Shahr-i Sokhta: Drill-heads; a, b, c, d, not yet used; e, f, with traces of wear on the distal end (1:1).

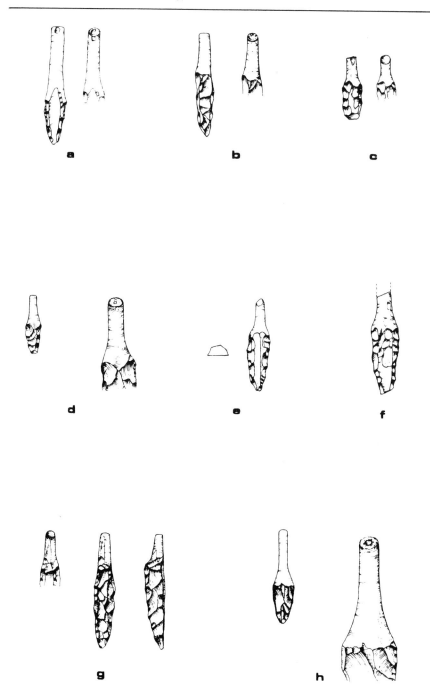

Figure 9.2 Shahr-i Sokhta: Drill-heads showing the characteristic cylindral shape
after very long use. (1:1, except for details of (d) and (h), 2:1).

Plate 9.1 Shahr-i Sokhta: Drill-head; on the Distal end the smoothing of the working end is clearly visible. (enlarged 3 times).

working of these drills, and we are led to the more likely conclusion that the cylindrical form held by Mackay to be intrinsic to their design is on the contrary a result of the use to which they were put. A detailed analysis of the points of several of these instruments which still have retouch on their surfaces reveals that they were used as drill-heads independently of the polishing of their own surfaces. The point of some of these tools shows the beginning of a rounding and bevelling of the flaking, probably through their being gradually worn down as they were rotated against the object being drilled (Pl. 9.1).

There is another characteristic of the drill-construction which gives strength to the theory of their use apart from the smoothing of their surfaces. In many of the examples, as we have seen, the working end of the tool has been narrowed more than the rest of the piece; if the whole tool had been designed to be smoothed down for its complete length, then this initial sharpening would be inexplicable, whereas it must instead have allowed the drill to begin its boring.

Mackay's mistaken interpretation can perhaps be explained by the fact that the drills found at Chanhu-daro are either roughly-flaked (as far as one can see in the photo reproduced by the author), or are fragments of which only the perfectly smooth parts remain, in fact, only the working end of the complete tool, after it had been broken through heavy use.

In his article Mackay refers to the experiments conducted by Dr C.H. Desch, Director of the National Physical Laboratory at Teddington, on one of the perfectly worn drills which came from

Chanhu-daro. In twenty minutes, using emery powder and water, Desch made a hole 1 mm deep in a fragment of cornelian. The wear on the drill was stated to be 'very slight'.

Some experiments made on drills from Shahr-i Sokhta in which they were used for a longer period (a little more than two hours) seemed to demonstrate that in fact the wear was fairly evident.

One tool chosen from the unworn ones, simply retouched on all its surfaces and narrowed to the working point, was fitted into a wooden rod and submitted to a continual rotation by hand. By this method five holes were bored to a depth of about 2 mm each in two alabaster fragments and one of basalt, without using any kind of abrasive but wetting both the drill head and the hole from time to time to prevent the pieces overheating. After two hours in use, the point of the tool appeared completely rounded and the polishing began also to extend to a small area next to the working tip of the drill.

We can therefore assume that the use of the tool for drilling deeper holes would spread the wear over the used part and give it the characteristic smooth cylindrical form.

Besides confirming the hypothesis of the use of the drill-heads before they become worn and smooth, this experiment shows that the wearing-down is more or less apparent to the extent of the depth the drill reached in its boring.

However, even if we accept, on the basis of these considerations and the tests made, that the implement described as a drill was used before becoming polished and that the polishing was a result of the use to which it was put, there still remains another feature to be explained, a characteristic noticeable on the majority of the very smoothed pieces. This is the minute hemispheric depression visible at the centre of the tips of many tools (pl. 9.2). In a good number of the beads where boring is not complete, and in some of the seals, it is possible to see a minute elevation like a pimple at the centre of the hole which corresponds to the depression on the drill.

Mackay considers this depression something essential to drill-making, and alleges that the cavity probably served to hold some type of abrasive. But having examined the Shahr-i Sokhta implements, this explanation does not seem to me convincing.

In the first place the absence of the depression on many intact and well-smoothed examples indicates that this was not an integral part of these tools. Mackay's explanation is based on observation of the lack of this depression on the drills that he considered unfinished and that, in fact, as the traces of polishing on the tips of many Shahr-i Sokhta products show, have rather come to be considered as drills ready for use and just in an initial stage of their employment.

Plate 9.2 Shahr-i Sokhta: Macro-photographs of two very used drill-heads, showing the little depression at the tip of the working end.

In the second place, the possibility that the depression was used to hold an abrasive seems unlikely considering how small it is; indeed, in some pieces it can only be clearly seen with the aid of a microscope.

Mackay himself also found some difficulty in explaining the formation of the pimple visible in the unfinished beads, matching the depression which, according to his theory, held an abrasive and which therefore ought, on the contrary, to have increased the drilling capacity right in the centre of the hole.

If we accept that there is no functional reason for the presence of these minute cavities, their origin must be considered as a result, once again, of the way in which these implements were used. A convincing explanation of the factors contributing to the formation of these depressions is, however, extremely difficult at present.

The lack of data on the type of drill-holder in use at Shahr-i Sokhta makes any attempt at reconstructing the system of drilling in its entirety quite hypothetical. Ethnographic comparisons (McGuire, 1896) show a great variety of solutions adopted to explain the problem of drilling. The characteristic common to these explanations leads back to the use of the 'bow drill' or the 'pump-drill' which revolved the point of the drill in an alternating rotatory motion.

The presence at Lothal in the Cambay Gulf (Rao, 1962) of a helicoidal bronze drill which requires a continual rotating motion, however, would seem to indicate that this fundamental innovation in drilling technique had already been introduced in the region under study from the beginning of the third millennium B.C. If we assume the use of a continually rotating drill at Shahr-i Sokhta as well, because of the perfection and regularity achieved in certain drilled holes, then we can explain how the depression was formed by considering the mechanical laws of the movements made by the drills.

The cutting speed of a drill, that is its rotation round its own axis, is in proportion to the distance of the rotating axis; therefore, it is theoretically nothing in relation to the height and greatest in relation to the periphery of the axis. Because of its small speed in relation to the height, the Shahr-i Sokhta drills meet their greatest resistance from the object they are boring right at the central part of the tip. Consequently they suffer particularly heavy use at this point which could cause the formation of such a depression, and this heavy use that is probably further increased by the considerable heat created at the area of major friction.

This explanation (put forward here only as a supposition) is reinforced by the fact that the depression has been observed only on some of the used drills, those employed for a longer period, whereas in the little-used pieces it is invariably absent; the successive stages of formation of the depression and the different depths it reaches on the tip of the drills are clearly visible in the tools illustrated in Pl. 9.3.

A tool of the kind described, well defined and highly specialized, demonstrates, when we consider its frequency in the lithic production at Shahr-i Sokhta, that activity connected with micro-drilling, and with working hard stone in general, represents a particularly important factor in the economy of this site.

The absence or rarity of similar instruments in contemporary settlements indicates a concentration of producing beads and, more particularly, stone seals in this very site, and it would appear that this craftmanship represents at least one of the reasons for the economic prosperity of Shahr-i Sokhta, which was based on full-time craftsmen who were released from agricultural labour.

The first range of products that may be connected with the use of these drill-heads is found in the beads, principally of alabaster, steatite, cornelian, agate, lapis-lazuli and turquoise.

The occurence of plentiful fragments of these stones roughly-hewn and of unfinished beads suggest a strong network of commercial relations in which Shahr-i Sokhta assumes the function of a centre to which there flowed the raw materials and from which the finished products were distributed.

Although bead making was one of the activities most closely associated with the employment of those drills examined above, nevertheless these tools were certainly not the only ones to be used in the micro-drilling operations. In fact, an examination of beads made of semi-precious stones like turquoise, cornelian and lapis-lazuli reveals much more accurate work than the alabaster beads show, suggesting too the use of a drilling technique that required very different instruments from the stone drill-heads.

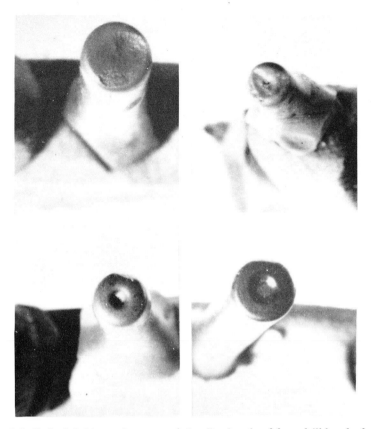

Plate 9.3 Shahr-i Sokhta: close-ups of the distal ends of four drill-heads showing the different depth and shape of the depression.

Two elements indicate the existence of a drill probably made of bronze, modified and more efficient than the stone one: in the first place, the holes bored in the beads that were made from more precious and imported materials are always of a diameter less than 1 mm, and this is smaller than the minimum achieved by the stone-drills found so far at Shahr-i Sokhta. In the second place, the shape of these holes is sometimes biconical and differs from the invariably cylindrical shape made by the stone drills. Frequently, in spite of the small size of these beads, a double hole has been bored (starting at opposite ends) to avoid the probable fracturing if the piece were bored into deeply from only one end. The double piercing has the advantage of limiting the width to the smallest possible hole, and this advantage becomes more evident when the element to be bored is very tiny, especially when a conical instead of a cylindrical point could be used to achieve a biconical bore, diminishing the amount of material to be removed.

If it becomes clear from these assumptions that a great number of

Plate 9.4 Shahr-i Sokhta: Steatite round seal. The employment of a lithic drill-head to obtain the motif of the seal is quite evident.

the Shahr-i Sokhta beads were made with the use of a micro-drilling technique which does not involve the drills examined in this work but depends instead on other tools whose exact nature cannot be established for the moment, there is another range of objects represented by the many steatite and alabaster seals discovered at Shahr-i Sokhta which are definitely connected with these drills.

The tablets, varying in thickness between 2 and 4 mm, that were used for the seals were first reduced to the required shape, often triangular or circular, and all the surfaces smoothed. The geometric motif was then cut out on one side with a series of holes about half the thickness of the particular tablet. After the outline of the design had been cut in a series of perforations close to each other, it was sometimes finished off by evening and polishing the holes so that almost no trace remained of the drill.

In some seals which have not been completely finished off the series of holes cut into the tablet is still clearly visible. In the circular one reproduced in pl. 9.4, for example, the traces left by the drill-heads show more than 150 perforations.

From all this it is evident that the level of technical performance reached in this micro-drilling work was peculiar to a class of highly-specialized craftsmen who must have enjoyed a considerable social and economic position in the life of Shahr-i Sokhta.

There were probably other objects connected with this craft which the excavations at Shahr-i Sokhta have brought to light. Among these we may recall some rectangular wooden tablets with a series of irregularly placed holes which could have been used to support the beads during drilling, (Tosi, 1969: fig. 257) and the conically shaped alabaster objects with a concave base, which may have been used by the craftsmen to support the rod into which he had fixed the drill, during its rotation (Tosi, 1969: figs. 254-6).

These latter objects have been suggested by Soviet authors to be a candle-holder or cruse (V.I. Sarianidi to M. Tosi, personal communication). Chemical analysis now in progress on the material found inside the cavities of these tools should soon clear up the mystery of their function.

REFERENCES

Mackay, E. (1936) Bead making in ancient Sind. *Journal American Oriental Society*, 47, 1-15.
Mackay, E. (1943) *Chanhu-daro excavations 1935-6.* New Haven.
McGuire, J.D. (1896) A study of the primitive methods of drilling. *Report Smithson. Institute for 1894*, 623-756. Washington.
Piggott, S. (1946) The chronology of prehistoric North-West India. *Ancient India*, 1, 11-25.
Rao, S.R. (1962) Further excavations at Lothal. *Lalit Kala* Akademi, II, 14-30.
Tosi, M. (1968) Excavations at Shahr-i Sokhta, a Chalcolithic settlement in the Iranian Sistan. Preliminary report on the first campaign, October-December 1967. *East and West*, XVIII, 9-66.
Tosi, M. (1969) Excavations at Shahr-i Sokhta. Preliminary report on the second campaign, September-December 1968. *East and West*, XIX, 283-386.

10

Archaeological field surveys in Afghan Seistan 1960-1970

KLAUS FISCHER

Introduction

Many explorers, MacMahon and Curzon for example, agree that Seistan offers a special phenomenon which puzzles students of comparative geography and archaeology. The shallow lakes alternately swell, recede and disappear, and the rivers are constantly shifting their beds. Consequently settlements were created and abandoned in short periods. While the country owes to the abundant alluvium its wealth and fertility, it also contains more ruined cities and habitations than are perhaps to be found within a similar space of ground anywhere in the world.

This fact is a challenge to archaeological field work. When we were allowed to continue researches started in 1959 we tried to place the problem of ancient and modern Seistan into the framework of current exploration in Afghanistan.

An archaeological map of Afghanistan (fig. 10.1) shows the major sites of historical and artistic interest explored so far: the prehistoric mound of Mundigak with pottery ornamented both in ancient Iranian style and with the Indus valley patterns, the provincial capital of Kandahar in the vicinity of which were discovered Greek and Aramaic versions of Ashoka inscriptions; Buddhist monasteries, stupas and caves embellished by Gandhara-style sculpture and painting, namely Bamiyan, Fondukistan, Hadda, Qunduz; the 'mother of cities' from Zoroastrian to Islamic times – Balkh; a dynastic sanctuary of the Kushanas to be connected with the art of Mathura – Surkh Kotal; places with remains of Hindu-Shahi temples and images, for example Gardez and Chigha Sarai; centres of Islamic architecture and decoration – Lashkari Bazar, Ghazni and Herat. Seistan, known to the Greek and Roman world as Drangiane, is just being explored. The vast desert is covered by mud-brick remains.

Figure 10.1 Afghanistan, Archaeological Sites. (after *Fischer*)

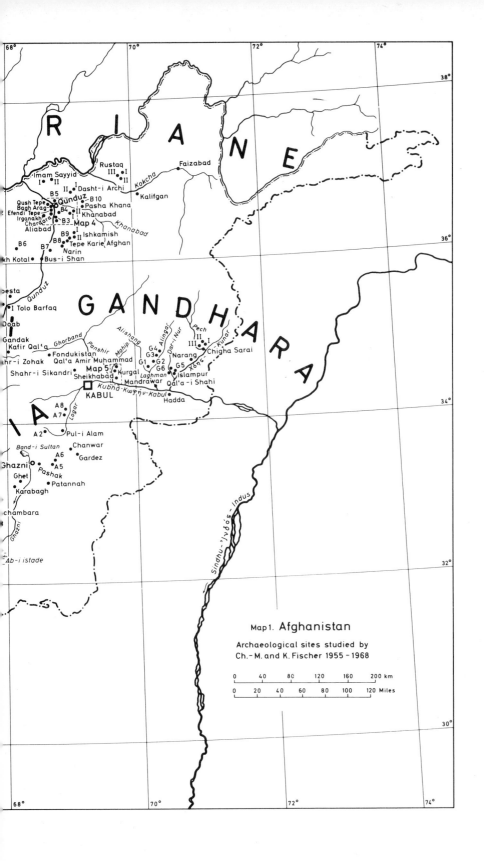

Map1. **Afghanistan**

Archaeological sites studied by
Ch.-M. and K. Fischer 1955-1968

| 0 | 40 | 80 | 120 | 160 | 200 km |

| 0 | 20 | 40 | 60 | 80 | 100 | 120 Miles |

Moving sand dunes encircle old fortresses, like that of Sangar. Recently we have located prehistoric and early historic tepes, mounds and wall systems deriving from the periods of the Parthians, Sakas and Sasanians, and abandoned Islamic cities with soaring mud-brick walls and towers.

Seistan was in prehistoric times a densely populated country. Inhabitants and intruders utilized the water of the river in various canals and made the land in the beginning of the Christian era into a rich and wealthy district. Seistan was crossed by Alexander the Great in the autumn of 330 B.C. As heir of the Achaemenid empire, he wanted, as no ruler before or after him, to unite East and West not only politically but also culturally. Parthian, Sasanian and early Islamic rulers are said to have reigned over a blossoming country. Roads from east to west and north to south crossed great and rich cities.

During the thirteenth and fourteenth centuries the inhabitants opposed the Mongol invasion, were conquered and totally destroyed. The irrigation works were wasted, the cities burnt and life seemed to end. But in the half-millennium from the Mongol invasion till recently life and art in Seistan have remained. The water of the Helmand was again used in canals and carried to distant points in the country; new canals were built and old ones repaired. Natural changes in climate and reduction of water supply seem to have restrained people from settling far from the river. Finally the population was forced to keep cattle and fields in the plain near the Helmand. Mighty rulers settled in new spots with large administrations and created Islamic art forms in various centuries. Today the mud-brick *qalas* of the native sovereigns still show monumentality, decorated with all kinds of Oriental ornaments, from Sasanian forms to Islamic patterns.

Orientalists and archaeologists have frequently studied the historical geography of the Near East, of Central Asia and of the Indian peninsula. They have interpreted ancient and mediaeval texts by epigraphic material, extant ruins, excavations and numismatic finds. Thereby they have explained the historical interrelations between Mediterranean and Eastern countries of different geological, hydrological and geographic conditions. During recent years, important archaeological publications have dealt with Iranian Seistan: Scerrato 1962, 1966 and Tosi 1968-9 gave preliminary reports on their prehistoric and early historic excavations. At the same time I have continued my earlier archaeological explorations of Afghan Seistan which were initiated by British, French and American scholars. (Dales, 1968, 1969, this vol.; Fairservis, 1961; Fischer, 1961, 1967, 1969/70, 1970a,b, 1970/71; Hammond, 1970; Herzfeld, 1932;

Kohzad, 1953; M.D.A.F.A., 1959; Rawlinson, 1873; Schlumberger, 1952; Tate, 1912.)

We were concerned with the main problems of topography in Seistan, faced by the first surveyors since the beginning of the nineteenth century, namely by Pottinger, Conolly, Bellew, Ferrier, J. Huntington, McMahon, Tate, Hedin, Stein; with the hydrography and history of the Seistan basin and especially the oscillation of the Helmand delta (now represented by old Iranian references in Gnoli's study), and with the direction of the caravan routes and the movements of immigrations leading from the Mediterranean coast through Seistan towards Central Asia in the early centuries of our era, recently described by Daffinà 1967. We wished to study the history of urbanization during the early Islamic period, which was a topic of Bosworth's 1968 work. On the evidence of archaeological remains we have to discuss the question of whether the whole of Seistan has been a cultural unity or whether there existed regional varieties to the west and east of the Helmand.

Environs of Khwaja Siah Posh

We shall now study various regions of Afghan Seistan and start in the area between Farahrud and Khashrud. Fig. 10.1 shows the stretch between these two rivers where no ruins have yet been recorded. The discovery of a minaret will therefore be of interest to the student of Islamic art history. In contrast to the masses of mud-brick ruins of south-western Afghanistan it consists of burnt brick.

A vast field of mud walls and mud-brick ruins at the site of Khwaya Siah Posh was dominated by a mosque with a baked brick minaret, the stump of which reveals traces of its original beauty.

While certain pillar-like constructions which consist of basements in baked brick and uperstructure in sun-dried brick and several examples of 'Towers' (pl. 10.1) have been constructed entirely from mud brick and only been reinforced or embellished by baked bricks, the traditional lofty Islamic religious structure of a minaret, praying tower of a mosque, had to be built only with the solid building material of burnt brick. Tate has illustrated two remarkable specimens of ruined minarets in baked brick and mortar and the beginning of the second millennium A.D. and Rawlinson mentioned on his map a place 'Minar Khwaja Siah Posh' to the south of the lower dry Khuspas river. We located the ruined minaret marking the site of a nearly totally vanished mud-brick mosque in the centre of an extensive deserted Islamic city. As in the case of the Mil-i Kasimabad, the upper part of the tower seems to have been less

Plate 10.1 Mud brick tower, ruins of the so-called Burj-i Samad.

affected by the vehemence of the wind-borne sand. There are indications that the sand or dust does not attain a height of more than a few metres above ground level even when impelled by the strongest wind. The people of the country say that the strength of the wind is greatest close to the ground, and that the minaret of Khwaja Siah Posh has been especially affected in the first 3-4 m above ground level.

We realize the importance of recently discovered Islamic ruins in Afghan Seistan in the evolution of Islamic architecture in Central Asia, Eastern Iran and North-West India. Again, we observe the phenomena of mutual influences between East and West. Minarets were conceived in early mediaeval Islamic art of Iran on a round plan, as for example at Damghan, erected about A.D. 1058. Another tradition of the tomb tower derives from polygonal or star-shaped ground forms, as preserved at Bostam, dated A.D. 1313. The old capital of the Ghaznavids is marked by two towers on the star-plan, erected during the earlier part of the twelfth century. The Ghorid minaret of Jam, on the other hand, rises on a circular plan. It belonged to a mud-brick mosque at the capital site of Firuzkoh. Its elevation in four storeys and the combined star-shaped and polygonal plan of Khwaja Siah Posh seem to have supplied the model for the Qutb al-manar of Delhi, at the end of the twelfth century. The variety of the circular plan is reflected in later Timurid monuments: on Afghan soil at Herat, and beyond the Amu Darya in the Registan monuments of Samarkand.

Environs of Zaranj

One of the two above-mentioned Seistan towers illustrated by Tate has recently collapsed: the minaret of the great mosque of Zaranj. This place name indicates the original capital of the country of the Irangae = Zarangai. A view from the protohistoric mounds of Nad-i Ali reveals the decay of this old residence and the site of the ruin of a modern fortress on the top of a historic tepe. To the south of the remains was re-created the contemporary capital of the province. Nowadays old Drangiane = 'land of the Zarangae', or old Sakastana = 'land of the Sakas' = Sigistan = Seistan has been renamed after the Iranian term Nimruz = 'land in the south', while the present capital has received again the traditional name of 'Zaranj'.

Now let us examine the mud-brick ruins of the area to the north and south of Chakhansur (see fig. 10.2) according to the names on the 1:50,000 sheets.

The 1:50,000 sheet is named after the main settlement in the northern part of Afghan Seistan, the seat of an administrative centre with a bazar, mosque, school, telephone station, and halting place for the motor bus to the south-western border of Afghanistan at Nimruz, to the north at Farah and to the east at Dilaram. Chakhansur and the neighbouring villages on the lower course of the Khashrud and its channels possess deep wells that supply water to the inhabitants throughout the year. Since the river of Khashrud is dry for the greater part of the year, the villagers look for new means of irrigation, for example new channels bringing water by electric pumps from the Aŝken—Am lake. To the north of this stretch of villages and cultivated fields extends an area of ruins. On the aerial photograph as well as on the spot we can rexognize abundant water courses of the past that have once fed populous cities. During the first season of archaeological survey we usually started on the track leading from Chakhansur towards the north-west, i.e. to Farah. The first 10 km of the track are frequently crossed by old irrigation

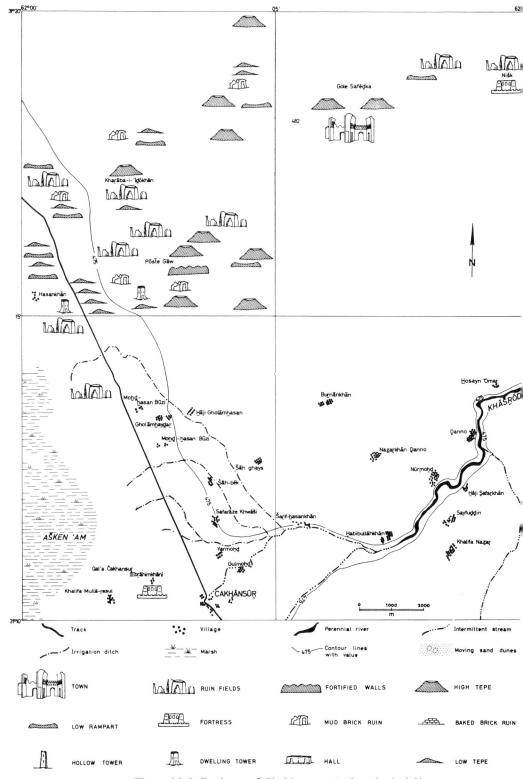

Figure 10.2 Environs of Chakhansur, Archaeological Sites.

Plate 10.2 Mud brick ruins of mediaeval Islamic buildings at Gole Safedka.

systems, for example in the area of the ruined Qala Chakhansur Ebrahimkhan. Later on we reached the open plains where we followed old channel courses to the various ruins. The first impression is of a multitude of 'ruin fields', low tepes and low ramparts on both sides of the track. They start to the north of the present village Hasankhan west of the track. East of the Chak-hansur-Farah track the whole plain is covered with these mounds of ruins. As I have already mentioned, further cartographic surveys and sondages can serve to interpret the function and age of these settlements indicated by low 'ruin hills'. Here in the plain between the lower Khash and Khuspas rivers they seem to mark by mud-brick ruins the main buildings of small villages grouped in a similar way to the modern villages immediately to the north of Chakhansur. From time to time high tepes constitute conspicuous land marks. They lie isolated or are combined with low ramparts and are crowned by mud-brick ruins and indicate what were probably important ancient administrative centres. Sometimes they rise near other extensive antiquarian remains: to the north and east of Poste Gaw and in the area of Gole Safedka (pl. 10.2). Poste Gaw refers to ruins of crumbled earthen masses of a square measuring approximately 500 m on each side. The square with its strong bastions has one corner pointing north. Thereby the interior of the habitation site is protected by one uninterrupted flank against the north-west, i.e. towards the direction of the wind which blows for 120 days during the summer from north-west to the south-east. The direction of the strong summer gales has apparently remained unchanged in the

Plate 10.3 Region of Kordu: ruins in the moving sand dunes.

prehistory and history of Seistan, and proved by the shapes and paths of the moving sand dunes (pl. 10.3). Consequently the layout of early mediaeval Islamic settlements follows the same pattern. It is for instance to be recognized in the south-eastern limits of the town of Gole Safedka. The wall decoration with corbelled niches in horse-shoe shape and the structural features of the pointed squinches transforming the square into the round are known on Afghan soil from Ghaznavid examples. Arabian and Persian geographers and historians mention caravanserais, bazars, fortified places etc. on the way from Iran through Afghanistan towards India. A famous site Qala-i Nisk may be recognized in the ruin fields and the fortress of Nisk. The technique and the style of the mud-brick fortifications persisted through the centuries, for instance in the later fortress of Wala Chakhansur Ebrahimkhan which has been described by European travellers of the early nineteenth century. Towns, fortresses and the political centres marked by some high tepes were ostensibly connected by a chain of dwelling towers examples of which we observe near Hasankhan and Poste Gaw.

To the east of Poste Gaw and south of Gole Safedka are situated the ruins of Dewal-i Khodaydad. Here we studied the type of a village-like settlement with remarkable remains of vaulted chambers (pl. 10.4), barrel-vaulted halls and arrangements of rooms on the basis of iwan-houses (pl. 10.5, fig. 10.10).

Plate 10.4 Dewal-i Khedaydad, arch of main hall in mud brick iwan house.

Plate 10.5 Dewal-i Khedaydad, one-storeyed and double-storeyed vaulted towers.

A well-irrigated region between the present villages of Mulla Musa and Amirkhan gave the name to the 1:50,000 sheet *Aliabad.* The fields and the villages are situated to the east of the Hamun-i Seistan, i.e. in the Area of Aŝken-Am and A Aŝken-Ghaybana. Further east the remains of the Joye Kuhna and the Joye Zarkano-zurkan canal systems indicate the ancient sources of prosperity. Near the northern edge of the map are situated small villages belonging to the cultivated area of the lower Kashrud described on the above-mentioned map of Chakhansur. During our survey we noticed several habitation sites that are not indicated on the map and may have sprung up recently wherever and whenever peasants discovered new means of livelihood. Thus we found people living in huts among the ruins of the town of Sawal (pl. 10.6).

The main archaeological vestiges on this topographical sheet are the pre-Islamic town and fortress of Sawal and the early mediaeval Islamic towns of Qalca-i Cegini and Cegini. The ruin fields near Sawal demonstrate a later re-occupation of the region during Islamic times. During the past 10 years I have observed a rapid decay in the mud-brick remains of Sawal and its environs. With the help of aerial photographs taken during various seasons one can realize that owing to the rainfall in the Central Afghan mountains and the climate in Seistan proper the water level of the Hamun-i Seistan changes considerably between spring and winter of one year and during successive years.

Ruins that we have found covered by water in our field survey in 1961 could be photographed in 1969 on dry ground. The activity of the water and possibly effects of the earthquakes in Chorasan had made mud-brick pillars of outstanding height collapse. Again one notices lines of dwelling towers connecting and protecting in pre-Islamic as well as in Islamic times the ancient tracks between the towns and fortresses I have just mentioned, in the surroundings of Qala-i Chegini and at Burje (Dewale) Gunde. Possibly also low ramparts, for example elevations in the eastern border of the Asken-Am, 31°07′N/62°03′E, to the north of the Joye Kuhna 31°01′N/62°04′E, and to the west of Qala-i Chegini are remains of old fortifications. The canal systems required special protection; watch towers have been studied for example together with the irrigation works of Chorasmia. Baked-brick ruins on a spot where a modern track crosses the Joye Kuhna at about 31°01′N/62°06′E seem to mark a fortified post that in antiquity protected south-north traffic and the maintenance of the water courses. While tepes, wall systems, ramparts or deserted Islamic towns have general architectural features known from Central Asian, Eastern Iranian or North-West Indian monuments, some structural remains seem to indicate regional developments in Afghan Seistan. A similar type of dwelling tower occurs in Chorasmia. But I have so far observed a variety of minaret-like square or octagonal hollow towers only in the part of Seistan under discussion. They are constructed in mud brick and display structural or ornamental details in burnt brick, for

Plate 10.6(a)   One of the central buildings in the ruinfield of Sawal.

Plate 10.6(b)

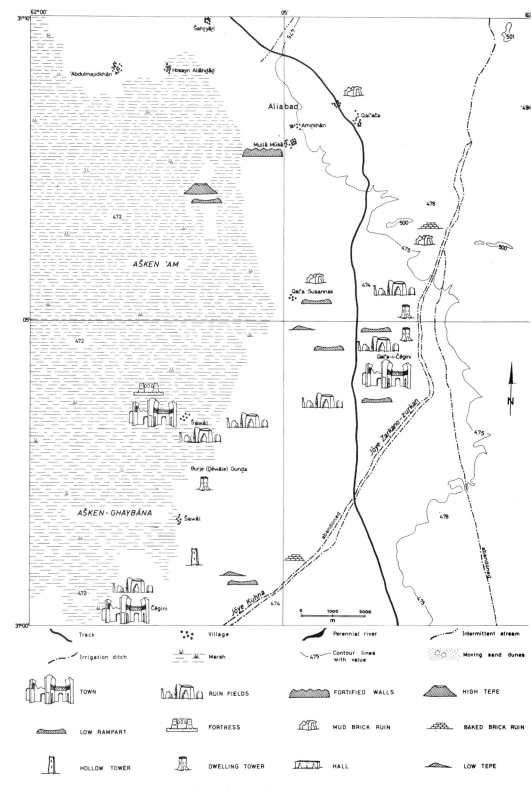

Figure 10.3 Environs of Aliabad, Archaeological Sites.

example, one ruin at the intersection of the present camel tracks to the south-west of Burje (Dewale) Gunde or to the north-east of Chegini at about 31°02'N/62°04'E. Ruins at Chegini (south-west corner of fig. 10.3) preserve especially interesting types of squinches forming the transition zone between square and circle.

The map shown in fig. 10.4 is named after the only present habitation site in this desert area. Ziyarate Amiran Saheb is a modest village round a sanctuary which constitutes a centre for Muslim pilgrims. Ruin fields to the north-east of the village remind us of the antiquity of the site.

An octagonal hollow tower near the present mosque was in better state of preservation about half a century ago. The place is situated on a gravel plain at the crossing point of camel tracks used by pilgrims from west (Nimruz), north (Chakhansur) and east (Dilaram). The same lines of communication also serve motor traffic. The tracks from Ziyarate Amiran Saheb towards south-west, south and south-east, that lead to vast series of ruins, are now obliterated. They followed abandoned irrigation works on which depended many villages and cities. Their remains cover the desert, the region of the barchanes, and the moving sand dunes to the south. Nowadays one follows tracks from one ruin to the other: from a polygonal wall to the structures of Chakhansurak.

To the north of the main ancient water source, the Nahre Kalane Kuhna, the ruin fields and towns of Chigini stretch over more than 1 km north to south. A richly decorated hall represents the early Islamic type of an ivan; fortified wall and mud-brick ruins indicate various stages of the settlement. To the south of the Nahre Kalane Kuhne we can observe another north-south line of ruins which also seem to contain regional architectural types of Afghan Seistan. For example, in the ruin fields and mud-brick ruins of Mirali we find rare specimens of baked-brick ruins, probably pillars marking an ancient gateway. Then there is a double-storeyed hall in mud bricks of various sizes. Beyond the abundant canal systems the ruins extend further towards the south-west immediately up to the present northern border of the moving sand dunes. The fortress of Dewale Lawur contains among other remains the mud-brick structures of adjoining vaulted halls, a building type known from early pre-Islamic Iranian architecture. In the vast ruin fields extending between the fortresses of Dewale Lawur and Dam we find another example of a hall the superstructure of which may be reconstructed as a barrel vault of elliptical section in Parthian/Sassanian style. A later re-occupation of the site is attested by masses of glazed Islamic pottery. To the north of these two important pre-Islamic and Islamic sites of Dam and Dewale Lawur we observe further vestiges of a rich past:

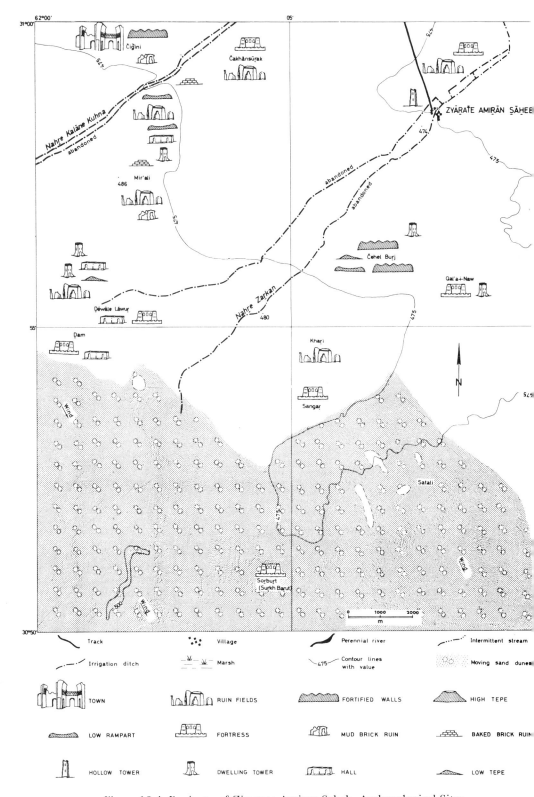

Figure 10.4 Environs of Ziyarate Amiran Saheb, Archaeological Sites.

Plate 10.7 Many-storeyed building near Kordu.

Plate 10.8 Double-storeyed watch tower in ruin fields of Kordu, Islamic period.

Plate 10.9 Pre-islamic mud brick fortress near Kordu.

kilns and baked-brick ruins and another vaulted hall. To the east of
the north-south line Chegini-Chigini-Mir'ali-Dewale Lawur-Dam one
observes another large area of ruins: square and round fortified walls
and dwelling towers at Chehel Burj, the Burj-i Samad (pl. 10.1), an
ancient dwelling tower connected with a later fortress at Quala-i Naw
and further east both pre-Islamic and Islamic ruins of Quala-i Surkh.

As far as we could ascertain during our first campaign masses of
ruins extend further south right into the area of the moving sand
dunes. To begin with we located huge Islamic fortresses at Sangar
and Sorburt.

Owing to the constant sand-drifts, the old and modern maps of
Seistan contain various, changing information on habitation sites and
their subsequent ruined state. Moreover, they may lie buried under
sand for centuries and later they may reappear and be noted by
travellers. Elphinstone has described how the Mullah Jaffer had to
abandon his village because of the moving sand dunes. When mapping
ruins in the above-mentioned places of Sangar and Sorburt we noted
at a certain distance the abandoned walls of Patandak that we
reached by landrover. From here we observed further fields of
antiquarian remains in the belts of barchanes (= Regawan = moving
sand dunes) (pl. 10.3). We had to walk through the dunes and

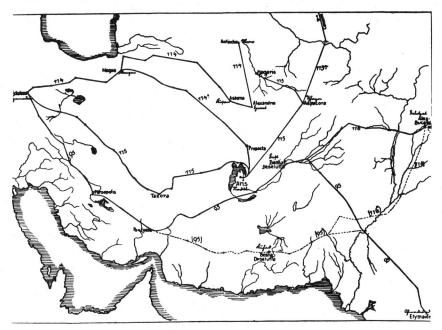

Figure 10.5 Seistan on the Tabula Peutingeriana.

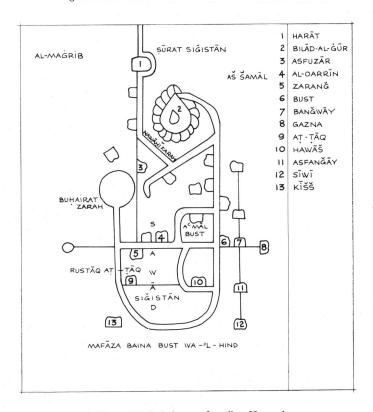

Figure 10.6 Seistan after ibn Hauqal

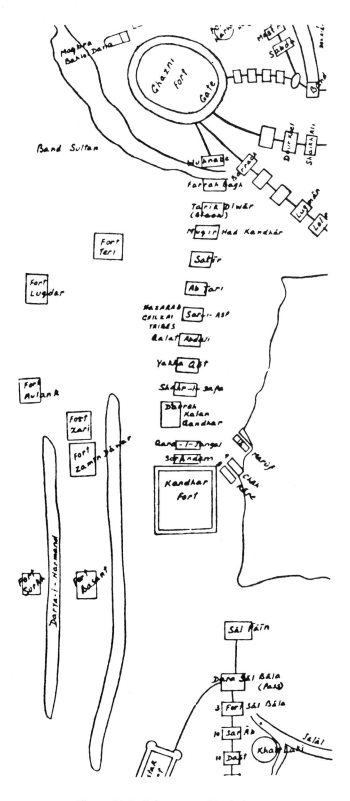

Figure 10.7 Seistan on a Mughal map.

discovered multi-storeyed buildings (pl. 10.7), old irrigation systems, abandoned fields, Islamic watch towers (pl. 10.8) of small mud bricks and remains of a fortress in large-size mud bricks of Sassanian type (pl. 10.9) in a region called Kordu.

Conclusion

In the next few years we hope to locate and to excavate further ruins indicating well-known towns of the pre-Islamic and mediaeval past. The Graeco-Roman world learnt about Drangiane through historians and geographers describing the march of Alexander the Great from Iran to India in 329 B.C. A sketch adopted by Miller from the Tabula Peutingeriana (fig. 10.5, about middle of first millennium A.D.) shows Aris = Zaranj and Propasta = Farrah. In the tenth century A.D. ibn Hauqal described the frontiers of Sigistan = Seistan (fig. 10.6) with Zarah = Hamun-i Sistan, Zaranj and the region of Farrah. Phillimore interpreted a Mughal map of the seventeenth or eighteenth century A.D. (fig. 10.7): it gives an itinerary from Ghazni fort to Kandahar fort, shows the forts of Zari and Zamin Dawar and finally indicates in the south-west of Afghanistan the Darra-i Harmand = the Hilmend river; we notice a 'Fort Surkh' and this may correspond to our ruin Qala-i Surkh. At the same time Delisle reported to the European public what was known about the Zare-lake, Parra = Farrah and Zaranj = Seistan (fig. 10.8). In the beginning of the nineteenth century Edward Conolly explored Seistan (fig. 10.9) and supplied information on the position of Farrah, Chakhansur or Nad-i Ali; the latter is to be found in the ruins of Zaranj and its environs. We are preparing further archaeological maps enabling us to identify the recently discovered ruins with place names mentioned by Greek, Roman, Arabic, Persian and European historians or geographers.

REFERENCES

Bosworth, C.E. (1968) Sistan under the Arabs, from the Islamic conquest to the rise of the Saffarids. Rome, 30-250, 651-864. IsMEO *Memoirs, XI* Rome.
Daffinà, P.D. (1967) *L'immigrazione dei saka nella Drangiana.* Rome.
Dales, G.F. (1968) The South Asian section. *Expedition,* 11, No. 1.
Dales, G.F. (1969) On tracking woolly Kullis and the like. *Expedition,* 12, No. 1.
Dales, G.F. (this vol.) Archaeological and Radiocarbon Chronologies for Proto-historic South Asia.
Fairservis, W.A. (1961) Archaeological studies in the Seistan basin of South-Western Afghanistan and Eastern Iran *A.M.N.H. Anthrop. Papers,* Vol. 48, Part I. New York.

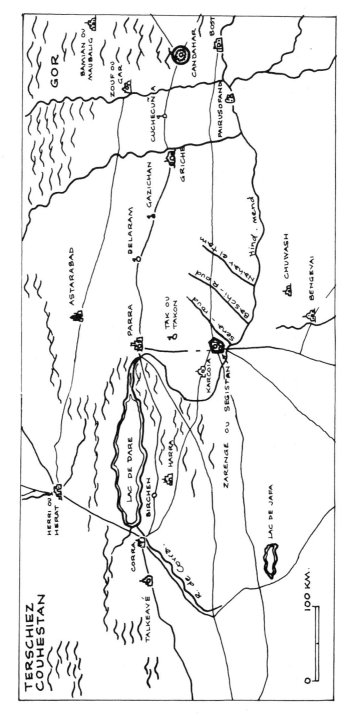

Figure 10.8 Seistan in Delisle's Atlas, 1724.

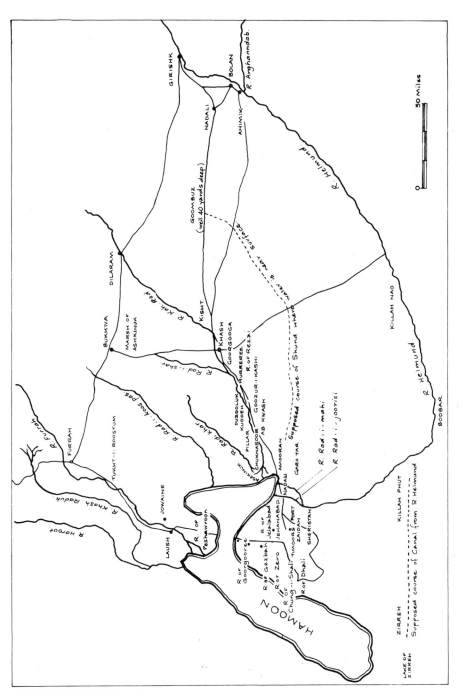

Figure 10.9 Seistan after Edward Conolly, 1840.

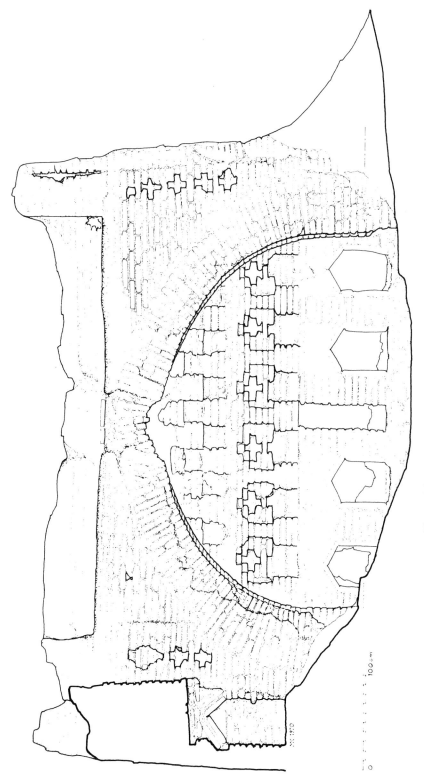

Figure 10.10 Drawing of mud brick iwan at Dewai-i Khodaydad.

Fischer, K. (1961) Recent research in ancient Seistan. *Afghanistan*, 16, No. 2.

Fischer, K. (1967) Der spätsassanidische Feuertempel-Typus in Obergeschob eines Lehmziegel-Turmes in Afghanisch-Seistan und die indo-islamische Baukunst, in *Festschrift für Wilhelm Eilers*. Wiesbaden.

Fischer, K. (1969/70) Archaeological studies in Seistan and adjacent areas. *Afghanistan*, 22.

Fischer, K. (1970*a*) Interrelations of Islamic architecture in Afghanistan. Marg, December 1970, No. 1.

Fischer, K. (1970*b*) Projects of archaeological maps from Afghan-Seistan between 31°20′ to 30°50′N and 62°00′ to 62°10′E., in *Zentralasiatische Studien*, No. 4. Wiesbaden.

Fisher, K. (1970/71) Rapport préliminaire sur la prospection archéologique du Seistan septentrional en octobre 1970. *Afghanistan*, 23.

Hammond, N. (1970) An archaeological reconnaissance in the Helmand Valley, South Afghanistan. *East and West*, 20.

Herzfeld, E. (1932) Sakastan, geschichtliche Untersuchungen zu den Ausgrabungen am Kuh-i Khwadja. *Archäologische Mitteilungen Aus Iran*, 4.

Kohzad, A.A. (1953) Nimrouz ou le bassin inférieur de l'Hilmend. *Afghanistan*, 8, No. 4.

M.D.A.F.A. (1959) Mémoires de la Délégation Archéologique Française en Afghanistan, VIII (J.-C. Gardin, R. Ghirshman, J. Hackin).

Rawlinson, H. (1873) Notes on Seistan. *Journal of the R. Geographical Society of London*, 43.

Scerrato, U. (1962) A probable Achaemenid zone in Persian Sistan. *East and West*, 13.

Scerrato, U. (1966) Excavation at Dahan-i Ghulaman (Seistan-Iran), first preliminary report. *East and West*, 16.

Schlumberger, D. (1952) Le palais Ghaznévide de Lashkari Bazar. *Syria*, 29.

Ta'rih-i Sistan. Ta lif-i-dar-hudud 445-725. Ed.: Malik as-su'ara Bahar. Teheran 1935 (1314).

Tate, G.P. (1912) *Seistan. A Memoir on the History, Topography, Ruins and People of the Country*. Calcutta.

Tosi, M. (1968-9) Excavations at Shahr-i Sokhta, a Chalcolithic settlement in the Iranian Sistan. Preliminary report on the first campaign, October-December 1967. *East and West*, 18, 1968 and 19, 1969.

ACKNOWLEDGMENTS
Figs. 10.1-9: Mrs. H. Pinschke
Fig. 10.10: Dr.-ing. M. Klinkott

11

Archaeological and Radiocarbon Chronologies for Protohistoric South Asia

GEORGE F. DALES

The early chronology of the Indus Valley and the eastern half of the Iranian plateau has been fraught with problems since the discovery of the Indus civilization in the 1920s. Until recently the tendency has been to derive the initial cultural impetus for the rise of civilization in South Asia from the Near East — mainly Mesopotamia. Mesopotamian chronology and dating were also imposed on the cultural development of South Asia and the intervening regions on the Iranian plateau. But by now the increasing quantity and quality of archaeological investigations in the East is making it possible to develop the chronologies of these regions on their own internal evidence (Allchin and Allchin, 1968; Casal, 1969; De Cardi, 1965; Wheeler, 1968). Also, the use of radiocarbon dating has added an important new dimension to the solution of the chronological problems (Agrawal, 1964; 1966; Dales, 1965; 1971).

This concern with chronology and dating is of more than academic importance at this stage of our knowledge. For example, as emphasized by Colin Renfrew (1970), new and more accurate cultural and historical configurations are possible to discern as chronologies and temporal interrelationships are refined. This is especially vital here as we learn more about the extent and complexity of 'international' trade and other inter-cultural contacts.

The purpose of this paper is to review the current status of the chronology and dating of the fourth and third millennia in the eastern Iranian plateau region and the greater Indus Valley. This will be done first from the standpoint of traditional comparative archaeology (fig. 11.1). Secondly, the pertinent radiocarbon dates are tabulated and discussed (fig. 11.2). Thirdly, the new correction factors proposed by the physicists for radiocarbon dates are tabulated and evaluated in relation to the first two mentioned types of chronological frameworks. Although it is not my intention to

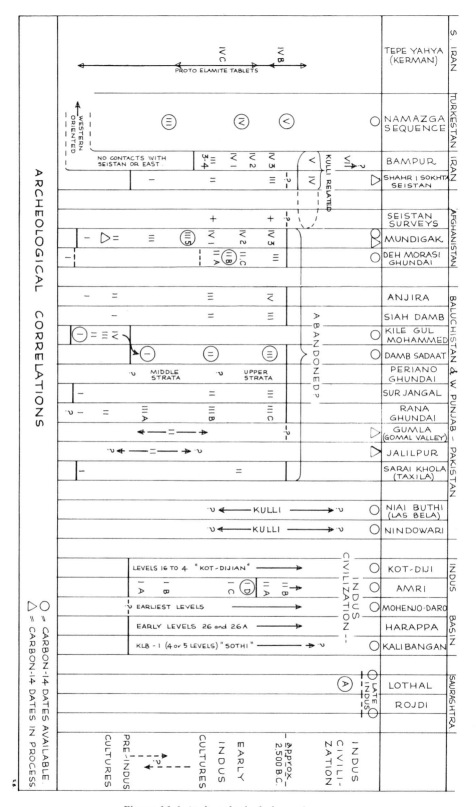

Figure 11.1 Archaeological chronology.

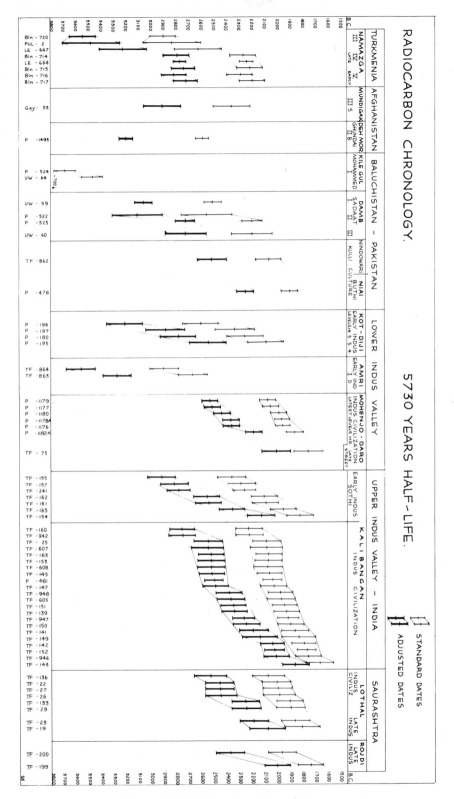

Figure 11.2 Radiocarbon chronology.

delve deeply into matters of interpretation and reconstruction, a few patterns emerge from the raw chronological data that are suggestive and of potential historical and cultural importance. Finally, the role of Seistan, that once rich and productive region that now straddles the desolate border between south-western Afghanistan and eastern Iran, is discussed.

The archaeological chronology

Fig. 11.1 summarizes the primary correlations between the early sites of the greater Indus Valley, Baluchistan, southern Afghanistan, Seistan, and Turkmenistan (see fig. 11.3). There are, and always will be, differences of opinion about specific correlations, but in general I believe the figure has practical validity. The correlations suffer badly from the fact that archaeology in this part of the world is still ceramic typology bound and only a few sites have received more than preliminary trenching. Two of the sites on the chart, Gumla and Jalilpur, have been too recently excavated to be generally known through published reports. Gumla, in the Gomal Valley on northern Baluchistan, was excavated by Professor A.H. Dani of Peshawar University. Jalilpur, in Multan District, Pakistan, was excavated during the summer of 1971 by Dr Rafique Mughal of the Pakistan Department of Archaeology. Both of these sites are extremely important for the new information they are shedding on contacts between the Indus region, Afghanistan, and Turkmenistan. Radiocarbon samples from both sites are being tested.

A word concerning terminology is necessary. South Asia's earliest civilization, centred in the Indus Valley, is known to us only through its mute archaeological remains. Its writing system has yet to be convincingly deciphered. Thus the civilization has been called either Harappan (after the modern name of one of its major cities) or the Indus civilization. Both names have drawbacks. To use a single site name focuses undue attention on a settlement of unknown significance and function in the total civilization. The discovery of impressive ancient settlements of this culture outside the Indus Valley — especially in Saurashtra — has put into question the propriety of using the label Indus civilization. Even more troublesome is what to designate those occupation levels and sites having cultural materials that are stratigraphically and typologically earlier than what is generally accepted as the mature manifestation of this civilization. The term 'pre-Indus' begs the question and conveys the impression that we know more about the origin of the civilization than we do. Recently, a detailed review of all the evidence from the

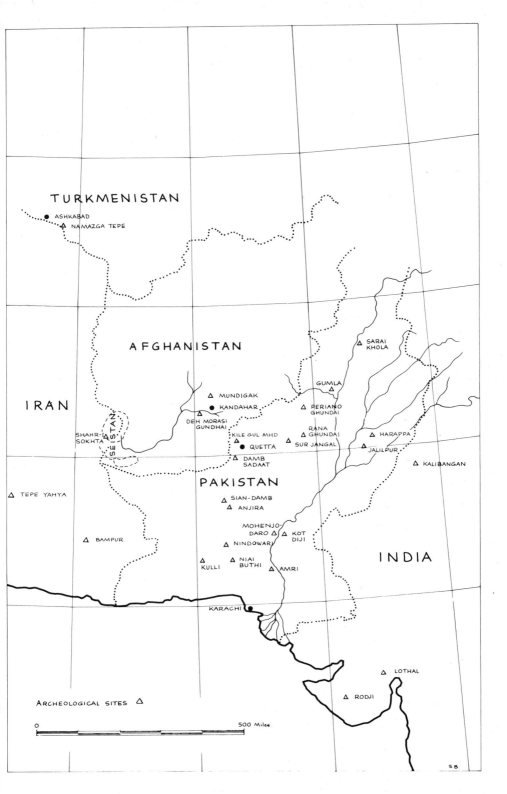

Figure 11.3 The location of sites mentioned in the text.

early sites of the Indus Valley and northern Baluchistan has produced convincing criteria for recognizing what may have been the early formative phases of the civilization (Mughal, 1970). Mr Mughal has proposed the terminological scheme 'Mature Harappan', 'Early Harappan', 'pre-Early Harappan'. But one can object that his use of 'Early Harappan' implies that all the early settlements in the greater Indus Valley and northern Baluchistan dating from about 3000 B.C. to 2400 B.C. were participating in the general development towards the mature urbanized civilization that is so dramatically exemplified by the city-sites such as Mohenjo-daro, Harappa, and Kalibangan. This terminology question was informally discussed among several members of the 1971 Cambridge conference (R. Allchin, B.K. Thapar, J.-M. Casal, B. de Cardi, and myself). Final agreement was not reached but there was general satisfaction expressed for a scheme such as this for the greater Indus Valley:

Indus Civilization: Designates the 'mature' maximal stage of the culture as exemplified by the major city-sites and described most eloquently by Sir Mortimer Wheeler (1966 and 1968). Despite the objection raised about the name 'Indus', it is thought best to retain it because of its wide and popular usage.

Early Indus Cultures: Designates those various cultural deposits either stratified directly beneath remains of the Indus civilization or found at smaller sites otherwise dated before the period of the Indus civilization. Some of these — e.g. the early levels at Kot-Diji (Khan, 1965; Mughal, 1970), the 'Sothi' levels at Kalibangan (Indian Archaeology, 1960-5), and the 'pre-defence' material at Harappa (Wheeler, 1947) qualify for Mughal's definition of an early formative phase of the Indus civilization. On the other hand, the early levels at sites such as Amri (Casal, 1964) do not contain material that anticipates that of the Indus civilization and should be classified as belonging to an early Indus culture of still undetermined affinity. Even those sites that belong to the early formative phase of Indus civilization should, on present evidence, be regarded as relatively independent from one another. They shared certain common traits, styles and techniques that eventually coalesced to form the mature Indus civilization, but originally these sites had other traits that were peculiar in their own micro-region.

Pre-Indus Cultures: Designates those sites or early levels of sites that are temporally much earlier than the first discernable settlements that developed into the Indus civilization. The dividing line — temporally and artifactually — has yet to be determined through extensive and intensive new excavations in Baluchistan and the greater Indus Valley.

This tripartite classification is admittedly gross. New and more extensive excavations will hopefully increase our knowledge not just of ceramics and artifacts, but of settlements, settlement patterns, and environmental details that will allow us to understand better the processes involved in the development of South Asia's earliest civilization. The terminology just discussed does not apply to those regions west of the present western border of Pakistan. For southern Afghanistan and eastern Iran it is still necessary to identify cultural groups by site names (Dales, 1971). If the present work of the Italian archaeologists in Iranian Seistan continues (Tosi, 1968; 1969; 1970a, b) we should soon be able to develop a more meaningful classification of the occupational sequence. The importance of the Seistan region can not be overemphasized. Historically, and now archaeologically, it is evident that Seistan was at the hub of 'international' trade and other contacts between South Asia, Central Asia, and the Near East as early as the middle of the fourth millennium B.C. Although Seistan did not apparently have first-hand contacts with the Indus civilization, it did have strong contacts with some of the Early Indus Cultures and areas such as south-eastern Afghanistan (Mundigak, Deh Morasi Ghundai) and Turkmenistan. Thus a stronger chronological framework for Seistan is essential to that of the entire region covered in this paper.

The radiocarbon chronology (fig. 11.2)

The shortcomings and abuses of C14 dating are becoming proverbial in archaeological literature. However, from the standpoint of the South Asian evidence, the main thing to be discouraged about is the lack of enough dates and the dismal prospects of obtaining many in the near future. What few dates are available must be carefully and consistently analysed. Here I have converted all the published dates to the 5,730 years half-life as is the standard practice at the University of Pennsylvania Radiocarbon Laboratory. Certain dates have been excluded, namely, those derived from the old solid-carbon samples, dates with inordinately large tolerances, and dates that are logically inconsistent. The narrow vertical bars in the upper part of fig. 11.2 show the maximum range of each date as published in *Radiocarbon*. Dates belonging to the same phase or period of a site are enclosed by solid lines so as to emphasize the total block of time represented by the dates rather than the limits of any single date. The laboratory numbers are given for each date so that details of their publication can be found in *Radiocarbon*. On fig. 11.1, circles are placed around those site periods or levels that have provided radiocarbon dates. The triangle signs indicate those sites that have provided new carbon samples that are currently in the process of being dated.

Comparison of the relative temporal position of the blocks on the radiocarbon chart (fig. 11.1) and the corresponding cultural phases or levels on the archaeological chart (fig. 11.2) shows a generally consistent correspondence. There are some anomalies, e.g. the radiocarbon date for Deh Morasi Ghundai seems too early and that for Mundigak III, 5 too late, but single samples are dangerous to rely on at any rate. The Amri dates — only two — also appear to be too early. The Tepe Yahya dates so far published are too inconsistent and out of line with accepted archaeological parallels to be meaningful (Lamberg-Karlovsky, 1970; 1971). New dates are presently being calculated from this very important site in southern Iran that may help clarify some of the chronological relationships between southern Iran and Seistan. Finally, a puzzling situation is presented by the almost total overlap of the radiocarbon dates from the 'Sothi' and Indus civilization levels at Kalibangan. Preliminary reports on the excavations (*Indian Archaeology*, 1960-5) give the impression that the 'Sothi' phase proceeds the mature Indus civilization occupation and has been regarded by Mughal (1970) as belonging to the general early formative phase of Indus civilization.

New adjustments for radiocarbon dates

As if many archaeologists were not already confused and discouraged by the apparent unreliability of radiocarbon dating, the physicists are now proposing major adjustments to bring radiocarbon dates more in line with historical reality (Michael and Ralph, 1970 and 1971; Renfrew, 1970). Correction factors have been determined from inconsistencies between radiocarbon and denrochronological chronologies. For the B.C. era, the correction factors that should be added to the standard radiocarbon dates grow progressively larger as you go earlier in time — from plus fifty years at 300 B.C. to plus 650 years at 2700 B.C. The most recent calculations for the time period covered in this paper are as follows. (Michael and Ralph, 1971).

Time period represented by radiocarbon dates (5,730 half-title)	Average correction to be added
1551 B.C. − 1750 B.C.	200 years
1751 B.C. − 1900 B.C.	300 years
1901 B.C. − 2050 B.C.	400 years
2051 B.C. − 2225 B.C.	500 years
2226 B.C. − 2450 B.C.	550 years.
2451 B.C. − 2650 B.C.	550 years
2651 B.C. − 2850 B.C.	650 years

Thus, for example, a published radiocarbon date of 1950 B.C. should be corrected to 2350 B.C.

These correction factors have been added to each date in fig. 11.2 and are represented by the heavier vertical bars on the lower part of the figure. Note that because of the progressive increase in the size of the correction factors, the blocks of dates for each site phase or level are elongated and encompass a longer time span than do the blocks for the unadjusted dates. At first glance this appears to make the dating for any particular phase or period less precise than the unadjusted dates seem to indicate. Actually, however, given the innate variables of any radiocarbon determination, the broader range suggested by the adjusted dates may be more realistic. This emphasizes even more strongly the desirability of treating C14 dates in blocks and units with rather large overlapping tolerance levels rather than placing much reliability on single isolated samples.

Comparison of the adjusted dates with the archaeological correlations presents us with a chronological structure that seems to fit much better than that using the unadjusted dates. For example, using the adjusted dates (with the 5,730 half-life) for the Early Indus Cultures, we get close agreement with the archaeological parallels that link phases such as Mundigak IV, Bampur IV, Namazga IV, Susa D (south-western Iran) and the Mesopotamian Early Dynastic period. Similarly, the adjusted dates for the Indus Civilization bring the Indus chronology directly in line with the historical chronology of Mesopotamia. The adjusted Indus dates compare closely with the accepted historical dates for the Mesopotamian Old Akkadian and Ur III periods. These were the periods of considerable seafaring activities by the Mesopotamians and of the presence of Indus-type artifacts in southern Mesopotamia. The adjusted dates also allow for a late slowing down and eventual disappearance of the classic Indus civilization by about 1900 B.C. This coincides favourably with the latter part of the Mesopotamian Isin-Larsa period and the cessation of Mesopotamian seafaring activities.

The adjusted dates also correlate better with the archaeological parallels between the Early Indus Cultures, Afghanistan, Seistan, and Turkmenistan and add support to the Russians' comparative dating of their Namazga III period (Mesopotamian Ubeid-Uruk periods) and Namazga IV (Jamdat Nasr) (Dyson, 1968; Masson, 1961 and 1968, Mellaart, 1967; Frumkin, 1970). The importance of the new radiocarbon dates from Shahr-i Sokhta, Mundigak II (collected by G. Dales in 1969; note at end of paper), Gumla, Jalilpur can not be over-stressed. They are expected to strengthen the framework of South Asian chronology so that it can be brought to bear on some of the unresolved problems of Iranian chronology and inter-cultural contacts.

Some historical patterns

Although the chronological framework is still very slight, a few patterns are beginning to emerge from a study of the archaeological parallels and the radiocarbon charts that go beyond the mundane timetables.

First, the archaeological parallels, reinforced by the adjusted radiocarbon dates, suggest that for several centuries before 3000 B.C. there were strong overland cultural and economic contacts ranging from Turkmenistan (Namazga III) through Seistan (Shahr-i Sokhta I), south-eastern Afghanistan (Mundigak III), through northern Baluchistan and into the sphere of the Early Indus Cultures of the middle and upper Indus basin (Dales, 1971).

The archaeological contacts are quite convincing, including not merely ceramic analogies but virtually identical female figurines, art motifs, and especially significant, the widespread presence of lapis lazuli. Workshops, with raw and finished lapis beads are reported at Shahr-i Sokhta (Tosi, 1970a) and large quantities of lapis have recently been discovered at the Early Indus site of Jalilpur (Mughal, personal communication). During this period, Seistan and the lower Helmand valley provided the south-western limit of this cultural sphere. There is no evidence of contact between Seistan and Bampur or Tepe Yahya in southern Iran. Bampur's cultural gaze was cast westward, past Yahya to as far as southern Mesopotamia (de Cardi, 1970).

However, it should be noted that the Period I levels of Shahr-i Sokhta had not yet been published when Miss de Cardi made the above suggestions. Now with the publication of the second season's work (Tosi, 1969), she does see several specific parallels in the painted designs between Shahr-i Sokhta I and her Bampur I and II. Also, there was the common tendency at both sites to apply painted decorations to both the interior and exterior of the rims. The cultural significance of these few parallels, if any, remains to be determined.

Then, at approximately 3000 B.C., we see the first evidence of contact between Bampur (III, 3-4) — with its southern Iranian culture — and Seistan. This heralds the start of dramatic changes in 'international' contacts and spheres of contact and influences that culminate by approximately 2500 B.C. in the following new patterns:

(*a*) Archaeological evidence for contacts between Turkmenistan and the greater Indus region cease and we see the independent development of urban civilization in each region.

(*b*) The reasons for this break in contact are unknown but a look at fig. 11.1 shows that some serious disruption had apparently taken place along the land routes between Turkmenistan and the Indus. Every site, from Mundigak through northern Baluchistan, was abandoned at this time (Dales, 1965 and 1971).

(*c*) The result of this unexplained abandonment of the northern land routes is a dramatic shift in the avenues of contact to the south, into southern Baluchistan and along the Indian Ocean Coast. This is the period of the 'mature' Indus civilization in the east and of the apparently flourishing seafaring activities of the Mesopotamians in the West (Akkadian and Ur III periods) (Bibby, 1969; Dales, 1968; Oppenheim, 1954). Contacts between Bampur, southern Iran, and the Persian Gulf were also maximized during this period. Seistan's role changed. Its relations with Mundigak and northern Baluchistan had ceased, but its contacts with Turkmenistan and southern Iran continued. The lapis trade continued but only with the Near East. Very little lapis is found in Indus civilization contexts. Seistan may well have been a major source of raw materials for the Near East. Large quantities of alabaster and other stone are present, both in the raw state and in the form of bowls and other objects. Copper smelting was carried out on a vast scale as is witnessed by the miles of slag and furnaces in the Gardan reg part of southern Afghan Seistan. (Dales and Flam, 1969; Fairservis, 1961.) These areas and materials will receive intensive study during the University of Pennsylvania's 1971-2 project in Afghan Seistan.

Summary

The use of the adjusted radiocarbon dates fits best with the comparative archaeological chronology for South Asia and the eastern Iranian plateau. It also fits well with the archaeological evidence for contacts between the Indus and Mesopotamia. The current field work in Seistan (especially at Shahr-i Sokhta) and in the northern Indus region (Gumla and Jalilpur) is essential to both chronological and dating problems and to the further documentation of cultural and economic contacts between South Asia, Central Asia, and the Near East.

Three Mundigak dates received while this paper was in press are: Period I, 2-3: 3145 ± 110 BC (TF-1129); Period I, 5: 2755 ± 105 BC (TF-1131); Period II, 1 or I, 5(?): 2995 ± 105 BC (TF-1132). 5730 half life; on wood charcoal from Mound A.

REFERENCES

Agrawal, D.P. (1964) Harappan culture: new evidence for a shorter chronology. *Science*, 143, 950-2.
Agrawal, D.P. (1966) Harappan chronology: a re-examination of the evidence, in *Studies in Prehistory*, Calcutta.
Allchin, B. and Allchin, R. (1968) *The Birth of Indian Civilization*. Harmondsworth.
Bibby, G. (1969) *Looking for Dilmun*. New York.
Casal, J.-M. (1961) *Fouilles de Mundigak*. 2 vols. Paris.
Casal, J.-M. (1964) *Fouilles de Amri*. 2 vols. Paris.
Casal, J.-M. (1969) *La civilisation de l'Indus et ses énigmes*. Paris.
Dales, G.F. (1962) Harappan outposts on the Makran coast. *Antiquity*, 36, 86-92.
Dales, G.F. (1965) A suggested chronology for Afghanistan, Baluchistan and the Indus Valley, in *Chronologies in Old World Archaeology*. Chicago, 257-84.
Dales, G.F. (1968) Of Dice and Men. *Journal of the American Oriental Society*, Vol. 88 (1), 14-23.
Dales, G.F. (1971) Early human contacts from the Persian Gulf through Baluchistan and southern Afghanistan, in *Food, Fiber, and the Arid Lands*. University of Arizona, 145-70.
Dales, G. and Flam, L. (1969) On tracking wooly Kullis and the like. *Expedition*, Vol. 12 (1), 15-23.
de Cardi, B. (1965) Excavations and reconnaissance in Kalat, West Pakistan. *Pakistan Archaeology*, No. 2. Karachi, 86-181.
de Cardi, B. (1970) Excavations at Bampur, a third millennium settlement in Persian Baluchistan, 1966. *Anthropological Papers of the American Museum of Natural History*, Vol. 51, Part 3. New York.
Dyson, R.H. (1968) The archaeological evidence of the second millennium B.C. on the Iranian Plateau. Revised Edition of the *Cambridge Ancient History*, Vol. II, Chapter XVI.
Fairservis, W.A. (1961) Archaeological studies in the Seistan Basin of Southwestern Afghanistan and Eastern Iran. *Anthropological Papers of the American Museum of Natural History*, Vol. 48, Part 1. New York.
Frumkin, G. (1970) *Archaeology in Soviet Central Asia*. Leiden.
Indian Archaeology: A Review. Archaeological Survey of India. New Delhi. Yearly.
Khan, F.A. (1965) Excavations at Kot Diji. *Pakistan Archaeology*, No. 2, 11-85.

Lamberg-Karlovsky, C.C. (1970) Excavations at Tepe Yahya, Iran (1967-69). Progress Report I. American School of Prehistoric Research, Peabody Museum, Harvard. *Bulletin* 27.

Lamberg-Karlovsky, C.C. (1971) The Proto-Elamite Settlement at Tepe Yahya. *Iran*, IX: 87-96.

Masson, V.M. (1961) The first farmers in Turkmenia. *Antiquity,* Vol. XXXV 203-13.

Masson, V.M. (1968) The Urban Revolution in South Turkmenia. *Antiquity*, Vol. XLII, 178-87.

Mellaart, J. (1967) The earliest settlements in Western Asia. Revised Edition of the *Cambridge Ancient History*, Vol. 1, Chapter VII.

Michael, H.N. and Ralph, E.K. (1970) Correction factors applied to Egyptian radiocarbon from the era before Christ, in, *Radiocarbon Variations and Absolute Chronology*, Olson, I.U. (ed.) Nobel Symposium, 12th Uppsala University 1969, Proceedings, 109-20. New York.

Michael, H.N. and Ralph, E.K. (1971) (in press) *Dating Techniques for the Archaeologist.* Boston, Mass.

Mughal, M.R. (1970) The Early Harappan Period in the greater Indus Valley and northern Baluchistan. University of Pennsylvania, Philadelphia, Department of Anthropology, Ph.D. dissertation.

Oppenheim, A.L. (1954) The seafaring merchants of Ur. *Journal of the American Oriental Society*, Vol. 74, 6-17.

Radiocarbon Vol. 1, 1959, to date annually. New Haven, Conn.

Renfrew, C. (1970) New configurations in Old World archaeology. *World Archaeology*, Vol. 2, No. 2, 199-211.

Tosi, M. (1968) Excavations at Shahr-i Sokhta, a Chalcolithic settlement in the Iranian Sistan. Preliminary report on the first campaign, October-December 1967. *East and West*, Vol. 18, Nos. 1-2, 9-66.

Tosi, M. (1969) Excavations at Shahr-i Sokhta. Preliminary report on the second campaign, September-December 1968. *East and West*, Vol. 19, Nos. 3-4, 283-386.

Tosi, M. (1970a) On the route for lapis lazuli (in two parts). *Illustrated London News, 24 Jan*, 24-5; *7 Feb*, 24-5.

Tosi, M. (1970b) A Tomb from Damin and the problem of the Bampur sequence in the third millennium B.C. *East and West*, Vol. 20, Nos. 1-2,9-50.

Wheeler, R.E.M. (1947) Harappa 1946: the defences and Cemetery R.37. *Ancient India*, No. 3, 58-130.

Wheeler, R.E.M. (1966) *Civilizations of the Indus Valley and Beyond.* New York.

Wheeler, R.E.M. (1968) *The Indus Civilization* (3rd ed.) Supplementary Volume, Cambridge History of India.

12

Excavations at Pirak, West Pakistan

J.-M. CASAL, Mission Archéologique de l'Indus

Discovered in 1957 by R.L. Raikes, Pirak lies in the plain of Baluchistan, on the western side of the road from Quetta to Jacobabad, about 12 miles south of Sibi (fig. 12.1). It is a low mound, about 300 x 200 m in size. Its highest point is only 8 m above the level of the plain (pl. 12.1a). Among the surface finds, the most noticeable were fragments of bichrome painted pottery of a kind hitherto unknown (pl. 12.1b). It is handmade and crude and the decoration consists of geometric patterns painted black or dark brown with red fillings on a buff background. There were also many small flint blades, with one carefully serrated edge, probably sickle elements (pl. 12.1c).

Finding together these two categories of objects led the discoverer to look for related sites. Having found no similarities with any of the sites so far known in Pakistan, he looked further afield, and finally discovered that the designs painted on the Pirak pottery were the same as some of the motifs painted on the Samarra ware of Mesopotamia. The conclusion he came to was that Pirak could have been the oldest seat of a sedentary life in Pakistan (R.L. Raikes, 1963: 67-68; and 1965: 76).

In 1967, as we had no possibility of carrying on the excavations undertaken at Nindowari in Southern Baluchistan, we asked the Pakistan authorities for permission to excavate Pirak. The license was granted early in 1968 and work started immediately.

For the first season a trial trench was dug in steps from the top of the mound on its western side, to a length of 43 m, down to the virgin soil which was reached some 10 m below, and 1.75 m below plain level (pl. 12.2a). From the first season, it was possible to learn that there was no apparent break in the occupation of the mound, but that three phases could be distinguished.

The bichrome painted ware, of which so many sherds had been

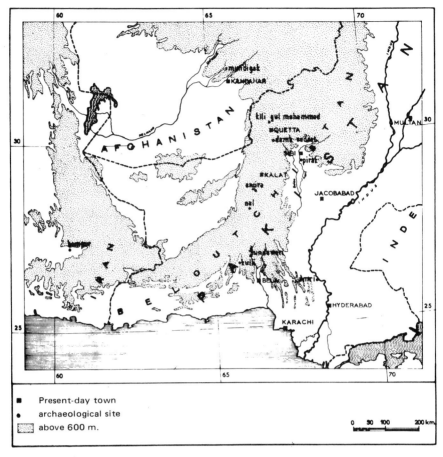

Figure 12.1 The locations of sites mentioned in the text.

Plate 12.1(a) Pirak. General view from the east.

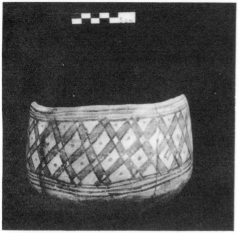

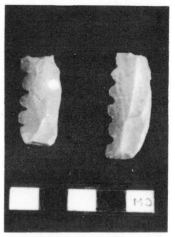

Plate 12.1(b) Pirak. Bichrome painted pottery.

Plate 12.1(c) Pirak. Flint blades with serrated edge.

Plate 12.2(a) Pirak. Trial trench, seen from west.

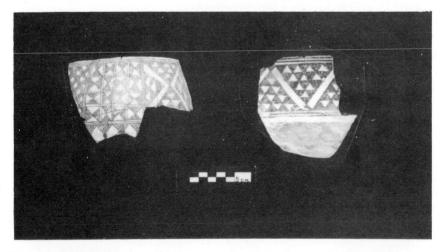

Plate 12.2(b) Pirak. Monochrome painted pottery; left, red on buff; right, dark brown on buff.

Plate 12.3(a) Pirak. Sherds of black pottery.

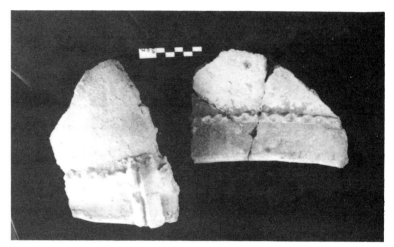

Plate 12.3(b) Pirak. Specimens of crude white pottery.

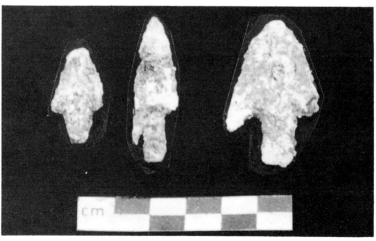

Plate 12.3(c) Pirak. Iron arrow heads.

collected on the surface, was mostly to be found in the middle phase, although stray specimens of it were present in the upper levels too. The lowest layers yielded only specimens of a buff pottery decorated with one colour (pl. 12.2b). And it was obvious that a majority of the motifs of the bichrome painted ware originated in the monochrome decoration.

As for the upper third of the mound, the majority of the pottery collected in its levels was a black or greyish ware of which a few specimens had been turned on the wheel (pl. 12.3a).

Besides these three main categories of pottery there are a few others such as a plain red-painted ware which occurs mainly in phases 2 and 3. Another is a crude plain whitish pottery often decorated with relief bands bearing incisions or fingertip impressions (pl. 12.3b). This last category consists mostly of jars or similar big vessels, and it has been found from the lowest layer above virgin soil throughout all subsequent occupations, up to the end of the site, thus displaying a rare continuity in fashion.

But the most astonishing discovery came with that of wrought iron in the last phase, that of the black pottery (pl. 12.3a). With it vanished the anticipated great antiquity of the site. Two samples of charcoal tested by the Tata Institute of Bombay for the layers corresponding to the oldest level with iron gave dates between 875 and 610 B.C. (955-685 B.C.). Correlatively with such dating, it has been noticed that all layers, from top to bottom, yielded besides the various wares of Pirak which are hand-made a few typical sherds which had been part of wheel-turned vessels, probably imports.

It is obvious, then, that no such antiquity can be attributed to Pirak as its discoverer had first suggested. But another point of importance is revealed: Pirak is, so far, the first site excavated in Pakistan which gives indications of the passage from the Bronze Age to Iron Age.

Unfortunately, the community sheltered at Pirak seems mainly to have lived rather in isolation, sticking for hundreds, and probably even thousands, of years to its own traditions. This is clear from the permanent use of the whitish pottery from the beginning to the end. But the same applies to the way in which houses were built. A peculiarity of Pirak was indeed soon noticed when, in the upper levels, rooms were found with small niches in the walls (pl. 12.4a). It has since been ascertained that such a process was a long-lived feature at Pirak (pl. 12.4b). Some ten levels have now been successively cleared, and all of them have shown the same niches, sometimes disposed on all four walls of a room.

It seems therefore that the inhabitants of Pirak remained permanently rather conservative, and this, together with the absence

Plate 12.4(a) Pirak. Room with niches in the upper levels.

Plate 12.4(b) Pirak. The same room partially excavated showing previous stages of building with the same niches in the walls.

of any well-identified pottery in the excavated layers, makes it difficult to assess the total duration of the site.

In these circumstances, the discovery on the surface of the site of a few sherds clearly painted in the fashion of Baluchi Chalcolithic sites raised the question of the layers they had come from (pl. 12.5a). None had been found in the trial trench made in the first year, so that I decided in the last season to open a small sondage on the northern slope of the mound where a few ancient sherds had been collected. The result was nil. We were outside the main settlement there; the structural remains were very scarce, and the layers obviously consisted of refuse and debris which had run down the slope. The order of deposition and the classification of the sherds collected in that sondage roughly agreed with the classification previously established in the trial trench, but no Chalcolithic pottery was discovered. Ironically enough, the head of a broken Mother-Goddess figurine had been found on the surface of the spot excavated! (pl. 12.5c).

As for the virgin soil, it was found at the same level as in the main trench. It consisted of alluvial sand. We dug for more than a metre without success, and then gave up in order to concentrate on the main excavation.

Finally, in the last week of the season, a few sherds apparently from the Chalcolithic period were found in stratified deposits, some 1.50 or 1.80 m above virgin soil (pl. 12.5b). The next season will thus be of exceptional interest if a number of such sherds turn up in the lowest layers.

If this is the case, the conclusion would be that the oldest phase of Pirak, with monochrome decorated pottery, might be con-temporaneous with, at least, the last phase of the Quetta period, and in fact a few sherds of the monochrome decorated ware of Pirak could support such a suggestion. But this conclusion would raise another problem for which there is no adequate answer. It would indeed be difficult to reconcile such a long duration, let us say from 2500 or 2200 B.C. to *c.* 600 B.C., which means 1,900 or at least 1,600 years of continuous occupation with an accumulation of debris 10 m deep, which does not represent more than 40 to 60 cm per century.

Moreover one anyway must always remain cautious, as is shown by the following story. During the last season, I was very pleased when several fragments of a single vessel, obviously Harappan, turned up on an intermediate layer (fig. 12.2). It was the only specimen we have ever found of an identifiable import. But this feeling soon turned into disappointment when it became evident that that layer really belonged to a late phase and that iron was still present in a

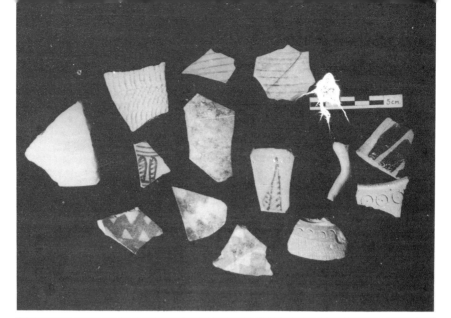

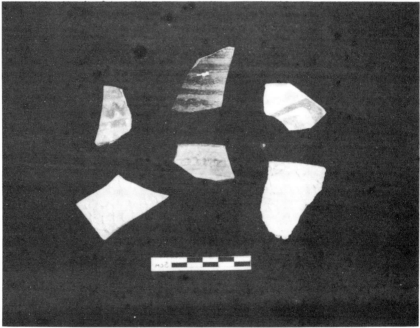

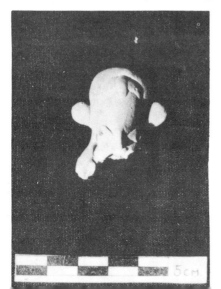

Plate 12.5(a) Pirak. Sherds of Chalcolithic period collected on the surface.

Plate 12.5(b) Pirak. Sherds of Chalcolithic period found in stratified context.

Plate 12.5(c) Head of a Mother-Goddess figurine found on the surface.

Figure 12.2   Fragments of a single Harappan vessel from Pirak.

lower level. It was just one of those pitfalls in archaeology of which Sir Mortimer Wheeler warned us years ago!

Rather than giving a provisional report of the levels and layers excavated, I have preferred to dwell on the various problems encountered in the course of excavations at Pirak. Samples of charcoal from the upper layers of the first phase have been sent for radiocarbon dating, but no result is yet available. Let us hope that the thorough exploration of the lowest layers down to virgin soil, as well as fresh C14 datings will help give a total vision of Pirak and make clear its full significance in the archaeology of Pakistan.

REFERENCES

Raikes, Robert L. (1963) New prehistoric Bichrome ware from the plain of Baluchistan (West Pakistan). *East and West*, New Series, Vol. 14, Nos. 1-2, March-June 1963, 56-68.

Raikes, Robert, L. (1965) A Supplementary Note on Pirak Bichrome ware. *East and West*, New Series, Vol. 15, Nos. 1-2, Jan. 1964-March 1965, 69-78.

13

Chalcolithic pottery from four sites in the Bolan area of Baluchistan, West Pakistan

J.F. ENAULT and J.F. JARRIGE

The area where the Bolan Pass debouches into the Kacchi lowland is one of the most interesting regions in Pakistan from the archaeological point of view (fig. 13.1). It is the connecting point between the Quetta Valley, well known for its Chalcolithic settlements, and the Indus plain where the Harappan civilization flourished. Geographically, the Bolan Pass does not merge directly into the Kacchi plain: before Bibi Nani levy post, the pass widens and forms a plateau of alluvial soils mixed with rubble, where, owing to the perennial Bolan river, cultivation is possible. Then, after a last narrowing at the foot of the Kohan Spur, the Kacchi lowland begins, a few miles west of Dadhar.

Merghar

Merghar, the first site visited, stands in the fertile alluvial plain itself, 9 miles south of Dadhar. It is a low mound divided in two parts of about 150 m x 150 m each. The surface of the mound and adjoining plain is covered by a large number of potsherds. Stone implements were found in plenty — most of them parallel-sided blades in chert — along with a few arrowheads (pl. 13.1). Among the small finds in terracotta were many fragments of bangles, some with traces of painting, and a few lower parts of female figurines (pl. 13.2). These figurines have a slim waist, broad hips, inflected legs and naturalistic toes. Most of the time one finds only broken legs; such legs were previously collected from the surface of Pirak mound, also at Damb Sadaat, in the Quetta Valley (Fairservis, 1956: 225) and at Sur Jangal, in Loralai (Stein, 1929, pl. XVI). The only animal figurine from Merghar is a very fine bull with a prominent breast, like an almost identical specimen from Pirak (pl. 13.3). Two fragments of

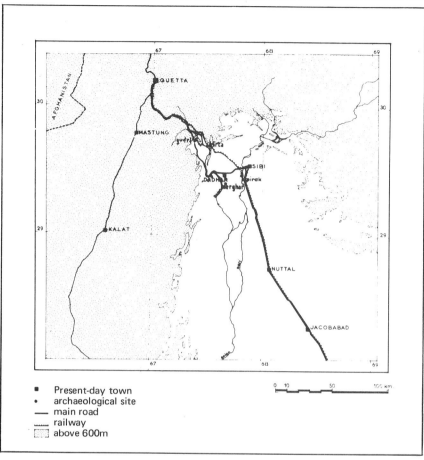

Plate 13.1 Sites in the Bolan-Sibi area of Pakistan.

Plate 13.1 Chert blades from Merghar

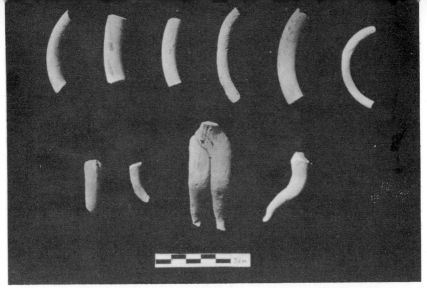

Plate 13.2 Pottery bangle and figurine fragments from Merghar

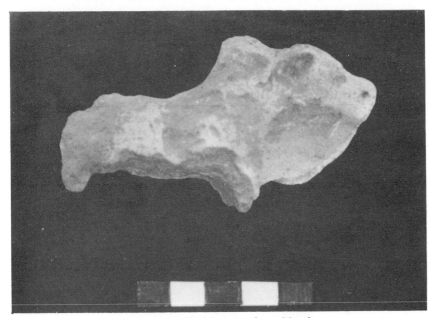

Plate 13.3 Ball figurine from Merghar

alabaster bowls were collected.

A large number of potsherds belongs to a grey ware, very often decorated in black. This ware is fine-grained, thin with a firing-reduced hardness, and when struck, gives a metallic sound. The surface is porcellanous and, when slightly over-baked, becomes greenish. Technically this ware is identical to what Fairservis (1956: 263) calls Faiz Mohammad greyware. The shapes are mostly shallow bowls, or dishes on ring foot or beaded-concave base. The external profile is often concave with a tapering rim (fig. 13.2, 14) or a beak rim (fig. 13.3, 1). A cap-shaped bowl is also a common type (fig. 13.3, 10). The other sherds come from beakers or small jars.

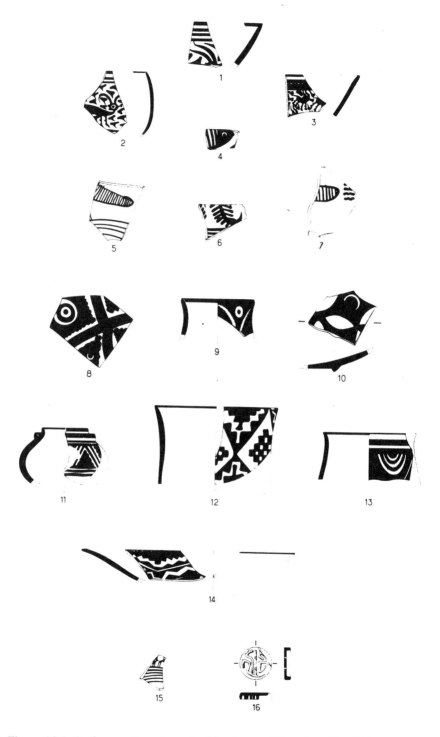

Figure 13.2 Surface pottery from the Merghar and Kot sites. No. 16 is a pottery seal.

Figure 13.3 Surface pottery from the Merghar site.

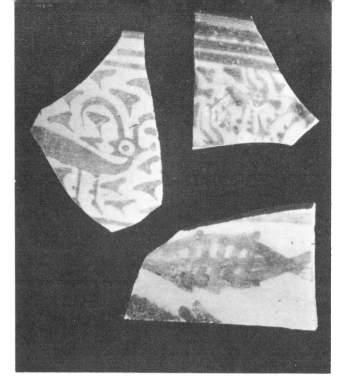

Plate 13.4 Fish and caprid on sherds from Merghar

Plate 13.5 Aquatic plants on sherds from Merghar

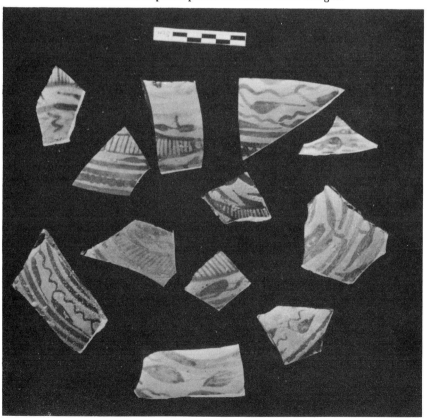

Plate 13.6 Plants on sherds from Merghar

This black-on-grey ware shows a wide range of decorative motives. Zoomorphic designs are of special interest; some of them have not yet been met at other sites. Most noticeable are representations of caprids (fig. 13.2, 1, 2, 3 and pl. 13.4), with long horns, very big eyes and a hammer-like muzzle; they stand on a background filled with stylized pipal leaves; in one case, the animals are shown in a herd, running freely on the surface. Fish are a very common motif, with a hatched body (fig. 13.2, 4 and pl. 13.4; sherds are numbered from top left). Very often they are depicted among aquatic plants (pl. 13.5). These plants with long leaves, associated with fish, are reported from Pathani Damb, in Kacchi district, or without fish from Sharh-i Sokhta (Tosi, 1968: 33), Periano Ghundai and Dabar Kot (Stein, 1929: pl. V and XIV). The same type of plant appears vertically on the inside of bowls (pl. 13.6). Other vegetal motifs are hatched pipal leaves (fig. 13.2, 5) and ball-like fruits, found on many sherds, sometimes on a large scale, showing the almost complete pattern (pl. 13.7). Some ball-like fruits appear on a sherd from Pathani Damb (de Cardi, 1964: pl. III, 16) and on another from Periano Ghundai (Stein, 1929: pl. V, 35). But the majority of potsherds bear geometrical patterns, well known in the Quetta Valley, like chevrons, stepped ovals, triangles with denticulate edging etc., (fig. 13.2, 8, 9, 10 and pl. 13.8).

A few potsherds in grey-ware are decorated in red; they show mostly pipal leaves, groups of sigmas or comb-like motifs

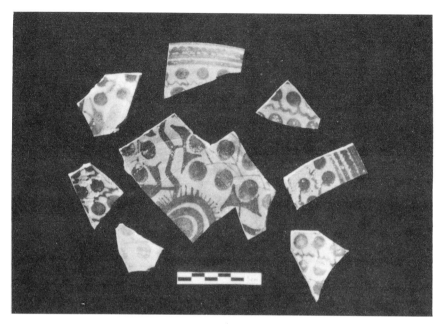

Plate 13.7 Plants on sherds from Merghar

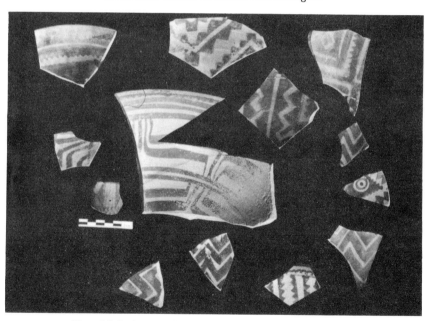

Plate 13.8 Geometric designs on sherds from Merghar

(fig. 13.2,7). Potsherds in buff ware are also present; many of them bear geometrical designs painted in brown or dark red. A fragment of a large basin has a motif of alternating brackets (pl. 13.8), which can also be met at Nal and at Nindowari, in layers earlier than the typical Kulli occupation (Casal, 1966: 19). Fragments of beakers are

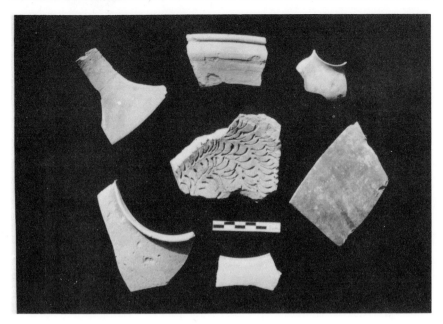

Plate 13.9 Incised and other sherds from Merghar

decorated by a combination of geometric designs in the Quetta style (fig. 13.2, 12) or with semi-circles (fig. 13.2, 13). Triangles with denticular edging appear on a globular pot with a flange around the neck to receive a lid (fig. 13.2,1). Some sherds also in buff ware belong to large globular jars, with slightly flaring tapered rim, sometimes underlined by horizontal painted bands (fig. 13.3,7).

A high proportion of sherds are in Wet ware, many of them coming from circle-stamped jars (fig. 13.3, 2).

A few potsherds occur in red ware, among them a small globular straight-neck jar (fig. 13.3, 6) and a jar with flaring mouth (fig. 13.3, 5). A sherd in pink ware shows a palm painted in dark brown (fig. 13.2, 6). Two finds are of interest for they are closely related to Harappan types; the first is an incised fragment of a dish-on-stand, (pl. 13.9) and the second is a part of a cream-slipped carinated basin with a nail-head rim in a sturdy red fabric (fig. 13.3, 11; pl. 13.9).

Kot

On the western slope of the first narrowing leading from the Kacchi plain to the Bolan plateau, four miles north of Kot, potsherds are spread on the rocky surface. Most of them are in wet-ware and very often circle-stamped. One sherd shows a frieze of caprids (fig. 13.2, 15), in a style recalling that of Sur Jangal (Fairservis, 1959: 392), but

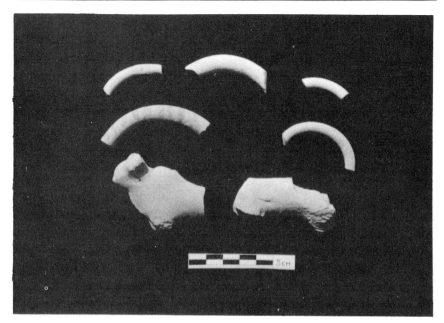

Plate 13.10 Pottery bangles and bull figurines from Kirta

here the painting is red on grey. At the same place was found a circular button-like seal in terracotta with geometrical incisions (fig. 13.2, 16).

The Bolan plateau

The two sites we visited in the Bolan plateau were discovered by Fairservis (1956: 200).
Kirta. The first site, on the route from Dadhar to Quetta, is located five miles north of the village of Kirta, and one mile from the railway line running against the eastern slope of the valley. It is a large mound standing more than ten metres above the plateau level. On the eastern part of the summit is a Muslim cemetery.

No stone implements except for a few shapeless flakes were found. The only small finds in terracotta are fragments of bangles and two broken figurines of bulls (pl. 13.10).

Some potsherds, found in a very small quantity, are in grey-ware with a geometrical decoration painted in black (pl. 13.11, 7, 8, 9, 11, 12, 13); they are associated with a few sherds in buff ware with geometric designs (pl. 13.11, 4, 5, 6, 14, 15). Some straight tapering rim of bowls in pink with painted lines or festoons were also found (pl. 13.13). The most interesting pattern in black-on-buff ware appears on an upper part of a jar showing two flowers which look like

Plate 13.11 Geometric designs on sherds from Kirta

stylized tulips (pl. xxx, 3; pl. xxx,1), closely comparable with specimens from Mundigak, in a mixed layer (Casal, 1961: fig. 128), Kulli (Stein 1931: pl. III), Nindowari and Bampur IV, Phase 1 (de Cardi, 1970: 290) etc., but here the oblique position of the flowers is exceptional. The circle-stamped Wet ware is also represented.

More characteristic of Kirta is a sturdy red ware, sometimes buff, very often covered by a bright red slip, related to Harappan or Kulli pottery. One notices a carinated basin with a nail-head rim (pl. 13.12, 1: fig. 13.4, 6) of a type already found at Merghar, fragments of perforated vessels (pl. 13.12, 2, 3), an incised part of a dish-on-stand, (pl. 13.12, 4), a splayed-out rim of dish-on-stand with Indus-like graffiti (pl. 13.12, 5; fig. 13.4, 5). Many stands were found, some in red-slipped ware, others in buff ware with, in a few cases, a dark brown slip (fig. 13.4, 9, 10). One also meets carinated basins with an externally-thickened rim (fig. 13.4, 7), or carinated and strongly inflected red-slipped basins with a beak rim, decorated with a horizontal and a wavy line (pl. 13.13, 2; fig. 13.4, 8) or with parallel lines and points (pl. 13.13, 1). This type of basin is often found in Kulli culture sites. Jars with an externally thickened rim were also found in large quantities (pl. 13.13, 3).

Several sherds bear Harappan designs, such as the intersecting circles (pl. 13.12, 6), or hatched pipal-leaves associated with a palm-tree in black on a bright slip (pl. 13.12, 7); this last motif is also found on Kulli culture sites, like the fish-scale design on buff or red

Plate 13.12 Perforated, incised and other sherds from Kirta

Plate 13.13 Painted sherds from Kirta

ware (pl.13.12, 8, 9, 10). Some patterns are specially related to Kulli pottery, among them the hatched-wavy line (pl. 13.13, 3, 4), fragments of a palm-tree (pl. 13.13,10) and other vegetal designs (pl. 13.13, 8, 9), a frieze of small caprids (pl. 13.13, 11) and the back of a bull (pl. 13.13, 12).

Plate 13.14 Circle-stamped and other sherds from Gudri

Gudri. Instead of being south of Bibi Nani Levy post as reported by Fairservis (1956: 200), the site is north-east of it, controlling the entrance into the Bolan plateau of one of the small valleys leading to the Bolan pass. The site is divided into two mounds lying against the rocky slope of the mountain.

The only finds were potsherds. The black-on-grey ware with geometric designs is more abundant than in Kirta; as at Merghar, this ware is associated with red-on-grey ware and with wet-ware, in many cases with stamped-circles (pl. 13.14). A group of sherds is in buff ware with geometric designs painted in black (pl. 13.15, 3, 5, 6, 11). Several potsherds in buff ware bear a bichrome geometrical decoration in red and black (pl. 13.15, 8, 9, 10). In a light red ware, one can see cap-shaped bowls, sometimes flat-bottomed (fig. 13.5 6: pl. 13.15, 1, 2), often internally decorated with horizontal lines and festoons, or with groups of parallel vertical lines (pl. 13.15, 5); one also finds basins with everted-tapering rim (fig. 13.5, 9). One of the most frequent motifs seen on red ware is a frieze of animals, most probably caprids, at various stages of stylization (fig. 13.5, 3, 4, 5); hatched pipal leaves in black on red are also commonly found (fig. 13.5, 1); a big palm appears on the bottom of a basin standing on a beaded concave base (fig. 13.5, 8); an upper part of a canister (fig. 13.5, 7) recalls some complete specimens from Kulli (Stein, 1931: pl. XXIII) and from other sites of south Baluchistan. Resembling the Kulli-like pottery from Kirta, one sherd with a very bright red slip

Plate 13.15 Painted sherds from Gudri

shows a pipal leaf and a group of festoons (fig. 13.5, 2).

Conclusion

This surface collection of potsherds and small artifacts from four sites located on the southern foot of the Bolan Pass shows the importance of this area in throwing light on the relations between the Chalcolithic cultures of the Quetta Valley and the Helmand Basin with the Harappan Civilization and the sites of south Baluchistan like Nal and Kulli.

In any case, Merghar appears as a dynamic production centre of greyware. This ware is closely related to the Faiz Mohammad greyware, but is remarkable in the originality and the variety of its naturalistic designs. Pathani Damb (de Cardi, 1964: 28), which was also a large Harappan settlement, has given many potsherds in black or red-on-grey ware, with shapes and decoration commonly found at Merghar. This fact is interesting as Pathani Damb, in the southern part of the Kacchi plain, also occupies a very important position, at the foot of the Mula pass, one of the main routes leading to Kalat.

Harappan influences seem very slight at Merghar, as far as the pottery is concerned, but a few potsherds show definite contact with Harappan ceramics. At Kirta, the situation is different, the greyware is not abundant, but one can feel a very strong Kulli-Harappan influence, in a way recalling the last occupation period at Nindowari. It is interesting to see that the period showing a mixture of Harappan and Kulli elements at Nindowari is preceded by layers containing basins in buff ware decorated with alternating brackets, a motif met at Nal and at Merghar (pl. 13.8). Let us hope that in the future excavations at Kirta or Merghar will establish the respective stratigraphic position of the greyware and pottery related to the Harappan civilization and South Baluchistan cultures. It would be quite interesting to know the process of contact in the ceramic industries between Harappan civilization and the sites in the Bolan area. It is not impossible that these contacts might have gone through different stages, the first one visible at Merghar, in association with greyware, and the second one at Kirta, mixed with Kulli elements obviously absent from Merghar. Gudri seems the only site with a large proportion of pottery with a bichrome decoration. But these sherds appear to be rather different from the well-known polychrome Kechi Beg ware, found in the Quetta Valley (Fairservis, 1956: 259); we do not find at Gudri the very fine and delicate line drawing on small vessels, characteristic of Kechi Beg. Here, too, only excavation will reveal the position of polychrome ware from Gudri relative to the black-on-grey ware.

Acknowledgments

The authors wish to thank J.-M. Casal, Director of the French Archaeological Mission, for his help in this survey done in the winter 1970-1, Miss de Cardi for her kind help and Mr Saeedur Rehman, Representative of the Department of Archaeology in Pakistan, who took an active part in the field work.

REFERENCES

Casal, J.-M. (1961) *Fouilles de Mundigak*. Mémoires de la Délégation Archéologique Française en Afghanistan, XVII. Paris.
Casal, J.-M. (1966) Nindowari — A Chalcolithic site in South Baluchistan. *Pakistan Archaeology*, 3, 10-21.
de Cardi, B. (1964) British expeditions to Kalat, 1948 and 1957. *Pakistan Archaeology*, 1, 20-9.
de Cardi, B. (1970) *Excavations at Bampur, a Third Millennium Settlement in Persian Baluchistan, 1966*. Anthropological Papers of the American Museum of Natural History, Vol. 51, Part 3. New York.
Fairservis, W.A., Jr. (1956) *Excavations in the Quetta Valley, West Pakistan*. ibid., Vol. 45, Part 2. New York.
Fairservis, W.A., Jr. (1959) *Archaeological Surveys in the Zhob and Loralai Districts, West Pakistan*. ibid., Vol. 47, Part 2. New York.
Stein, M.A. (1929) *An Archaeological Tour in Waziristan and Northern*

Baluchistan. Memoirs of the Archaeological Survey of India, No. 37. Calcutta.

Stein, M.A. (1931) *An Archaeological Tour in Gedrosia.* ibid., No. 43. Calcutta.

Tosi, M. (1968) Excavations at Shahr-i Sokhta, a Chalcolithic settlement in the Iranian Sistan. Preliminary report on the first campaign, October-December, 1967. *East and West*, 18, No. 1-2, 9-66.

14

Inhumation and Cremation in North-West Pakistan at the end of the Second Millennium B.C.

GEORGIO STACUL

Research in the last few years in the Swat Valley and in the surrounding hilly areas — where the Italian Archaeological Mission of IsMEO has conducted several excavations — attests to a range of cultures, in the protohistoric period, that has probably no equivalent in other regions of the Indo-Pakistan sub-continent (Tucci, 1962a; 1963b;Silvi Antonini, 1963; Faccenna, 1964; Stacul, 1966a; 1966b; 1967a; 1967b; Castaldi, 1968; Silver Antonini, 1969; Stacul, 1969a; 1969b. 1970a).

Excavations carried out in the rock shelter near Ghaligai, have in the first place provided proof of the great differences through the various chronological phases between the second half of the third millennium and the first half of the second millennium B.C. Pottery vessels dating back to a period probably coeval with the Indus civilization are very different from those of the periods immediately preceding and immediately following, in shapes and decoration and in the production techniques of the vessels (Stacul, 1967b: 190-211; 1969a: 46-57).

Similar well-defined differences, indicating varying influences and most likely the overlap of different ethnic groups, are attested also in subsequent protohistoric periods; by the florescence of the phase marked by the burnished black-grey ware, then of the phase characterized by grey and red vessels with disk- or button-base, followed by one with a prevalence of grey vessels with thin sides and lastly of the red fine ware phase (Stacul, 1970b).

In the course of this brief survey, we shall examine some distinctive aspects of the Fifth Chronological Period in the Swat Valley, which, on the basis of the data supplied by the radiocarbon analyses, and of various typological comparisons, we assume can be assigned to the last centuries of the second millennium B.C. This period, chiefly documented by the cemeteries of Loebanr and

Katelai and, judging from some trial trenches by some settlement sites in the same Swat Valley, seem to us of especial interest, because of the varying cultural components it reveals.

At Loebanr and Katelai, this period is identified with the earliest use of these cemeteries. During the course of the period, the rite of inhumation, in which the inhumed body lies on one side with the lower limbs contracted, exists together with the rite of cremation, where the ashes are deposited in urns (pl. 14.1, a-d).

The components of the grave furniture, vessels and other objects, show remarkable differences in shape as well as in technique of manufacture. Among the vessels, there should be noted the grey and red vases with a disk-base, the red ones on a conical pedestal, the cinerary jars of anthropomorphic character and the terracotta box-shaped cinerary urns.

In many graves of this period, these elements of grave furnishing are found in association, in a single complex, but, in the majority of cases, it is possible to establish a clear distinction between the furnishings belonging to the inhumation graves and those of the cremation graves. The former are in fact mostly furnished with grey vessels, chiefly of a type with a high disk-base that present various analogies with distinctive shapes of Phase V of Hasanlu, in Iran the first period of the Iron Age (Stacul, 1970b: 97).

It is more difficult to establish comparisons for cremation graves of the same period, which probably reflect an autonomous cultural component, and ethnic groups may have differed from those practising the rite of inhumation in the Swat Valley, and neighbouring valleys.

In the area surrounding the north-western regions of the Indo-Pakistan sub-continent, cremation cemeteries have recently been found in Soviet Tadjikistan, in the Kafirnigan Valley, near the Amu Darya river. These graves have been dated around the end of the second millennium and the beginning of the first millennium B.C. (Frumkin, 1970: 68). However, furniture and other features of these graves do not seem to indicate affinities with the graves found in Northern Pakistan. On the contrary, the cremation graves and grave goods of Swat allow more significant comparisons to be established, which we shall now briefly consider.

In the first place, we should note that the type of vase that occurs most commonly in these graves, the red cup standing on a conical pedestal (with the profile of the body of various forms) is clearly derived from analogous shapes in black, black-grey and buff burnished ware found in the same region in the preceding period, for which, we have only fragmentary data from excavations in some settlement sites. The fact that these burnished vases — distinctive of

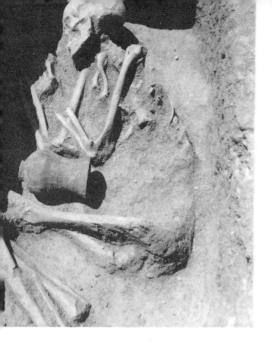

a. Katelai, grave no. 216.

b. Katelai, grave no. 207.

Plate 14.1 Inhumation and Cremation Graves of the Swat Valley, N.W. Pakistan (Cultural Period V).

c. Katelai, grave no. 167 and no. 168.

d. Cinerary urn from Loebanr, grave no. 47.

the Fourth Chronological Period in the Swat Valley — show close analogies with common types of Phases IIB — IIIB of Tepe Hissar may be significant (Stacul, 1970b: 93-95).

Secondly, there are other typological relationships, in some cases very definite, with pottery and other objects of funerary furnishings from cremation graveyards of Eastern Europe, chiefly from graves dating to the Early and Middle Bronze Age in the Middle Danube Basin: this is an area that for a long period, in the course of the second millennium B.C., is noted for the prevalence of the cremation rite, remarkably in advance of the European Urnfield cultures.

The possibilities of establishing comparisons are supplied not only by general analogous features between vessels and other objects, numerous enough by themselves, but also by the fact of their having in common elements of a rather peculiar and specific nature. One such element comprises the terracotta box-urns, occurring both in the cremation graves of the Swat Valley and in cremation graves of the Hungarian Plain, the latter of the North Pannonian Incrusted Pottery culture. Another element is that of the urns decorated with bosses and holes, clearly of anthropomorphic inspiration, that, found in the Pakistani regions of Swat and Dir, are peculiar also to the Danubian cultures of Harvan, Kisapostag and Vatya in the Hungarian Plain. The concept of the 'face-urn', so common in Swat and Dir in cremation graves, has a significant previous occurrence in Hungary, in the latest phase of the Pečel-Baden Culture, that testifies to the first important concentration of cremation graveyards in the area of the Middle Danubian Basin (Stacul, 1971).

Considering the great distance separating the cultural areas that have been compared and the lack — for the moment at least — of intermediate occurrences of this type of grave and funerary furnishing, we cannot rule out the possibility that the relationships are entirely fortuitous, or result from environmental causes. On the other hand, we cannot rule out the possibility of some relationship between these occurrences. made possible by the peculiarity of the events that took place in the Middle Danube Basin in the Middle Bronze Age, when the so-called period of migration was already in progress. We cannot ignore the possibility that human groups, large or small, probably coming from Eastern Europe, may have been responsible for extensive displacement eastwards, perhaps in con-sequence of the increasing pressure exerted in the Middle Bronze Age by the peoples of the so-called *Hügelgräbenkultur.*

Such displacement might have anticipated the wider tribal movements that many scholars attribute to the Late Bronze Age, when Central and Eastern Europe would have become an epicentre of outward cultural movements, and probably also ethnic ones. One could perhaps link this to the displacements of the so-called 'Sea-Peoples' in the eastern area of the Mediterranean, and farther east to the so-called 'Pontic migration', the latter being detectable as far as the region of the Ordos and Northern China.

REFERENCES

Castaldi, E. (1968) La necropoli di Katelai I nelle Swat (Pakistan). *Memorie della Accademia Nazionale dei Lincei*, XIII, 7, 485-641.
Faccenna, D. (1964) *A Guide to the Excavations in Swat (Pakistan) 1956-1962.* Rome.
Frumkin, G. (1970) *Archaeology in Soviet Central Asia.* Leiden.
Silvi Antonini, C. (1963) Preliminary notes on the excavation of the necropolises found in Western Pakistan. *East and West*, XIV, 13-26.
Silvi Antonini, C. (1969) Swat and Central Asia. *East and West*, XIX, 100-15.
Silvi Antonini, C. and Stacul, G. (1971) *The Protohistoric Graveyards of Swat (Pakistan).* Rome. In press.
Stacul, G. (1966a) Preliminary report on the pre-Buddhist necropolises in Swat (West Pakistan). *East and West*, XVI, 37-79.
Stacul, G. (1966b) Notes on the discovery of a necropolis near Kherai in the Gorband Valley (Swat, West Pakistan). *East and West*, XVI, 261-74.
Stacul, G. (1967a) Discovery of four pre-Buddhist Cemeteries near Pacha in Buner (Swat, West Pakistan). *East and West*, XVII, 220-32.
Stacul, G. (1967b) Excavations in a rock shelter near Ghaligai (Swat, West Pakistan). *East and West*, XVII, 185-219.
Stacul, G. (1969a) Excavation near Ghaligai (1968) and chronological sequence of protohistorical cultures in the Swat Valley (West Pakistan). *East and West*, XIX, 44-91.
Stacul, G. (1969b) Discovery of protohistoric cemeteries in the Chitral Valley (West Pakistan). *East and West*, XIX, 92-9.
Stacul, G. (1970a) An archaeological survey near Kalam (Swat Kohistan). *East and West*, XX, 87-91.
Stacul, G. (1970b) The grey pottery in the Swat Valley and the Indo-Iranian connection (*c.* 1500-300 B.C.). *East and West*, XX, 92-102.
Stacul, G. (1971) Cremation graves in north-west Pakistan and their Eurasian connections: remarks and hypotheses. *East and West*, XXI, in press.
Tucci, G. (1963a) *La via dello Swat.* Bari.
Tucci, G. (1963b) The Tombs of the Asvakayana-Assakenoi. *East and West*, XIV, 27-8.

15

The Mahisamardini image from Tapa Sardar, Ghazni

MAURIZIO TADDEI

Tapa Sardar is a hillock in the vicinity of Ghazni, Afghanistan on which a Buddhist sanctuary was discovered by the Italian Archaeological Mission. The general outlines of the site have already been described by me in my 'First preliminary report' (Taddei, 1968: 109-24).

Here I intend to illustrate only one of the large chapels or viharas which are aligned along the right (south-west) side of the main stupa. This chapel, which bears the number 23 (pl. 15.1), was excavated in 1969 and belongs to the last phase of building activity at Tapa Sardar, i.e. the eighth century A.D., according to my tentative chronology. Moreover the unbaked-clay sculpture of this period has been partially illustrated in the above-mentioned 'Preliminary report'.

Only the base survives from the central image of Vihara 23, along with part of side-walls of the base which must have formed two arched passages connecting the vihara with the corridor running along the back. On the surviving portion of the upper surface of this base there was no trace of any image or other object. Since an empty throne is not what one would expect in an eighth-century Buddhist chapel in Afghanistan, the problem did not seem to have any obvious solution. It was only the excavation of another vihara (No. 37) in 1970 that enabled us to understand what the central decoration of Vihara 23 looked like. It must indeed have been a rather elaborate composition, in which a Buddha image was seated on a lotus flower supported by two nagas; these were represented as if emerging from the waters, i.e. from the upper surface of the basis, following a pattern which is also found in the famous group of Fondukistan in the Kabul Museum (Hackin, 1959: 55, fig. 182).

Against the left wall of the vihara there was a standing Buddha image, larger than natural size. Only its square pedestal with a lotus

Plate 15.1 Tapa Sardar (Ghazni, Afghanistan), Season 1969. General view of Vihara 23.

Plate 15.2 The Mahisamardini group.

flower and the Buddha's feet remains *in situ*: the rest of the image, which was of the bejewelled type (Hackin, 1959: 54 ff., fig. 179; Rowland, 1961: 20-4), had fallen on the ground and the shape of the fragments had been destroyed by the weight of the vault which collapsed at a later date (soon after I presume).

Facing this Buddha, against the right wall of the vihara there was another image which suffered even greater damage because of the surface erosion of the hill slope on this side, but what survives is more than enough to allow us to identify the image (pl. 15.1). On a rectangular base there is the body of a buffalo, still in the attitude of raising itself by pressing the ground with its left front leg. Its head (pl. 15.2) is represented as severed from its body, resting on the

Plate 15.3 A detail of the Mahisamardini group showing the Buffalo's head and
  Durga's foot.

Plate 15.4 A detail of the Mahisamardini group showing the lion's paw.

Plate 15.5-6 Durga's head, as found in front of the Buddha pedestal.

Plate 15.7 One of Durga's forearms.

ground (i.e. on the base), and turned towards the onlookers; a lion's paw is still visible on the hind portion of the buffalo (pl. 15.3) and a human foot survives on the right, above the buffalo's head (pl. 15.4).

This is obviously an image of Durga Mahisasuramardini, which is confirmed by the fragments we found in front of the base. Amongst them the most interesting and clearly recognizable are the head (pl. 15.5-6), four forearms (pl. 15.7), one of the right hands of the goddess, holding a vajra (pl. 15.8), and a fragment of the lion's head, found near the left side of the base.

The head of the goddess (pl. 15.5) is without doubt one of the most beautiful pieces of sculpture ever found in Afghanistan and it is also noteworthy for the fairly well-preserved polychromy; her forehead is decorated with a crescent-shaped simantika (V.S. Agrawala, 1947-8: 134, pl. XLVII B, No. 124) hanging above the vertically placed third eye; her hair is bound by a garland.

That the cult of Durga was widespread in Afghanistan in the Sahi period is a fact well documented by several though sporadic finds. We may recall the well-known 'Scorretti Marble', now on loan to the National Museum of Oriental Art, Rome (Schlumberger, 1955: 112-9; Goetz, 1957: 13 ff.; Barrett, 1957: 54 ff.), the marble group of Mahisamardini from Gardez (Fischer, 1967: 25; Auboyer, 1968: 56 f., fig. 99), the head, also from Gardez (Schlumberger, 1955: fig. 2; Fischer, 1967: 168, note 150; Cat. London, 1967, 27, No. 65, pl. 11b; Dupree, 1968: 27, case 4, No. 4, and plate; Hallade, 1968: 226, fig. 179), 'usually but probably wrongly interpreted as head of god Shiva' (Fischer, 1969: 340), and the head from Qalca Amir Muhammad, Tagao Valley (Cat. Tokyo, 1963: No. 177; Fischer, 1964: 35-42; Cat. Tokyo, 1964: 194; Cat. London, 1967, 27,

Plate 15.8 One of Durga's hands, holding a vajra.

No. 64), all of them in the Kabul Museum. I would also tentatively suggest adding to this list of pieces found in the Afghan territory the stylistically cognate marble female bust from the North-West Frontier Province, in the British Museum, No. 1902, 10-2, 46 (Barrett, 1957, 56: fig. 2). It has also been pointed out that the cult of the devi as Mahisamardini or in related forms had deep roots in the north-west of India and clear evidence has been provided for this (Tucci, 1963: 148-82).

The Durga from Tapa Sardar is the first image of this goddess found in a regular excavation in Afghanistan and it is at the same time sure proof of the intrusion of an originally non-Buddhist deity into a purely Buddhist sanctuary. One should not forget that the religious and iconographic evidence from Tapa Sardar as a whole probably reflects the ideology of an economic and cultural elite; nevertheless this phenomenon of syncretism has a parallel in Swat, where Tucci (1963, 155) points out that 'Buddhism did not succeed in completely overthrowing the original belief of the inhabitants of Swat and surrounding countries; on the contrary, the dakinis and the dakas . . . are but the last remnants of old, pre-Buddhistic cults which resisted what I should call traditional Buddhism to such an extent that, when it began to collapse, they took again the upper hand and found their way into Vajrayana'.

In so far as the iconographic details of the Tapa Sardar image are concerned, we must wait for the completion of the delicate work of consolidation and partial reconstruction of the various fragments, which is now being undertaken. For the time being we may safely point out that the goddess had not less than four arms, one of the right ones holding a vajra (pl. 15.8) with red and black paint, the shape of which may be compared with a fragment from Siksin, Karasar (Ol'denburg, 1914: 7, fig. 4); indeed, four forearms (pl. 15.7) have been found in the debris. Nevertheless we cannot discount the possibility that Durga's arms were more than four, and must remember in this connection that the vajra — though explicitly cited in the Devimahatmya of the Markandeyapurana, LXXXII 21, as a gift from Indra — is not to be listed among the essential attributes of Mahisamardinis and is seldom found in four-armed images: it is absent in both four-armed and six-armed images from Ahicchatra. According to the texts cited by Rao (1914: 345 ff.), the vajra appears only in the twenty-armed form, but M.-th. de Mallmann (1963: 143-7), besides the description from the Visnudharmottara, relates also the one of the Agnipurana, in which the 29-armed goddess holds also a vajra. Nevertheless a parallel to the Tapa Sardar Mahisamardini is to be found in a much earlier terracotta plaque from Nagar, Rajasthan, mentioned by R.C. Agrawala (1955: 56, 72-4; 1958: 124-7; 1965: 11) and Odette Viennot (1956: 372), the date of which is still to be fixed (Iyer, 1969: 180, note 9). Here the goddess holds in her upper right hand an object that appears to be a vajra: R.C. Agrawala has described it as a trisula (1955-6: 74; 1958: 127), but has correctly identified it as a vajra in his latest article on the subject (1965:11).

It is not easy to establish whether there was also the human aspect of the daemon coming out from the buffalo's neck or whether Mahisa was only represented in his animal form (compare the marble group from Gardez and the 'Scorretti Marble' for two parallels in the same period), because that part of the Tapa Sardar group has been

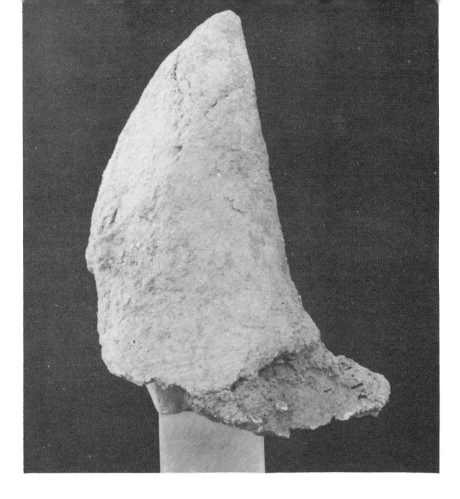

Plate 15.9-10 The horns of Mahisa in human form.

Plate 15.11 A fragment of a clay sculpture or wall decoration showing an animal skin, from Room 36 at Tapa Sardar.

washed away down the hill slope. Nevertheless a suggestion comes to us from two fragments which were found near the right corner of the base, i.e. near the buffalo's head, one of them a bovine horn (pl. 15.9), the other a larger fragment in very poor condition, but clearly including another horn (pl. 15.10). We can rule out the possibility that these are the buffalo's horns, since one of the latter is still preserved in its original position, i.e. on the buffalo's head, while the second was not even represented, being completely hidden by one of the buffalo's front legs (pl. 15.4). We can therefore assume that there was also the daemon in human form and that it was horned. The presence of two bovine horns on the head of Mahisa in human form appears to be an unusual feature in the iconography of Mahisamardini whenever the daemon is represented in the attitude of emerging from the slain buffalo's neck.

The problems which I would submit to your attention can be summarized as follows: (1) Is the Tapa Sardar image a real Mahisamardini or is it some 'Buddhist' deity which has taken over the outward appearance of the Hindu goddess? (2) If it is Mahisamardini, does this image bear witness to a tolerant attitude of Buddhism towards other cults on the same lines which were followed by Gandhara Buddhism? (3) Can our Mahisamardini be equated with the so-called Saiva images from Pjandzikent?

In this connection, another clay fragment from Tapa Sardar (pl. 15.11) should also be taken into consideration, though it was not found in the same chapel as Mahisamardini. It is a part of an animal skin (?Hayagriva; ?Siva) which somehow recalls to our mind the tiger skin worn by the dancing god from Pjandzikent — 'Siva' according to P. Banerjee (1969: 73-80); cf. Kabanov, 1971: 249 ff.), 'unknown god' according to Belenickij and Marsak (1971: 3 ff.). The two Soviet scholars believe that the images from Pjandzikent are not to be labeled as 'Saiva', because many of their features do not find any counterpart in the Indian prototypes; moreover, 'rien de ce que nous savons de la religion en Sogdiane ne nous permet de considérer les Sogdiens comme civaites'. They further confirm their opinion by pointing out that 'les prêtres du culte local ont fait leur les formes elaborées par les hindouistes, pour exprimer leur conceptions religieuses' (Belenickij and Marsak, 1971: 10 f.).

The social and cultural background of Afghanistan was certainly different, but it is also possible that the Durga at Tapa Sardar is some local deity that has found an iconographical definition thanks to the emergence of Hindu cults in that area. The old problem of Hindu-Buddhist syncretism in the north-west and Afghanistan will be much helped in its way towards solution by the new excavations now being carried on also by other archaeological mission. In my opinion, much is to be expected from the Japanese excavations at Tapa Iskandar, north of Kabul. The image of Siva and Parvati from that site, which was kindly shown to me and other colleagues by the Japanese archaeologists, is no doubt an adaptation of a Hindu iconography (and probably also of a Hindu concept) to a religious subject which had deep roots in the north-west, namely Pancika and Hariti.

For the Tapa Sardar Mahisamardini we have the Indian prototype but no local precedent, though one of the names of the goddess, Gandhari, that already appears in the Vanaparvan of the Mahabharata (Tucci, 1963, 20 f.), certainly points to some special connection of the devi with the north-west.

REFERENCES

Agrawala, R.C. (1955-6) A terracotta plaque of Mahishamardini from Nagar, Rajasthan. *Lalit Kala*, 1-2.
Agrawala, R.C. (1958) The goddess Mahisasuramardini in early Indian art. *Artibus Asiae*, XXI.
Agrawala, R.C. (1965) Mahishamardini in early Rajasthani art. *The Researcher — A Bulletin of Rajasthan's Archaeology and Museums*, V-VI, 1964-5. Jaipur.

Agrawala, V.S. (1947-8) Terracotta figurines of Ahichchhatra, District Bareilly, U.P. *Ancient India*, 4.

Auboyer, J. (1968) *The Art of Afghanistan*. Feltham, Middlesex.

Banerjee, P. (1969) A Siva icon from Piandjikent. *Artibus Asiae*, XXXI.

Barrett, D. (1957) Sculptures of the Shahi period. *Oriental Art*, III.

Belenickij, A.M. and Marsak, B.I. (1971) L'art de Piandjikent à la lumiere des dernières fouilles (1958-1968). *Arts Asiatiques*, XXIII.

Cat. London (1967) *Ancient Art from Afghanistan at the Royal Academy of Arts*. London.

Cat. Tokyo (1963) *Exhibition of Ancient Art of Afghanistan*. Tokyo.

Cat. Tokyo (1964) *Ancient Art of Afghanistan*. Tokyo.

Dupree, A. *et al.* (1968) *A Guide to the Kabul Museum* (2nd ed.) Kabul.

Fischer, K. (1964) Une tête śivaite en marbre de l'Afghanistan oriental. *Arts Asiatiques*, X.

Fischer, K. (1967) *Alexandropolis metropolis Arachosias* — Zur Lage von Kandahar an Landverbindungen zwischen Iran und Indien. *Bonner Jahrbücher*, CLXVII.

Fischer, K. (1969) Preliminary remarks on archaeological survey in Afghanistan. *Zentralasiatische Studien*, 3.

Goetz, H. (1957) Late Gupta Sculptures in Afghanistan: the Scoretti Marble and cognate sculptures. *Arts Asiatiques*, IV.

Hackin, J. (1959) Le monastère bouddhique de Fondukistan. *Diverses recherches archéologiques en Afghanistan (1933-1940)*, Mémoires de la Délégation Archeologique Francaise en Afghanistan, VIII, Paris.

Hallade, M. (1968) *Inde: un millénaire d'art bouddhique*. Paris.

Iyer, K.Bh. (1969) An early Gupta seal of the Mahisasuramardini. *Artibus Asiae*, XXI.

Kabanov, S.K. (1971) Izobrazenie Sivy na ossuarii. *Sovetskaja Arheologija*, 2.

Mallmann, M.-Th. de (1963) *Les enseignements iconographiques de l'Agnipurana*. Paris.

Ol'denburg, S.Th. (1914) *Russkaja turkestanskaja ekspedicija 1909-1910 goda*. Sanktpeterburg.

Rao, T.A.G. (1914) *Elements of Hindu Iconography*. I, 2. Madras.

Rowland, B. (1961) The bejewelled Buddha in Afghanistan. *Artibus Asiae*, XXIV.

Schlumberger, D. (1955) Le marbre Scorretti. *Arts Asiatiques*, II.

Taddei, M. (1968) Tapa Sardar: first preliminary report. *East and West*, 18.

Tucci, G. (1963) Oriental notes, II: an image of a Devi discovered in Swat and some connected problems. *East and West*, 14.

Viennot, O. (1956) The Goddess Mahishasuramardini in Kushana Art. *Artibus Asiae*, XIX.

16

The Azes hoard from Shaikhan — Dheri: Fresh evidence for the context of Jihonika

DAVID W. MAC DOWALL

Through the kindness of Dr F.R. Allchin, I have been able to examine some enlarged photographs of the 9 round coins of Azes found in a pot in Trench A5(6) — period 1VB of the excavations at Shaikhan Dheri near Charsadda (Dani, 1965: 17 f.). The hoard contains two copper coins of Azes II, and two silver and five copper coins copying the types of Azes II, which indicate a subsequent stage in the coinage of this region (pl. 16.1).

Azes II round copper coins (2)

1.	Obv.	Indian humped bull to r.	
		Greek legend	ΒΑΣΙΛΕΩΣ ΒΑΣΙΛΕ ΩΝ ΜΕΓΑΛ□ΥΑΖ□Υ
	Rev.	Lion r.	
		Kharoṣthi legend	*Maharajasa rajatirajasa mahatasa Ayasa*
	Obv.	and Rev. symbols as	*BMC* Azes No. 143. Diam. 26 mm. Die position↓
2.	Obv.	and Rev. as 1 but with different symbols in field as *BMC* Azes No. 141.	
			Diam. 26 mm. Die position ↓

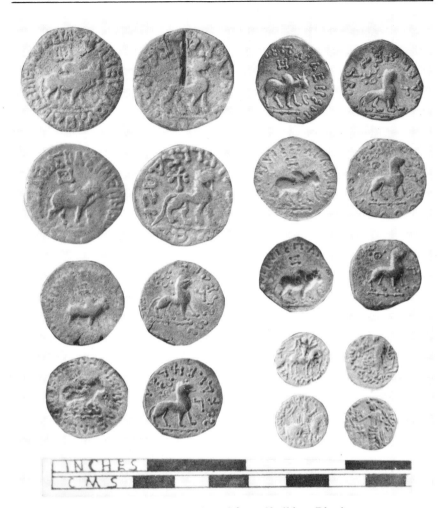

Plate 16.1 The Azes hoard from Shaikhan-Dheri.

Copies of Azes II round copper coins (5)

3.   Obv.   Indian humped bull to r.
                Blundered and misunderstood Greek legend
                derived from preceding type. Symbol above bull

        Rev.   Lion r.
                Literate Kharoṣṭhi legend, partly off flan,
                with smaller letters than 1, but reproducing
                the same legend. Above lion, triratna symbol
                                      In front of lion
                                          Diam. 21 mm.
                                          Die position ↓

4.-7.   Obv.   and Rev. as 3.

Diam. 20, 21, 20 and 18 mm.
Die positions ↑ → ↑ ↑
the last coin has a squarish shape and
may have been struck as a trimmed square flan.

Copies of Azes II drachms in silver (2)

8.   Obv.   Mounted king r., holding whip in raised r. hand.
Behind king's head — uncertain object —
possibly the long ribbons of his fillet.
Corrupt Greek legend.

Rev.   Zeus standing l., holding Nike in outstretched
r. hand and traces of long sceptre in l.
Kharoṣṭhi legend partly off flan but seems
ordinary legend of Azes II.
Ayasa clearly visible in exergue.
Symbols in l. and r. field as BMC Azes No. 10.

Diam. 13 mm.
Die position ↓

9.   Obv.   as 8, but behind king's head there seems to be
a Nike flying, about to crown the king.

Rev.   as 8, but only symbol to l. clearly formed
and distinct.

Diam. 12 mm.
Die position →

The first point about the hoard is that it consists entirely of
coins of Azes II and of copies of coins of Azes II. The distinction
between the coins of Azes I and Azes II suggested by Marshall (1951:
131) from his excavations at Taxila has now been refined by
subsequent numismatic analysis (Jenkins, 1955: 1 ff.). The sharp
debasement of silver occurs during the issue of tetradrachms of the
king mounted holding whip type. These are the coins that occur in
the later strata and in later associations at Taxila; and this is the
obverse type of the billon tetradrachms of the subsequent Pahlava
kings Indravarma, Aśpavarma, and Gondophares. In the mints of
Taxila and the Punjab we can safely distinguish the silver issues of
Azes I by their obverse type of the king mounted holding a
transverse spear, from those of Azes II which have the obverse type
of the king mounted holding a whip. As a large number of the
monograms are found on both the silver and the copper coins, we

can equally deduce the types of the copper issues of Azes I and those of Azes II.

The coins in this hoard reinforce the evidence from the excavations at Udegram and Mingora (Gullini, 1962; Faccena, 1962) that the copper currency of Azes II west of the Indus in Gandhara normally consisted of the bull and lion type, and not of the other copper types of Azes II that are reported in quantity from Taxila. Among the finds of copper coins of Azes II we should distinguish the genuine copper denominations from the debased tetradrachms and drachms which retain the types of the earlier silver. When we do this, we see that the bull and lion type, which amounts to only 4.5% of the copper denominations of Azes II at Sirkap (Marshall, 1951) is the sole type of copper denominations of Azes II found in Swat at Udegram and Mingora (Gullini, 1962; Faccenna, 1962), in this hoard from Shaikhan Dheri, and in the deposit from Mir Zakah in Afghanistan (Curiel and Schlumberger, 1953: 80).

COPPER DENOMINATIONS OF AZES II

	Bull/lion	other	Percentage of Bull/lion
Sirkap	49	969	4.5
Udegram	10	—	100
Mingora	3	—	100
Shaikhan-Dheri hoard	2 + 5 copies	—	100
Mir Zakah deposit	7	—	100

But the most significant feature about this small hoard is the presence of the coins copying the types of Azes II, which gives important evidence about a subsequent stage in the coinage of Gandhara.

The copper coins copying the types of Azes II clearly represent a continuation of the same copper denominations in part of the territory in which the originals circulated. But they represent a later stage in the series, when the Kharosthi remains, but the Greek is being copied mechanically, when the size (and presumably weight) of the denomination is being reduced, and when the obverse symbol has been deliberately replaced by a triratna symbol.

The silver coins seem to represent a corresponding stage in the contemporary silver denominations, when the symbols of Azes II Zeus Nikephoros coinage are being progressively misunderstood. The deliberate change in the type in this case seems to be the introduction behind the horseman's head of a flying Nike about to crown the horseman with a wreath — a Parthian motif that we find on several issues of the Pahlavas at the beginning of their rule in the Punjab — as on Gondophares (Whitehead, 1914: pl. xv No. 43).

Both groups of copies found in this hoard in association with orthodox coins of Azes II seem to represent an important stage in the development from the official coins of Azes II in the territories west of the Indus and north of the Kophen — which can throw light on the complex relationship of the coinages of the later Sakas, Pahlavas and Kusanas in this region, and in particular on the context of Jihonika the Satrap.

Theories about the context of Jihonika

Jihonika is known from the Taxila silver vase found at Sirkap, bearing his name with the date 191 and from his coins in silver and copper. Whitehead (1914: 96) considers him to be an Indo-Parthian, a subordinate number of the dynasty of Gondophares and perhaps the satrap of Taxila. Marshall (1951: 773 ff.) also regards him as an Indo-Parthian of the dynasty of Gondophares but thinks he was satrap of Chukhsa, a satrapy of which the primary purpose was to guard the northern frontier. On the other hand Ghirshman (1946: 140) and Van Lohuizen de Leeuw (1949: 376-81) both regard Jihonika as a satrap of the Kusana period between Vima Kadphises and Kaniska. But whereas Ghirshman explains yr. 191 as a date in the Vikrama era giving Jihonika a date of A.D. 134 and thus reconciling this context with his date of A.D. 144 for the era of Kaniṣka, Van Lohuizen de Leeuw refers yr. 191 to her era of c. 129 B.C. thus dating Jihonika to A.D. 62 and so reconciling the context with her date of A.D. 78 for the era of Kaniska.

The Taxila silver vase

Jihonika's name occurs in the Kharosthi inscription round the neck of the silver vase of duck shape found in Sir John Marshall's excavations at Sirkap in 1926/27.
Konow (1929: 82) reads the inscription as:

Ka 1 100 20, 20 20 20 10 1 maharaja [bhra] [ta Ma] [ni] [gula*] sa putrasa Jihonikasa Chukhsasa Kshatrapasa* Year 191 (during the reign) of Jihonika the kshatrapa of Chukhsa, the son of Manigula, the brother of the Great King.

The coinage of Jihonika

The coins of Jihonika are known in the following types:
1.   Base silver tetradrachm   25 to 28 mm
      Obv.   Horseman to r., with r. arm extended; behind him, a
              bow.
              To r., triratna symbol; below, Kharoṣṭhi letter
              Corrupt Greek legend, including ΣΑΤΡΑΠΥ
              ΖΕΙωΝΙΣΟΥ
      Rev.   Satrap standing on l., being crowned with a wreath by
              a figure standing on r., wearing a mural crown, and
              holding a cornucopiae (l.) To r., monogram, to l.,
              Kharoṣṭhi letter *mṣa*
              Kharoṣṭhi legend *Manigulasa chatrapasa putrasa
              chatrapasa Jihuniasa*
      British Museum   9.71, 9.03, 9.80, 10.03, 8.87, 9.77, 9.63,
              10.19 gm.   *BMC* Pl. xxiii.4.
      Punjab Museum   10.04 gm   and one other example
                          PMC Pl. xvi. 82
      Indian Museum   9.66 gm
                          IMC Pl. ix. 14.
2.   Base silver tetradrachms   27 mm plate 16.2 fig. c.
      Obv.   as 1.
      Rev.   Satrap standing facing holding a dependent club,
              being crowned by two standing figures; a winged Nike
              on l. and a wingless figure on r.
              Kharoṣṭhi legend as on 1.
      British Museum   9.03 gm
                          BMC Pl. xxxii. 11.
3.   Round copper denomination   23 to 27 mm
      Obv.   Bull standing r.
              corrupt Greek legend as 1.
              Above, triratna symbol. To r. Kharoṣṭhi letter *sa, pu,*
              or *va.*
      Rev.   Lion to r.
              Kharoṣṭhi legend *Manigula putrasa chatrapasa
              Jihuniasa.*
              In field monogram ⅂ , sometimes Kharoṣṭhi letter
              dhra or *tra.*
      British Museum   11.23, 10.49, 10.82, 10.02, 9.96, 9.77,
              9.69, 9.57, 8.97, 8.73, 8.32, 8.14, 10.93, 10.68,
              10.15, 9.21, 8.98, 8.77, 8.46 gm.
                          BMC Ol. xxiii. 5.
      Punjab Museum   13.15 gm and six other examples

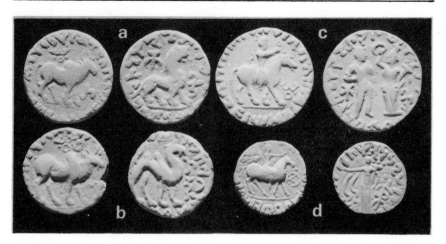

Plate 16.2   (a)   copper coin Jihonika   (c)   base silver tetradrachm Jihonika
             (b)   copper coin Kujula   (d)   billon tetradrachm Kujula

PMC Pl. xvi. 84.

Indian Museum   9.78, 9.78, 8.88, 7.19 gm and two other examples

4.   Round copper denomination (small)
     Obv. and Rev. as 3.
     British Museum   2.09 gm.

5.   Square copper denomination
     Obv.   Elephant to r.
     Rev.   Bull to r.
     White King Sale I. iv. 198.

6.   Square copper denomination
     Obv.   Bull to r. . . . . CAT
     Rev.   Lion to l. . . . . chatrapa
     Jenkins and Narain 1956: 25

Denominations and metrology

The pattern of the denominations of Jihonika is certainly not that of the Kuṣana period of Vima Kadphises and Kaniṣka. Jihonika's coinage consists of a base silver (but not billon) denomination *c.* 10 gm which is an Indian standard silver tetradrachm of the type struck by Hermaeus, Azes I and Azes II (Gardner, 1886: lxix; Whitehead, 1923: 296 ff.), round copper coins struck al marco between 8 and 11 gm again resembling the copper denominations of Azes II (see table of weights) and an extremely rare square copper denomination. The coinage of Vima Kadphises consists of gold denominations — a double dinar, dinar and quarter dinar, with no silver coinage, but with issues of copper tetradrachms (*c.* 17 gm) copper didrachms (*c.* 8 gm) and copper drachms (*c.* 4 gm). Kaniṣka issued no double dinars, but otherwise follows closely the pattern of the coinage of Vima Kadphises with a gold dinar and quarter dinar, and copper tetradrachms, didrachms and drachms (MacDowall, 1960: 63 ff.).

These denominations of Jihonika — an Indian standard silver tetradrachm, with copper coins to provide the small change — was the pattern of denominations struck at several mints south of the Hindu Kush by the Indo-Bactrian and Saka kings down to Azes II. On the other hand, the debased quality of the tetradrachms of Jihonika clearly establishes their place in the series right at the end of Azes II just before the quality of the coinage degenerated sharply into billon. The silver of Jihonika is debased, inferior to the normal silver of the tetradrachms of Azes II, but it is not yet the black billon of the Taxila coinage of Gondophares with Sasan (Whitehead, 1914: 148, Nos. 20-34) and Abdagases (Whitehead, 1914: 154, Nos. 64-5). Moreover the issues of Jihonika still have complementary copper issues which disappeared when the silver currency finally collapsed and was replaced by black billon.

Distribution of Jihonika's coinage

There is little positive evidence about the finds of coins of Jihonika. There was one of his round coppers compared with ten bull/lion coppers of Azes II among the excavation coins from Udegram (Gullini, 1962: 331 ff.). The B.M. coins mostly came from Cunningham and Whitehead, who were largely Punjab collectors. There is however some important negative evidence. Masson did not recover any coins of Jihonika among the enormous numbers he acquired from Begram, and they are not represented in the large deposit from Mir Zakah near Gardez (Curiel and Schlumberger, 1953: 67 ff.). Wilson (1841: 312 pl. viii, No. 17) reports only one example that belonged to General Court who collected round Rawalpindi and Peshawar. Whitehead comments that they are rare at Taxila, and only one silver coin of Jihonika is recorded among the numerous finds from Taxila (Marshall, 1951: 815). The little evidence we have suggests that the round coppers may belong to the satrapy west of the Indus — the satrapy where the round copper coins with the same lion/bull types of Azes II certainly circulated.

Table 16.1
TABLE OF WEIGHTS
ROUND COPPER DENOMINATIONS

GMS	AZES II			JIHONIKA	KUJULA
	Elephant Bull	Std. King Hermes	Bull Lion	Bull Lion	Bull Bactrian Camel
16					
15			xxxxxxx		
14	xxx		xxxxxxxxxxx		
13	xxx	x	xxxxxx		xxx
12	xxxxxxxxx		xxxx		x
11	xxxx	xxxxxx	xx	xxxxx	xxx
10	x	xxx		xxxxxx	xxxxxxxxxxxx
9	x	xxxxx		xxxxx	xxxxxxx
8	xx	xxx		xxx	x
7	x	x	xxxx		x
6	x	xxx	x		
5	x	xx	x		xx
4		xx			xxxxxxx
3	x	x			xxxxxxxxx
2	x				xxx
1					

Based on the weights of coins in the British Museum, London.

Epigraphy

The legends on the coins of Jihonika are in corrupt Greek on the
obverse, often blundered and never completely decipherable, but the
reverse legends in Kharoṣthi are clear, well formed and fully literate.
It is clear that the engravers understood Kharoṣthi but not Greek. In
this respect the coins of Jihonika are different from the main issues
of Azes II, but resemble the group of Azes II tetradrachms and
drachms of the Zeus Nikephorus type in base silver with a corrupt
Greek legend (Jenkins and Narain, 1956: 12), and the billon
tetradrachms of Aspavarma and of Sasan (Jenkins and Narain 1956,

20 and 23) with the reverse type of Zeus standing right. These last two series incidentally share with the coins of Jihonika the use of the triratna symbol. The scripts used for the legends further reinforce the attribution of Jihonika to the period between Azes II and the billon tetradrachms of the dynasty of the general Aspararma.

In contrast, the Greek legends on the coinage of Vima Kadphises (Whitehead, 1914: 183-5) and Kaniṣka (Whitehead, 1914: 186-7) are invariably literate, and while Kharoṣṭhi is still found on the coinage of Vima, Kaniṣka's coins have legends in Greek script only.

The use of Kharoṣṭhi letters as mint control marks in the obverse and reverse field of the coins of Jihonika, is a further argument for the early context. Kharoṣṭhi letters were used for this purpose in the issues of Azes II (Whitehead, 1914: 104-31) and are found on the billon tetradrachms of Indravarma, Aśpavarma, (Whitehead, 1944: 99 ff.) Sasan, Gondophares and Abdagases (Whitehead, 1914: 146 ff.). There is a Kharoṣṭhi letter *vi* in the field of the standing Zeus and helmeted head types of Soter Megas (Whitehead, 1914: 160 f.), but not on Soter Megas general coinage or on any of the copper tetradrachms, didrachms and drachms of Vima Kadphises, or the later Kuṣanas.

The letter forms of the Greek legends on the coins of Jihonika have the rounded omikron (*o*), sigma (*c*) and omega (ω). Van Lohuizen de Leeuw (1949: 378 f.) claims that the use of the round *o* and ς is a decisive argument and makes it impossible to insert Jihonika in the sequence of rulers before Vima Kadphises. But her argument is clearly invalid when it is seen that the bull and Bactrian camel issue of Kujula Kara Kadphises (Whitehead, 1914: 180) have these rounded forms — copied apparently from the issue of Jihonika himself and that the round *o*, *c* and ω is found as early as Vonones (Whitehead, 1914: 141 ff.) (A.D. 8/9-11/12) on the imperial Parthian series, the series from which the coronation motif of the tetradrachms of Jihonika seems to be derived. Numismatic epigraphy is a notoriously complicated subject. It is now extremely doubtful whether any absolute chronological significance can be attached to the introduction of any given letter form. In individual mints (Narain, 1957: 157-9 against Bachhofer, 1941: 233 ff.) we can indeed trace a coherent and consistent development. Once introduced a new letter form tends to become the norm until the next major change is made. But it is equally clear that the same changes were not introduced uniformly through all the mints even of the same sovereign. For example Gondophares has

- ▢ Γ ω   on his Parthian type silver drachms (Markoff, 1892: pl. iv. 25) struck in Aria
- ▢ Γ Ω   on his Nike type copper terradrachms (Gardner,

1886: 105, Nos. 13-21) struck in Arachosia

ο   c   ω   on his Pallas type billon tetradrachms (Whitehead, 1914: pl. xv. 1.) struck in Gandhara

The preference for rounded Greek letter forms by the moneyers of Jihonika may have been influenced by the more familiar forms of Kharoṣṭhi aksaras such as Ψ, *me* which is in fact the same as the cursive form of Greek omega, or it may have been simply that the limited knowledge they possessed was primarily of cursive Greek. Round forms of omicron, sigma and omega are used in both the cursive writing like the will of Demetrius of 237 B.C. (Maunde Thompson, 1893: 130 ff.) and in literary or bookhand of papyri from the third century B.C. onwards, as the invocation of Artemisia and the lines from Philodemus (Maunde Thompson, 1893: 119 and 124).

Derivatives in the Kuṣana coinages

There is a connection between the coinage of Jihonika and that of Vima Kadphises in the common use of the triratna symbol (Whitehead, 1914: 183 ff.). But this certainly does not tie Jihonika to the period of Vima Kadphises. The form is different on the coins of Jihonika, and the use of the symbol is a recurrent feature throughout a succession of black billon tetradrachms issues in western Gandhara. But whereas it is found alone on the base silver tetradrachms and copper coins of Jihonika, it is found with a dynastic symbol on the later billon issues — with ♀ (the Gondopharan symbol) on the billon Indian-standard tetradrachms of Aśpavarma, Sasan and Abdagases, ⵣ on the Indian-standard tetradrachms of the Zeus standing type of Soter Megas, and ⵦ on the copper Attic standard tetradrachms, didrachms and drachms of Vima Kadphises.

In one important respect the coinage of Jihonika is clearly linked to that of the early Kuṣana king Kujula Kara Kadphises. The round copper coins of the bull and lion type of Jihonika (pl. 16.2a, fig. a) seem to have been the model for Kujula Kara Kadphises' bull and Bactrian camel coins (pl. 16.2b), and Whitehead, 1914: (pl. xvii 18). He copied not only the denominations and the obverse type of the bull, but the corrupt and misunderstood Greek legend of Jihonika. The Greek legends of these coins of Kujula have not yet been fully deciphered, but a careful comparison of well-preserved specimens shows that there are the same elements in the legend, revealing that the issue copies that of Jihonika (Marshall, 1951: 840). The silver tetradrachms of Jihonika (pl. 16.2c) also seems to have been copied by the black billion tetradrachms bearing the Kharosthi legend of Azes II with the title *dhramikasa* and the type of King mounted holding whip/standing figure holding cornucopiae (pl. 16.2d) — an issue which has been attributed to the Kuṣanas (Jenkins and Narain, 1956: 13) and has the obverse symbol that is found on the Roman head issue of Kujula (Whitehead, 1914: pl. xvii 24). Although the *Dhramikasa* issue is of black billion, it still retains features of the base silver tetradrachms of Jihonika. It has Kharoṣthi mint control marks in the field; and like the coins of Jihonika it has a corrupt Greek legend on the obverse, but an intelligible Kharosthi legend on the reverse. It has the obverse horseman holding whip, common to the silver of Azes II, Jihonika and the Pahlavas in Gandhara and Taxila. Its reverse type has a standing figure holding a cornucopia, derived from the standing figure of Tyche with cornucopia on the base silver tetradrachms of Jihonika; and on well preserved specimens there is the same triratna symbol to the left of the standing figure.

Other type relationships

The other type relationships of the coinage of Jihonika reinforce the conclusions to be drawn from denominational pattern, metrology and epigraphy about its context. The horseman on the obverse of Jihonika's silver tetradrachms holds a whip in his extended right hand as on silver tetradrachms of Azes II, and the subsequent billon of Aśpavarma, Indravarma and Soter Megas. It is quite distinct from the horseman holding a couched lance which is the invariable type of Azes I (Jenkins, 1955: 1 ff.). There is no comparable horseman on any of the Kusana coins from Vima Kadphises to the end of the dynasty.

The more common form of the two coronation types found on the reverse of Jihonika's silver — showing the satrap being crowned by a Tyche or city goddess seems to be copying the recurrent type found on the Parthian silver tetradrachms, first used by Orodes I (57-37 B.C.) and subsequently employed by his successors Phraates IV (38-3 B.C.) Artabanus III (A.D. 10-40) Vardanes I (A.D. 41-45) and Gotarzes (A.D. 40-51) (Wroth, 1903: pl. xiv, xviii, xxv, xxvi) and points to a strong Parthian connection.

The types of the round copper coins of Jihonika
humped bull r.   /   lion r.
are the copper types used by Azes II in Gandhara, and Jihonika's copper coins seem to be copying both the denominations and types

of Azes II in that region. But while they are clearly derived in some way from the round copper coins of Azes II with the same types, they are different in three significant and puzzling respects:

1. Jihonika's coins are noticeably smaller and struck to a lower weight standard of 10-11 gm. In both diameter and weight standard they are much closer to the copper coins of the seated king/Hermes type of Azes II struck at Taxila and to the bull and Bactrian camel issue of Kujula than to the bull/lion type of Azes II from which their obverse and reverse types seem to be derived.

2. The Greek is badly blundered and only partly intelligible, whereas the Kharoṣṭhi is fully literate and clear. Such blundered Greek with literate Kharoṣṭhi is much closer to the billon of Indravarma and Aśpavarma and in particular to the bull/Bactrian camel issue of Kujula, which it resembles in other ways such as size and weight.

3. Instead of the monogram above the bull on the copper coins of Azes II of the bull/lion type they have the triratna symbol. This is found on several series of ancient India — the tribal coins of Kanauj, Kauśambi and Kuluta but it is also used in a similar way on the bull/Bactrian camel issue of Kujula and on Vima's copper coinage.

It is precisely in these respects that the copies of the round bull and lion coins of Azes II found with their prototypes in the Shaikhan Dheri hoard differ from their prototypes in the orthodox coinage of Azes II.

1. They show a progressive reduction in flan size and presumably in weight that bridges the gap between the two series.

2. The Kharoṣṭhi legend remains legible throughout and continues to read *Ayasa*; but the Greek legend while still retaining elements derived from the legend of Azes II becomes increasingly blundered.

3. In lieu of the monogram above the lion these copies substitute the triratna symbol.

From this small hoard, we can I think safely conclude that when the weight standard of the copper coinage of Azes II was reduced from 14 to 11 gm in Taxila to match the initial debasement of the silver tetradrachms and drachms, there was no fresh issue with new types in Gandhara. But this class of copies, to the same reduced size and weight standard as the new type at Taxila were issued in part of Gandhara. Their significance is that they mark the transitional stage between the regular Lion/Bull issue of Azes II and the copper issues of Jihonika with these types.

This reinforces the evidence of the appearance of the silver tetradrachms of Jihonika, which suggests that they belong to the stage when some debasement of the silver had started, but before the silver coinage had collapsed into the black billon of Aśpavarma and the dynasty of Gondophares.

The context of Jihonika

The numismatic evidence thus points clearly to the relative context of Jihonika. The pattern of his denominations, the quality of the silver, the types employed, the use of Kharosthi letters as mint control marks, the literate Kharoṣṭhi but corrupt Greek legends, and the triratna symbol without an accompanying dynastic symbol indicate the period after the good silver tetradrachms of Azes II and before the billon tetradrachms of Aśpavarma and the dynasty of Gondophares, to the period of transition when the silver coinage of Gandhara was beginning to collapse. Moroever the round coppers of Jihonika preceded the Bull and Bactrian camel issue of Kujula, for which they served as the prototype.

For this particular context of Jihonika there is a clear *terminus ante quem* A.D. 42 in an important passage in Philostratus *Life of Apollonius of Tyana* II, 7. Philostratus describes the journey of Apollonius the sage from Babylon to Taxila in that year, and says explicitly that the people who live between the Indian Caucasus, the River Kophen and Taxila have a coinage not of gold or silver but of orichalcum and black brass, with which 'all who come to the land of the Indians must purchase every thing'. The black brass is clearly the black billon coinage of the dynasty of Gondophares, and the orichalcum the more golden coloured *aes* denominations of that area, or the *aes* tetradrachms of the Kabul valley that seem to be contemporary with them. But whatever the precise series may have been, the point of the story turns on the fact that in the Kabul valley and Gandhara at this time there was no indigenous coinage of gold or silver. We can therefore safely conclude that the collapse of the silver denominations of Azes II and their replacement by black billon tetradrachms in Gandhara and Taxila had already taken place before A.D. 42.

It is more difficult to establish a close *terminus post quem* for the collapse of the silver denominations in Gandhara. There is however one piece of evidence that suggests the collapse must have been later than the second decade of the first century A.D. In Stupa No. IV at Taxila a Roman silver denarius of Augustus struck at Lugdunum in A.D. 11-13 was found with a silver drachm of Azilises of the Dioscuri type. The coins were found together with two decayed seed pearls, a tiny gold ornament and some glass beads. They were found in the Stupa with a tapering cubicle receptacle containing two steatite caskets, one within the other, and, inside, the enshrined relics enclosed in a tiny gold casket. The circumstances of the find show that both coins must have been placed at the same time deliberately in the position in which they were discovered. Neither coin is worn. The silver coin of Azilises cannot have survived in ordinary circulation beyond the reign of his successor Azes II, at the end of whose reign the silver debasement began. The Roman coin struck in A.D. 11-13 cannot have circulated long. This suggests that the deposit was in the second or third decade of the 1st century; and the comparable condition of the two silver coins suggests a general synchronism between Augustus and Azilises, the predecessor of Azes II. A.D. 11-13 is therefore the *terminus post quem* for this context of Jihonika, with the likelihood that the date was in fact a decade or two later.

Once we have established these limits for the context of Jihonika, we can establish with reasonable certainty the era of the date on the Taxila silver vase which has Jihonika's name in the genitive. The date of the era must lie after 180 B.C. (i.e. the *terminus post quem* of A.D. 11 minus 191 years) and before 149 B.C. (i.e. the *terminus ante quem* of A.D. 42 minus 191 years). The era cannot therefore be the Vikrama era (to which Ghirshman attributes it) or Van Lohuizen de Leeuw's era of 129 B.C.; but it does fit in remarkably well with the commencement of the old Saka or Indo-Bactrian era of *c.* 155 B.C. (Tarn, 1951: 494-502; Bivar, 1963: 489 ff.). A date of 191 in this era would in fact date the Taxila silver vase, the gift of Jihonika the Satrap to A.D. 36, and make A.D. 30-40 the decade of Jihonika's satrapy.

Implications for Kuṣana chronology

If Jihonika belongs to the decade A.D. 30-40 in the satrapy west of the Indus with a secure *terminus ante quem* of A.D. 42 and was succeeded in part of his territories by Kujula Kadphises and in other localities by the Pahlavas Indravarma and Aśpavarma, we have at last a date for the issue of Kujula's Bull and Bactrian camel copper coins to *c.* A.D. 40. Kujula had a long reign, but even so the possibilities are limited. His successors in the traditional view were Vima Kadphises and Kaniṣka. Between A.D. 78 and an early second century date for the era of Kaniṣka, this new evidence is indecisive. But it seems impossible that one or two Kusana kings can have spanned the period from Kujula (ruling *c.* A.D. 40) up of A.D. 231 — the date proposed by Göbl (1967: II, 269) or to A.D. 278 — the date proposed by Zeymal (1968) for the era of Kaniṣka.

REFERENCES

Bachhofer, L. (1941) On Greeks and Sakas in India. *Journal of the American Oriental Society*, 233 ff.

Bivar, A.D.H. (1963) The Kaniṣka dating from Surkh Kotal. *Bulletin of the School of Oriental and African Studies*, London, 498 ff.

Curiel, R. and Schlumberger, D. (1953) *Trésors monétaires d'Afghanistan.* Paris.

Dani, A.H. (1965) The excavations at Shaikhan Dheri *Ancient Pakistan* II, 17 f.

Faccenna D. (1962) *Reports on the Campaigns 1956-1958 in Swat (Pakistan):* Mingora site of Butkara I. Rome.

Gardner, P. (1886) *The Coins of the Greek and Scythic Kings of Bactria and India in the British Museum.* London.

Ghirshman, R. (1946) *Bégram, recherches archeologiques et historiques sur les Kouchans.* Cairo.

Göbl, R. (1967) Das Neue Datum des Kušankönigs Kaniṣka I. *Dokumente zur Geschichte der Iranischen Hunnen in Baktrien und Indien, II,* Wiesbaden, 269 ff.

Gullini, G. (1962) *Reports on the Campaigns 1956-1958 in Swat (Pakistan): Udegram.* Rome.

Jenkins, G.K. (1955) Indo Scythic Mints. *Journal of the Numismatic Society of India,* Vol. XVII, Part II, 1 ff.

Jenkins, G.K. and Narain, A.K. (1956) *The Coin Types of the Saka Pahlava Kings of India.* Varanasi.

Konow, S. *Corpus Inscriptionum Indicarum, Vol. II, Part I, Kharoshthi Inscriptions with the exception of those of Aśoka.* Calcutta.

Mac Dowall, D.W. (1960) The weight standards of the gold and copper coinages of the Kushana dynasty from Vima Kadphises to Vasu-deva. *Journal of the Numismatic Society of India,* 28 ff.

Mac Dowall, D.W. (1968) Soter Megas the King of Kings the Kusana. *Journal of the Numismatic Society of India,* 28 ff.

Markoff, A.K. (1892) *Unpublished Arsacid Coins.* Leningrad.

Marshall, Sir John, (1951) *Taxila.* Cambridge.

Maunde Thompson, E. (1893) *Handbook of Green and Latin Palaeography.* London

Narain, A.K. (1957) *The Indo-Greeks.* Oxford.

Philostratus. *Life of Apollonius of Tyana.*

Tarn, W.W. (1951) *The Greeks in Bactria and India.* Cambridge.

Van Lohuizen de Leeuw, J.E. (1949) *The 'Scythian' Period.* Leiden.

Whitehead, R.B. (1914) *Catalogue of Coins in the Punjab Museum Lahore, Vol. I: Indo Greek Coins.* Oxford.

Whitehead, R.B. (1923) Notes on the Indo Greeks. *Numismatic Chronicle.*

Whitehead, R.B. (1944) The Dynasty of the General Aspavarma. *Numismatic Chronicle.*

Wilson, H.H. (1841) *Ariana Antiqua.* London.

Wroth, W. (1903) *Catalogue of the Greek Coins in the British Museum, Catalogue of the Coins of Parthia.* London.

Zeymal, E.V. (1968) *Kushan Chronology.* Moscow.

17

Late Kusan, early Gupta: a reverse approach

J.C. HARLE

In the same way that when certain bridges are built a central gap remains until it is gradually closed by building out from either side, a large gap still remains in the history of Indian sculpture between the Kuṣan period at Mathura and the Gupta period. Yet the change in style between these two periods is a major one, in fact one of the two or three crucial articulations in the whole development of Indian sculpture over two millenia. The reason for so little being known with any certainty about this vital transition, how and when and where it took place, is because of the lack of firmly dated pieces from the century or two during which it must have occurred.

To continue with the bridge analogy, there is a good deal of evidence to extend the span from the Kuṣan side for 100-150 years beyond the accession of Kaniṣka: the abundance of sculpture from Mathura, a fair amount of it dated, the plentiful evidence of inscriptions and coins and the fact that the Kuṣan imperium was situated in a vast and varied cultural sphere. Epigraphers, historians, art historians and numismatists have disagreed as often as not on the conclusions to be drawn from this evidence, but for the purpose of this paper only two things need be born in mind: the span can be pushed out from the Kusan side up to another 66 years (Mac Dowall and Wilson: 221) or conceivably even more, (Zeymal: 22-27), depending on whether or not one opts for a date after A.D. 78 for the accession of Kaniska. There is, moreover, a telescopic effect of another 60 years or so to be added to this, or not, depending on whether one accepts the 'dropped hundred' theory of Professor van Lohuizen (van Lohuizen, 1949: 235 ff.) or a very similar extension proposed by Professor Rosenfield as an alternative (Rosenfield, 1967: 106). At its maximum extension on these two counts, a late date for Kaniṣka and a 'two century span' for the dated Mathura sculpture, the bridge, from the Kusan side, can be extended, in terms of dated sculpture to around the year 300 A.D. Unfortunately these dated sculptures, by and large a battered collection of poor quality Jina images, are moreover usually headless and often consist of nothing more than a base, from which style is difficult to deduce.

From the other side, the Gupta side, working backwards in time presents a very different situation. Not only is there no dated evidence enabling us to work backwards from A.D. 320, when the Gupta era begins, but the whole fourth century provides few inscriptions. It is sometimes forgotten that there are no inscriptions whatever of Candragupta I, the first of the Imperial Guptas, and only four, two of them copper-plates, belonging to his great son and successor Samudragupta. Of dated sculpture, until recently, there has been none properly speaking of the fourth century, or even early fifth, with the exception of some small and rather crude subordinate figures upon two stone carvings. The first is a pillar bearing an inscription of Candragupta II, dated A.D. 381 (Bhandarkar, 1931: 1-8; Joshi, 1966: pl. 76) which has a small nude figure with a staff, probably a mendicant form of Śiva. It is large bellied and dwarfish, its stylistic qualities blurred by these grotesque effects, but it appears to be in the Gupta rather than any recognizably earlier style. The other examples are two small male figures on a fragment of a base bearing a problematical date of 97 (van Lohuizen, 1949: fig. 65). The style of these mannikins appears to be a Gupta one. The sculptures in the caves of the Udayagiri Hill near Vidiśa in Madhya Pradesh have thus long been considered the first important dated sculptures of the Gupta period. For purposes of comparison, however, Mathura, in the Upper Doab and Vidiśa, in the eastern part of Malwa, are nearly three hundred miles apart, and each with a different artistic tradition.

Only three of the caves at Udayagiri have inscriptions containing either a date or the name of a known historical character, in this case Candragupta II (Fleet, Nos. 3, 6, 61). It is not certain, moreover, whether even the sculpture in or outside these three caves is strictly contemporaneous. It is possible that some of the sculpture is as early as the third quarter of the fourth century or even earlier: there are at least two discernible types of Durga images, one looking back to the Kuṣan period at Mathura, the other to Gupta and post-Gupta types, but at the same time this might simply be the result of two traditions more or less co-existing (Harle, in press). Until further evidence is adduced and analysed, it is safer to assume that all the Hindu sculpture of the Udayagiri Hill caves belongs to the time of the inscribed Hindu caves, i.e. around A.D. 408 and what remains in the Jaina cave to a decade or two later. Until very recently, these were then the earliest statues in the Gupta style which could be given even

Plate 17.1 Seated Jina (Gai 'B') — buff sandstone — Vidiśa — Vidiśa Museum.
Photo: Dept. of Archaeology, Govt. of India.

approximate dates with any assurance.

In the last few years, however, a number of works from this important period (the fourth century A.D.) have come to light. The excavations of the stupa at Devnimori have revealed a quantity of decorative ornament as well as a number of seated Buddhas, all in terracotta (Mehta, 1966: pl. 37-65). It seems possible to give these a fairly certain date around 375A.D. (Mehta, 1966: 28, 121, 122). Yet the location of the site in Northern Gujarat and the nature of the material make these finds, important as they are and of superb quality, difficult to relate directly to the transition from the Kuṣan style to the Gupta at Mathura.

More pertinent are the three practically identical seated Jina figures (pl. 17.1) recently dug up at Vidiśa and bearing largely similar inscriptions of Ramagupta (Agrawala, 1959: 252, 253). The historical authenticity of this personage as the short-lived successor to Samudragupta who was supplanted, because of a dastardly action, by his brother Candragupta II has long been debated (Gai, 1969: 247-51). It is of concern here only inasmuch as an historical Ramagupta in accordance with the old story enables us to date the new finds from Vidiśa around 370 A.D. The new inscriptions do, in fact, give powerful support to the claims for Ramagupta as an historical character. The rare coin finds, hitherto the only physical evidence of Ramagupta's existence, also come from Eastern Malwa. This locality, moreover, is the one where he would most likely have fought or staged the disastrous campaign against the Western Kṣatrapa which, according to tradition, culminated in the heinous deed for which he lost the throne. Further evidence from other parts of India to counter the argument that Ramagupta may simply have been a local ruler is still lacking, but the title *maharaja adhiraja* applied to him in these inscriptions goes far to prove that he was indeed one of the Imperial Gupta monarchs. All in all, the case for accepting Ramagupta as the ill-fated successor of Samudragupta is now a good one and these Jaina images can thus be dated, at least provisionally, around 370 A.D.

Fortunately, the damaged and missing areas in these sculptures are not all the same so that a fairly good idea of a complete figure can be obtained. From a comparative point of view, the following portions are of interest:

(*a*) *The base.* At each end, set in a panel, are small couchant lions, with highly stylized tail fronds, facing outwards. They are easily distinguishable from the outward facing couchant lions in Kuśan style sculptures from Mathura or from Kauśambi. What is more, in almost all of the later Kuṣan sculptures of seated Jinas from Mathura the lions are facing forward, as in the figure illustrated in pl. 17.2 (State Museum, Lucknow-J.15), dated in the Yr. 31 and, if one accepts the 'two century span', the latest dated seated Jina which has survived with its head and a large part of the halo intact (van Lohuizen, 1968: 129, 130). The general proportions of the bases are also different, wider and flatter than in the great majority of Kusan ones. Both the proportions of the base and the lions in the Vidiśa statues are in fact much closer to certain fifth century Jina images from Mathura (State Museum, Lucknow-J.36, J.121, J.122), one bearing a date of A.D. 432-33. One sign of a later date is the *cakra* seen end-on and without a pedestal, in the centre of the base, with swatches of (?) cloth falling on either side. The existence of bases with all these features at a relatively early date in Eastern Malwa is confirmed, moreover, by very similar ones on the defaced and barely recognizable images, so far unpublished, in the Jaina cave at Udayagiri. The inscription in the cave, which would appear to have been carved after the images, bears the date 426 A.D. (Fleet, 1970: No. 61).

Plate 17.2 Seated Jina — red sandstone — Mathura (Kankali Tila) — State Museum, Lucknow. J.15 — Yr. 31.
Photo: American Academy of Benares.

(b) The body. The style is closer to the Gupta than to the Kuṣan at Mathura, at least to the vigorous powerful style which seems to have continued for some twenty-five years after Kaniṣka's 'accession' and probably antedates his reign. On the other hand there are certain mannerisms which one associates with later Kusan work (cf.pl. 17.2), such as the squat body and its effect, combining with arms of exceptional length, in forcing the arms into a rather exaggerated akimbo position, arm and forearm forming an interior angle of 90° or less. This is, moreover, the first appearance, so far known, of the clearly marked fold of flesh, which appears almost as a line, below the breasts. It appears only in two of the images.

(c) The halo. A fairly elaborate degree of decoration has been attained. The scallops on the outer edge are delineated with a double line, there is then a beaded band, and a fairly complex lotus rosette. The crispness of execution makes the decoration appear more elaborate than it is (cf. pl. 17.2) and several of the features of developed Gupta haloes are missing, such as the wide bands of vegetal scrollwork with characteristic bias cutting or the rope-like band with small floral rosettes at wide-spaced intervals. Yet the latter is to be found in a seated Buddha image dated in the Yr. 36, now in the National Museum, New Delhi, and presumably of late Kuṣan date (Indian Archaeology: pl. 101 c; van Lohuizen, 1968: 130-2).

(d) The subordinate figures. They stand approximately level with the base, in contrast to both those in the Kuṣan style where such figures on either side of a seated Buddha or Jina, stand lower than the base, and the Gupta ones where they are raised. The faces, with their large eyes, as well as the general plastic feeling, are close to the Gupta style.

The sole surviving Jina head is very severely damaged. It would appear to have rather strong local characteristics; in fact the entire sculptures, particularly in their plastic quality are permeated by this local feeling. This must always be remembered when relating these figures to the productions of Mathura. Bearing this in mind, it can only be said that *if these Vidiśa figures were from Mathura* they would have to be placed, on grounds of stylistic development, earlier than the earliest dated Gupta Jain figures from Mathura (see above) and later than such presumably late Kusan figures as the one dated in the Year 31 (pl. 17.2). With a provisional date of c. 370 A.D., based on the Ramagupta inscriptions, for the Vidiśa *tirthankaras*, this is quite in accord with the more generally accepted chronologies for the Kusans. Assuming, however, that stylistically Mathura must have been in advance of provincial Vidiśa, it does not accord with such very late datings for Kaniska (A.D. 278) as Bhandarkar and more recently Zeymal (1968: 22-7) have proposed. Two unknown variables, however, the rate of stylistic change and the degree to which a place like Vidiśa lagged behind a great and ancient centre of sculpture, such as Mathura, stand in the way of using these important statues, working back in time, as evidence for an early or later date, within reasonable limits, of Kaniska, although it would seem impossible to still uphold both an A.D. 78 date for Kaniska and a 'single century span' for all the dated Mathura statues. Two hundred and sixty-one years (from A.D. 109 to A.D. 270) would then separate the sculpture of pl. 17.1 from that of pl. 17.2, which seems quite beyond the stretch of both the variables combined.

So far, with the unimportant exceptions noted above, not only have no statues from Mathura been discovered bearing fourth-century dates (although some of the dated images mentioned above may, if one accepts a 'two century span' for their own dates and a late one for Kaniṣka, conceivably be place in the fourth century) but no statues from Mathura so far suggest themselves, leaving fragments apart, as being of fourth-century date. The sculpture from this site generally accepted as being 'Gupta' would elsewhere invariably qualify for a later fifth- or sixth-century date. Mathura sculpture, stylistically may have been in advance of Eastern Malwa and Eastern Uttar Pradesh but not to such an extent. The fourth century at Mathura thus remains a blank, to all intents and purposes, as far as stone sculpture is concerned, but there is one image from there with good claims on stylistic grounds, to a fourth-century date. This is the yakṣa (pl. 17.3, 4), probably Kubera, from Ramghat now in the Mathura Museum (18.1506). A photograph was included in a book published over twenty years ago but the implication in the text was that it was of Kusan or pre-Kusan date (van Lohuizen, 1949: 154 and fig. 38). A close examination reveals that while earlier than any of the major pieces of 'Gupta' sculpture from Mathura it is at the same time unquestionably later than any of the Kusan sculputre from that site, with the possible exception of some of the Jina and Buddha figures, and therefore most probably was made in the fourth-century A.D.

The features of this sculpture which hark back to the Kuṣan style at Mathura are obvious: the hand raised in *abhaya* turned somewhat sideways and strengthened by a cushion-like support at the back, the continuous and relatively broad raised line of the eyebrows, the squinting appearance of the protuberant eyes with their heavy lower as well as upper lids (pl. 17.4), the general stance with the legs stiff and feet apart, and finally the whole arrangement of *dhoti*, waistband and scarf. On the other hand, the shape of the eye is longer and narrower than in Kusan heads. The way in which a ground is provided, flaring out in the lower part of the image, is a later feature never seen in standing figures of the Kusan period at Mathura. Necklaces or armlets of the type worn by the *yakṣa* are, moreover, quite unknown

Plate 17.3 Yaksa (Kubera?) — spotted red sandstone — Mathura (Ramghat) — Mathura Museum 18. 1506. Photo: Author.

Plate 17.4 Detail of above. Photo: Author.

Plate 17.5 Karttikeya — Cave 3, Udayagiri Hill (Vidiśa District, Madhya Pradesh.) Photo: American Academy of Benares.

in the earlier period. Conversely, however, armlets (*keyuras*) of this type, with the portions of cockades above them, appear in some of the Udayagiri Hill (Vidiśa) cave sculptures. They, together with a very similar treatment of the chest, swelling curves mounting to the over-broad almost circular shoulders may be seen in the Karttikeya (pl. 17.5) of Cave 3 at Udayagiri. Since the most likely date for this sculpture is around 408 A.D. and since it is difficult to believe that Mathura sculpture was not stylistically in advance of that produced at sites near Vidiśa, the most likely date for the Mathura Kubera seems to be in the fourth-century A.D.

REFERENCES

Agrawala, R.C. (1959) Newly discovered sculptures from Vidiśa. *Journal of the Oriental Institutes, M.S. University of Baroda*, XVIII, No. 3.

Bhandarkar, D.R. (1931) Mathura pillar inscription of Chandragupta II: G.E. 61. *Epigraphica Indica*, XXI.

Fleet, J.F. (1970) *Inscriptions of the Early Gupta Kings and their Successors.* Varanasi.

Gai, G.S. (1969) Three inscriptions of Ramagupta. *Journal of the Oriental Institute, M.S. University of Baroda*, XVIII, No. 3.

Harle, J.C. (in press). On the Mahiṣasuramardini images of the Udayagiri Hill (Vidiśa) Caves. *Journal of the Indian Society of Oriental Art, V.S. Agrawala Commemoration Volume.*

Indian Archaeology. 1957-8.

Joshi, N.P. (1966) *Mathura Sculptures.* Mathura.

van Lohuizen, J.E. (1949) *The 'Scythian' Period*, Leiden.

van Lohuizen, J.E. (1968) The date of Kaniṣka and some recently published images, in *Papers on the Date of Kaniṣka*, Basham, A.L. (ed.), Leiden.

Mac Dowall, D.W. and Wilson, N.G. (1970) The references to the Kuṣans in the Periplus and further numismatic evidence for its date. *Numismatic Chronicle*, X (7th Series).

Mehta, R.N. and Chowdhary, S.N. (1966) *Excavation at Devnimori.* Baroda.

Rosenfield, John M. (1967) *The Dynastic Art of the Kushans.* Berkeley.

Zeymal, E.Z. (1968) 278 A.D. – the date of Kaniṣka. *Abstract of Papers by Soviet Scholars. International Conference on the History, Archaeology, and Culture of Central Asia in the Kushan Era, Dushambe 1968.* Moscow.

18

Chinese Stoneware from Siraf: the Earliest Finds

DAVID WHITEHOUSE

This paper offers a preliminary account of the earliest Chinese export wares found at Siraf, the Sasanian and early Islamic entrepôt on the Persian Gulf (fig. 18.1). The earliest group of imported pottery, which comes from the Great Mosque, was buried in the first quarter of the ninth century A.D. It includes both storage vessels, presumably used as containers for perishable goods exported from the Far East, and table wares, notably bowls with painted ornament. The material forms the earliest datable group of Chinese ceramics in the Middle East. Two of the four main types have parallels elsewhere in the Middle East, in South Asia and East Africa, and the material is important not only for the study of T'ang dynasty export wares but also for the chronology of archaeological sites in South East Asia and on the shores of the Indian Ocean.

The excavations at Siraf began in 1966, sponsored by the British Institute of Persian Studies and supported by numerous institutions, including the British Museum, the British Academy, the Calouste Gulbenkian Foundation, the Royal Ontario Museum and a munificent anonymous trust. At the time of writing (July 1971), we have completed five seasons of excavations; a sixth and final campaign is planned for the winter of 1972-3. Interim Reports appear annually in *Iran* (Whitehouse, 1968, 1969, 1970a, 1971a and 1972). These have been supplemented by a summary of the results obtained in the first four seasons (Whitehouse, 1970b), and an account of the domestic buildings (Whitehouse, 1971c). The present paper is based on a contribution to the first *Colloquium* of the Percival David Foundation (Whitehouse, 1970c).

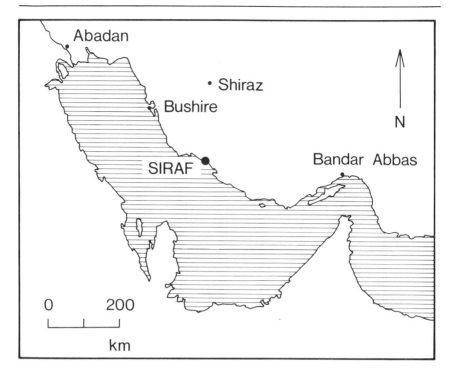

Figure 18.1 The Persian Gulf, showing the position of Sīrāf.

The site

In the ninth and tenth centuries A.D. Siraf was a leading entrepôt in the network of maritime trade which brought to the Middle East merchandise from India, China, South-East Asia, East Africa and the Red Sea. Contemporary writers agreed that Sirafi ships sailed all over the India Ocean and Sirafi merchants were notoriously rich. The earliest documentary sources refer to the mid-ninth century, while Istakhri (writing shortly before 950) describes the opulent houses of Siraf and the goods which passed through its bazaars, including pearls, ambergris, gemstones, ivory and spice. According to Muqqadasi, the city flourished until the late tenth century, when a sequence of events brought about a decline from which it never recovered. Earthquakes in 977, the rise of Qais as a rival port and anarchy in Fars following the collapse of the Buyid dynasty in 1055 combined to bring about an almost total eclipse. Ibn al-Balkhi (writing *c.* 1110) describes the results of this decline and to Yaqut, a century later, Siraf was a ghost town with only a small, impoverished population (Aubin, 1959; Whitehouse, 1968: 2-3 and 1970b: 141-3).

The excavations are throwing light on the origins of Siraf in the period before the earliest documents. Work at the Great Mosque,

described below, has established that the city was flourishing at the
beginning of the ninth century, while beneath the mosque are the
remains of a fortress-palace and other buildings of Sasanian and
Umayyad date (Whitehouse, 1972: 68-71 and fig. 3). Imported objects,
notably coins of Theodosius I (376-94), struck in Alexandria
(Whitehouse, 1971a: 3 and pl. VIIb), and Constans II (641-68),
minted in Constantinople in 651-9 (Whitehouse, 1972: 70 and
pl. XIIa), suggest that Siraf has a long history as an entrepot,
beginning in the Sasanian period (Whitehouse, 1971c). At the same
time, the excavations have revealed information about the decline of
Siraf and its replacement by a small settlement, known as Shilau
(Aubin, 1969).

The Great Mosque

The Great Mosque of Siraf is a composite building with several
periods of construction ranging in date from the ninth to the
eleventh centuries. The nucleus of the complex is a courtyard
mosque 51 m long and 44 m wide, with a plan characteristic of the
Umayyad and Abbasid periods; it consisted of a courtyard surrounded on three sides by a single arcade, with a triple arcade
forming the prayer hall in front of the *qibla* wall. The whole structure
rested on a platform nearly 2 m high, filled with earth and rubble
(Whitehouse, 1970a: 2-8 and 1971a: 2-4).

The filling of the platform contained a huge number of artifacts:
coins, small objects and pottery. The major part of this material
consisted of unglazed pottery, with a smaller quantity of pottery
with a green alkaline glaze (including Whitehouse, 1971a: pl. Xa and
1971: pl. Xb) and several hundred sherds of imported stoneware.
Most of the coins, including the latest datable pieces, were struck in
lead, probably at Siraf. Many are illegible, but others bear the date,
the name of the governor and the denomination (*fals*), which
suggests that they were local substitutes for small change made of
bronze. Two types occur: small pieces, 16-18 mm across, with neat
inscriptions in the style of the late Umayyad and very early Abbasid
periods (*c.* 700-60), and larger coins with clumsy legends of the full
Abbasid period. Among the latter group are the latest datable coins,
minted for the governor Mansur in 188/803-4. Several coins bearing
the name Ja'far have illegible dates but probably belong to the period
immediately after 803-4; Mr Nicholas Lowick of the British Museum,
who is studying the coins from Siraf, suggests that they were struck
before *c.* 810. Thus, the latest coins from the platform of the original
mosque belong to the opening years of the ninth century and we

suggest with confidence that the filling was deposited bwtween 803-4 and *c.* 825. It follows that all the finds from the filling, including the stoneware fragments, have a terminal date not later than *c.* 825.

The stoneware

Most of the stoneware from the original mosque falls readily into four categories:

1. Jars of 'Dusun' type and other vessels with a similar fabric and glaze.
2. Jars with a shiny black surface.
3. Bowls with patches of glaze removed from the interior.
4. Bowls with painted decoration.

'Dusun' jars and bowls with painted ornament are known from both finds in Eastern Asia and the Middle East and vessels in western collections; the other types, to the best of my knowledge, had not been described before their discovery at Siraf.

1. *'Dusun' jars and similar vessels.* By far the most common variety of imported pottery from the platform of the mosque consists of fragmentary 'Dusun' jars with an olive green glaze. The jars, which range in height from 40-60 cm, have a flat base, an ovoid or pear-shaped body, a rolled or low vertical rim and a row of between four and six horizontal handles on the shoulder. The fabric is a harsh, often granular stoneware which may be cream or grey, with pink or brown unglazed surfaces. The glaze is transparent and varies in colour from light brown to olive green, the predominant tint being olive. The jars are glazed on the outside and on the inside of the rim. On the outside, the glaze ceases shortly above the base and the top of the rim is never properly glazed, having instead a shiny purple-brown finish. Nearly all the fragments found at Siraf are plain, although a vessel from the well in front of House W at Site F (the residential quarter) bears incised ornament consisting of cloud scrolls, mountains, trees, birds and animals (Whitehouse, 1969: pl. VIc). The most important example of 'Dusun' stoneware from the mosque itself is a fragmentary jar bearing two moslem names, Yusuf and either Maymun or Mansur, incised *before* the vessel was glazed (pl. 18.1a, b). Evidently, the jar was made to order for a moslem trader with contacts, or possibly a factory, in a Chinese port.

In addition to the large jars, three other forms are found at Siraf which have the same fabric and olive green glaze. These are:

1. Barrel-shaped jars, 15-20 cms high, with four horizontal handles at the shoulder (pl. 18.1c).

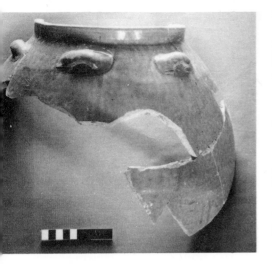

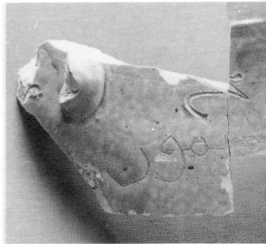

Plate 18.1(a-b) Fragmentary 'Dusun' stoneware jar with incised names.

Plate 18.1(c) Barrel-shaped 'Dusun' jar with horizontal handles.

Plate 18.1(d) Miniature 'Dusun' jar with vestigial handles.

2. Miniature jars with a spheroid body and two vestigial handles. (pl. 18.1d).

3. Large bowls with a flat base and straight, flaring side. The rim is relatively broad and the vessels have a series of vestigial handles shortly below the lip.

Sherds of 'Dusun' jars and similar vessels have a wide distribution in the Middle East, including Rishahr, Bibi Khatun and Tal-i Sabz on the Iranian coast of the Persian Gulf. Other find-spots include sites in Ceylon (Harrisson, 1965), Banbhore in West Pakistan (Anon., 1964), Socotra (Brian Doe, personal communication) and Manda in East

Africa (Chittick, 1967).

'Dusun' jars are best known from the researches of Ottema (1946) and Harrisson (1965, etc.) in South-East Asia. They take their name from the Dusun tribe of north Sabah in Borneo, who prize them sufficiently highly today to purchase all available examples found in ancient cemeteries. The place of manufacture of the jars, which were used to transport perishable goods, such as sauces and spice, is uncertain, although the fabric and glaze suggest a source in south China, a provenance which accords well with their wide distribution as a result of maritime trade.

For a long time the date of the 'Dusun' jars was open to doubt, although Ottema (1946: 128 and fig. 146) published an example allegedly found in a T'ang dynasty grave in Vietnam and Harrisson (1965) notes that the type is depicted in a temple at Burubadur, Java, which is earlier than *c*. 900. The finds from Siraf include not only abundant material from the platform of the mosque, but also a single sherd sealed by an eighth-century floor in one of the Sasanian and Umayyad buildings outside the fortress-palace. Clearly, therefore, Dusun jars were in use before *c*. 800 and by *c*. 825 large, medium and small vessels were imported to the Middle East, together with large, straight-sided bowls.

2. *Jars with a shiny black surface.* A second, but less abundant, type of storage vessel consists of fragmentary jars with a shiny black surface. The jars are 20-40 cms high, with a globular body and a high swelling shoulder. The base is flat and the vessel has a vertical or slightly everted rim. Four or five horizontal handles are attached to the shoulder at regular intervals. The vessels are remarkably coarse. The fabric is a dense grey or purple stoneware which contains numerous cream inclusions and striations. The outside of the sherds has an uneven, rather gritty surface with a shiny black finish. This distinctive finish does not appear to be a deliberate glaze and we await analyses to determine its composition. On the inside, the fragments have a black or, more often, pale grey surface with small horizontal striations, made when the vessel was turned. These, however, are partly obscured by groups of short parallel lines which may be straight or curved and are seldom horizontal. They appear to be the marks of a paddle or similar tool, suggesting that the jars were formed on a turntable, rather than a fast wheel, perhaps by the coiling technique and with the aid of a paddle. (pl. 18.2c, d).

We do not know where these vessels were made. While there is little doubt that they were imported from the Far East, I do not know of any coarse, coil-built wares of this type published from Chinese sites of the T'ang period and my colleagues tell me that kiln sites are unknown in South-East Asia. In Whitehouse (1970c: 31) I

Plate 18.2(a) Base of bowl with gouged foot-ring.
Plate 18.2(b) Interior of same bowl with patches of glaze removed.

Plate 18.2(c-d) Fragments of jars with a shiny black outer surface and internal marks suggesting the use of a paddle or similar tool.

suggested that a South-East Asiatic origin might be likely, but Dr Cheng has kindly pointed out to me that kilns in mainland China often produced coarse wares in large quantities.

3. *Bowls with patches of glaze removed from the interior* (pl. 18.2a, b). The third ware imported from China to Siraf *c.* 800 consists of bowls with a pale green or yellowish glaze on the inside, patches of which have been removed before firing with a broad implement. The bowls are 10-15 cms across. They have a thick, disk-shaped base, from which the potter has gouged a broad concentric groove, creating a clumsy foot ring with a central boss. The bowls have a curving side and a slightly everted lip. The fabric is a coarse buff or cream stoneware with a harsh granular fracture. The unglazed surfaces are smooth and may be cream or brownish pink. The glaze, which covers the interior and the outside of the rim, is pale and transparent, with streaks of green or yellow. The most

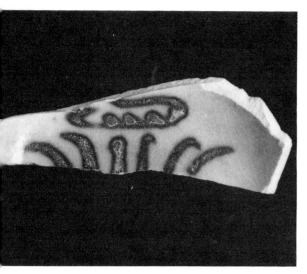

Plate 18.3(a-d) Fragments of bowls with painted decoration.

distinctive feature, however, is a group of four or five unglazed areas radiating from the centre of the bowl. Each area is roughly square and was made by removing the glaze before the vessel was fired. This had the double effect of decorating the bowl and providing unglazed surfaces on which props could be placed to aid stacking in the kiln. Indeed, scars or discolouration produced by the props are sometimes visible. The fabric and glaze of these vessels recalls the Dusun jars and, although wasters of this type have not been reported from the region, I suggest that the bowls, too, were made in South China.

4. *Bowls with painted decoration*. The only polychrome ware from the platform of the mosque consists of fragmentary bowls bearing ornament in green or green and brown. The bowls range in diameter from 10-20 cms. Many are thickly potted and all have a

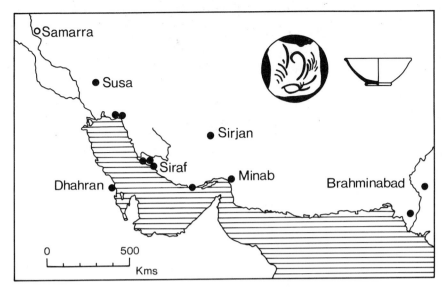

Figure 18.2   Find-spots of painted stoneware bowls in Pakistan and the Persian Gulf region.

heavy ring base, a curving side and slightly everted lip. The fabric is a coarse stoneware which varies in colour from light grey to buff, sometimes tinted with pink; indeed, a few fragments have a bright pink fabric with buff surfaces. Some vessels have a cream slip on the inside and the outside of the rim. The decoration is green or green and brown and consists of freely painted lines, occasionally forming a rosette, but more often making a purely abstract design. The vessels decorated in green tend to be small and have on the inside of the rim several groups of dots. The bichrome pieces include all the largest bowls and have on the rim four pendant arcs filled with brown. Both varieties are found in the platform of the mosque. In later deposits, the great majority of fragments are bichrome and it appears that the green variety may have gone out of use at Siraf some time before the two-coloured type. (pl. 18.3a-d).

Bowls of this type have attracted little attention in China, although one kiln site is known: at Wa Ch'a Ping in Hunan (anon., 1960). It is likely, however, that painted stoneware was made in several centres. Certainly, it was a popular export ware, with find-spots in the Far East and on the shores of the India Ocean.

Among the finds from South-East Asia are a bowl from the Kudus district of north-central Java (Orsoy de Flines, 1969: pl. 9) and a sherd from Takuapa in the Malay peninsula (British Museum; for the site, see Lamb, 1961). Mr Douglas Barrett and Mr Ralph Pinder Wilson tell me that several examples have been found in Ceylon. Farther west, the following find-spots are known to me (fig. 18.2):

West Pakistan Banbhore, perhaps medieval *Daibal* (Mr Leslie

Alcock, personal communication).

Brahminabad, *Mansura* (Hobson, 1928-30: pl. IX, 2).

Iran (1) inland:

Sirjan (Mr Andrew Williamson, personal communication).

Susa (Koechlin, 1928: ca. No. 105).

Iran (2) the Persian Gulf, from north to south:

Tel Moragh, *Hinduwan* (Hansman, 1970: pl. XXIVa).

Shah 'Abdullah, *Mahruban* (Hansman, 1970: pl. XXIVb).

Bibi Khatun, probably *Najiram* (Whitehouse, 1968: 18)

Tal-i Sabz, near Dayyir (Stein, 1937: 233 and pl. XXVII, 6).

Siraf

Bostaneh (Mr Andrew Williamson, personal communication).

Minab (Mr Andrew Williamson, personal communication).

Saudi Arabia   Dhahran (British Museum)

Kenya   Manda (public lecture by Mr Neville Chittick, June 1971: for the site, see Chittick, 1967).

At least two omissions from the list cause surprise: Samarra and Fustat, for enormous quantities of ninth- and tenth-century pottery are available from both sites. However, neither Sarre (1925) nor the anonymous author (1940) who reported on the excavations of 1936-9 mentions painted stoneware from Samarra and none of the sherd collections I have examined include a single sherd. Dr George Scanlon tells me that the type is unknown at Fustat. Although Hansman (1970: 197) advances the case for regarding some of the earliest bichrome wares of Khuzistan as imitations of painted stoneware, only one *close* copy is known to me: a sherd from Afrasiab in the Victoria and Albert Museum (Whitehouse 1970c: 32).

In conclusion, it is noteworthy that several painted stoneware vessels exist in museums in Europe and North America, including:

Great Britain   1. London, British Museum: a distorted bowl, reputedly from Szechuan.

2. Bristol, City Museum: Schiller Collection, N7888.

United States   3. Boston, Museum of Fine Art: a lobed bowl in the Hoyt collection (Anon., 1952)

4. Boston, Museum of Fine Art: a pillow in the Hoyt collection (Anon., 1952)

5. Buffalo, Museum of Science: inv. 288.

Discussion

It remains to place the sherds from the Great Mosque in the wider context of Chinese export wares to the Middle East. In the paragraphs which follow, I shall discuss: (1) the wares which occur not only in the platform of the mosque, but also in later deposits at Siraf; (2) three of the wares which do *not* occur in the platform, although they occur in later deposits, and, finally, (3) some of the literary evidence for T'ang stoneware in the Middle East.

Two types of stoneware from the mosque, jars with a shiny black surface and bowls with patches of glaze removed from the base, are extremely rare in later deposits and we conclude that they went out of use at Siraf at the beginning of the ninth century. The two other types, Dusun jars and bowls of painted stoneware, occur frequently in later deposits and clearly remained in use long after *c.* 825. However, stoneware vessels, which were both durable and costly, probably survived intact for some time after importation ceased and the occurrence of a ware in, say, twelfth century deposits does not necessarily mean that it was *made* in the twelfth century; the porcelain deposited by Shah 'Abbas at the Ardebil shrine in 1612 included numerous fourteenth-century vessels, as did the collection in the Topkapu Sarayi, Istanbul (Pope, 1952). At Siraf, several pieces of a large bowl of Dusun type were found in a refuse deposit outside the extension to the Great Mosque, associated with a 'late sgraffiato' ware bowl of the eleventh or twelfth century (Whitehouse, 1969: 46). According to Harrisson (1965), the latest Dusun jars were manufactured no later than the Sung period, which ended in 1280, but at present closer dating is impossible. Painted stoneware probably enjoyed a shorter currency. Thus, we found numerous examples in the earlier deposits at Site F, notably the wells back-filled when Houses E and N were built (Whitehouse, 1971: 9), but only a handful of fragments in the refuse and rubble which accumulated in Houses N, R and W after they had been abandoned in the eleventh century. Indeed, it seems probable that painted stoneware went out of use some time before *c.* 1000.

So far, three well-known types which occur in later deposits at Siraf are not represented in the platform of the mosque: green wares, white wares and ewers or jars with applied ornament. Bowls with a green or grey-green glaze, usually known as Yüeh ware (but see

Tregear, 1967) are the most common imported table wares throughout most of the ninth and tenth centuries at Siraf, where typical
vessels have a concentric ring of spur marks on the interior
(Whitehouse, 1969: pl. VIa and 1971: pl. IXa). Identical or similar
wares have a wide distribution in South Asia, the Middle East and
East Africa and Gray (1964-6: 24) hints that the earliest examples
from Ceylon may belong to the eighth century. It is interesting,
therefore, that a preliminary examination of the earliest imports
from Siraf does not reveal a single green ware fragment, a situation
which recalls Alcock's observation (personal communication) that at
Banbhore painted stoneware was present *before* the earliest green
ware bowls. White wares, too, are absent from the mosque, although
later deposits, such as the wells beneath Houses E and H at Site F,
contain both translucent porcelain and bowls with a coarse cream
fabric and a shiny glaze, comparable with Sarre's (1925: 60) Group E
of Far Eastern wares at Samarra.

Among the less frequent imports at Siraf are fragments of ewers or
jars decorated with applied reliefs, which are usually coloured brown
(Whitehouse, 1968: pl. VIa and 1971: pl. XIa). Vessels of this type
are represented in several western collections (Ottema, 1946: 77 and
figs. 78-9) and examples occur also in South-East Asia (Ottema,
1946: fig. 79; Orsoy de Flines, 1969: pl. 5). Although never
abundant in the Middle East, fragments have been found on several
sites in Iran, notably Bibi Khatun on the Persian Gulf (Whitehouse,
1968: 17), Tel Zibid in Khuzistan (Hansman, 1970: pl. XVIH) and
Nishapur (Mikami, 1969: 143). Islamic imitation are recorded from
Samarra, apparently with a blue alkaline glaze (Anon., 1940: Part II,
pl. LIII, 4 [line drawing] and pl. LIX [photograph]), and Susa, with
a tin glaze and lustre ornament (Koechlin, 1928: No. 158 on p. 108
and pl. XXII). In view of their presence in later deposits at Siraf and
their evident popularity in the Middle East, the absence at the
mosque of ewers with applied reliefs implies that they were not
imported until *after* the early ninth century.

The date of the finds from the Great Mosque corresponds closely
with the date of the earliest literary reference to Chinese wares in the
Middle East, the celebrated description by Baihaqi (writing in 1059)
of 'twenty pieces of Imperial porcelain (*chini faghfuri*) which had
never been seen before at a caliph's court', and more than two
thousand other vessels, sent by Ali b. Isa, a governor or Khurasan, to
Harun al Rashid (786-806) at Baghdad (for this and other literary
references, see Kahle, 1940-1 and Lane and Sarjeant, 1948).
Baihaqi's reference to Imperial porcelain suggests that fine wares
were unusual in the Middle East at this date — a deduction borne out
by the earliest finds from Siraf.

Several other writers refer to ninth-century Chinese imports. Sulaiman, for example, whose *Akbar as Sin wa l'hind* was probably written in 851 and annotated in 916, noted translucent pottery among the imports from China. Tanukhi mentions more than thirty Chinese jars (*hubb sini*) containing a perfume called *ghaliya*, the best of which was made during the caliphate of al-Wathik (842-7). One of the jars was so heavy that it had to be carried by several slaves. The only *large* Chinese jars known to have reached the Middle East in the ninth century are the Dusun jars mentioned above and it seems likely that these are the vessels in question. Al-Isfahani describes a bowl from China (*siniyat al-Sin*) with painted ornament (*tasawir*) which was broken during the reign of Mutawakkil (847-61). Al-Jahiz (d.869) also may have meant a painted vessel when he referred to a coloured Chinese vessel (*ghadar sini mulamma*), for *ghadar* means 'pottery' and *mulamma* has a variety of meanings, including 'coloured', 'variegated' or simply 'glossy'. In the past, these and other similar references have been taken to mean the mottled wares of the T'ang dynasty. However, Watson (1970: 39) has cast doubt on the Chinese origin of the mottled sherds from Samarra and Hansman (1970: 216-7) has pointed out the danger of attributing finds from Samarra to the period of caliphal occupation (836-83) without independent evidence of date. While *some* Chinese wares with mottled ornament certainly did reach the Middle East (e.g. Whitehouse, 1971: pl. XI), it is possible that the ninth-century wares mentioned by al-Isfahani and al-Jahiz are the painted bowls described above.

Acknowledgments

I have received invaluable help while studying the Chinese material from Siraf. Miss Jennifer Scarce, Mrs Barbara Stephen, Miss Mary Tregear, Dr Cheng Tê-K'un, Mr Basil Gray, Mr Peter Hardie, Professor Tsugio Mikami and Dr Yutaka Mino discussed the finds with me. Mr Leslie Alcock gave me information about his preliminary excavation at Banbhore. Dr George Scanlon told me much about his excavations at Fustat. Mr James Allan discussed with me the meaning of the Arabic sources quoted on p. 253 Mr John Ayers told me about the painted stoneware bowl in Buffalo Museum of Science. Mr Douglas Barrett, Mr Ralph Pinder-Wilson and Mrs Jessica Rawson gave me information on material in the British Museum collections and the occurrence of painted stoneware in Ceylon. Dr John Hansman permitted me to consult his doctoral thesis, which is not yet on open shelves. Mr Andrew Williamson discussed with me his important finds from Fars and the coast of the Persian Gulf. To all these colleagues I offer my warmest thanks. Needless to say, the errors are entirely my own.

REFERENCES

Anon. (1940) *Excavations at Samarra 1936-1939.* Baghdad, Iraq Government Department of Antiquities.

Anon. (1952) *Catalogue: Charles B. Hoyt Collection Memorial Exhibition.* Boston, Museum of Fine Art.

Anon. (1960) (Notes on the kilns at Wa Ch'a Ping) *Wen Wu* 1960, No. 3, 31.

Anon. (1964) Excavations at Banbhore. *Pakistan Archaeology*, I, 49-55.

Aubin, J. (1959) La ruine de Siraf et les routes du Golfe Persique aux XIe et XIIe siécles. *Cahiers de civilisation médiévale*, 2, 295-301.

Aubin, J. (1969) La survie de Shilau et la route du Khunj-o-Fal. *Iran*, VII, 21-39.

Chittick, N. (1967) Excavations in the Lamu Archipelago. *Azania*, II, 1-31.

Gray, B. (0000) The export of Chinese porcelain to India. *Trans. Oriental Ceramic Soc.*, 1964-6, 21-37.

Hansman, J.F. (1970) Urban settlement and water utilization in South-Western Khuzistan and South-Eastern Iraq from Alexander the Great to the Mongol conquest of 1258. Unpublished Ph.D. thesis, University of London.

Harrisson, T. (1965)'Dusun Jars': from Mayfair and Friesland through Cairo to Sabah. *Sarawak Museum J.*, NS XII, Nos. 25-6, 69-74.

Hobson, R.L. (1928-30) Potsherds from Brahminabad. *T.O.C.S.* 8, 21-3.

Kahle, P. (1940-41) Chinese porcelain in the lands of Islam. *Trans. Oriental Ceramic Soc.*, 1940-1, 27-46.

Koechlin, R. (1928) *Les céramiques musulmanes de Suse.* Paris.

Lamb, A. (1961) Kedah and Takuapa, some tentative historical conclusions. *Federation Museums J*, NS I, 69-88.

Lane, A. and Serjeant, R.B. (1948) Pottery and glass fragments from the Aden littoral, with historical notes. *J. Royal Asiatic Soc.*, 1948, 6-33.

Mikami, T. (1969) *Toji No Michi (Ceramic Road).* Tokyo.

Orsoy de Flines, E.W. van (1969) *Guide to the Ceramics Collection.* Jakarta, Museum Pusat.

Ottema, N. (1946) *Chineesche Ceramiek Handboek.* Amsterdam.

Pope, J.A. (1952) *Fourteenth-Century Blue and White: a Group of Chinese Porcelains in the Topkapu Sarayi Muzesi, Istanbul.* Washington, Freer Gallery of Art.

Sarre, F. (1925) *Die Keramik von Samarra.* Berlin.

Stein, A. (1937) *Archaeological Reconnaissances in North-Western India and South-Eastern Iran.* London.

Tregear, M. (1967) Early Chinese green wares in the collection of the Ashmolean *Museum, Oxford. Oriental Art*, XIII, No. 1, 1-7.

Watson, W. (1970) On T'ang soft-glazed pottery, in *Pottery and Metalwork in T'ang China.* Watson, W. (ed.), London, Percival David Foundation.

Whitehouse, D. (1968) Excavations at Siraf. First interim report. *Iran*, VI, 1-22.

Whitehouse, D. (1969) Excavations at Siraf. Second interim report. *Iran*, VII, 39-62.

Whitehouse, D. (1970a) Excavations at Siraf. Third interim report. *Iran*, VIII, 1-18.

Whitehouse, D. (1970b) Siraf: a medieval port on the Persian Gulf. *World Archaeology*, 2, No. 2, 141-58.

Whitehouse, D. (1970c) Some Chinese and Islamic Pottery from Siraf, in *Pottery and Metalwork in T'ang China*, Watson, W. (ed.), London, Percival David

Foundation, 30-4.

Whitehouse, D. (1971a) Excavations at Siraf. Fourth interim report. *Iran*, IX, 121-37.

Whitehouse, D. (1971b) The houses of Siraf. *Archaeology*, 24, No. 3, 255-62.

Whitehouse, D. (1971c) Siraf: a Sasanian port. *Antiquity*, XLV, No. 180, 262-7.

Whitehouse, D. (1972) Excavations at Siraf, Fifth interim report. *Iran*, X, 63-87.

19
Recent discoveries of the historical period in India

J.E. VAN LOHUIZEN-DE LEEUW

With a few exceptions the discoveries which I am going to mention all relate to the historical period and, apart from three items, they all refer to the years 1969, 1970 and the first six months of 1971. The selection is by no means a complete survey, and it might be prudent to give a word of warning, for my sources are practically all newspaper reports, the credibility of which is occasionally doubtful, either because the reporter may have misunderstood his source, or because certain news items are exaggerated to please local patriotism. A hilarious example of the latter is the following heading in the Poona Herald of 31 January 1971: 'Kondapuram another Mohenjo-daro in A.P.'.

The work at Sannothi began in 1966, when Dr Nagaraju of Mysore University explored a stupa at the site. Dr Nagaraju believes that this stupa is nearly 2000 years old as some of the Brahmi inscriptions which came to light can be dated between the first century B.C. and the third century A.D. (*India News*, 23 July 1966).

Although initiated by law in 1964, archaeology in Punjab took some time to get under way owing to technical difficulties, procedural delays and the splitting up of the State in Haryana and Himachal Pradesh. However, in 1967 an important site at Dholbaha, 30 km from Hoshiarpur, was discovered by the Archaeological wing of the Punjab State Archives. The excavations produced sherds of polished ware, Kushana coins and architectural remains and sculptures dating from the third-fifth centuries *A.D.*, besides several Hindu and Jaina temples, the latest of which was built during the Sikh period. In view of the importance of the site a proposal was made to build a site museum to house the finds (*Statesman*, 1 November 1967).

In the summer of 1967, the Directorate of Archaeology of West Bengal discovered fifteen smelting furnaces dating from the Gupta period, on the western flanks of the ancient defence works of Nalrajar Garh in the Mondabari forest, Jalpaiguri District. These furnaces are said to be curiously advanced in structure, resembling modern metallurgical furnaces (*Deccan Chronicle*, 27 May 1967; *India News*, 3 June 1967).

More furnaces for extracting and refining metals were found near Cave 25 at Kanheri in the summer of 1970 by Mr S.R. Rao. It appears that the Kanheri group consisting of over 100 caves, remained in continuous use from the first to the ninth century A.D. and was not deserted during the second-fifth centuries as was the case with other caves in the Decan. Mr Rao thinks that the monks smelted metal for the overseas trade which ran via Kalyana and Sopara, but I think that these furnaces served the needs of the very large monastic establishment which Kanheri must obviously have been (*Times of India*, 28 June 1970).

In 1968-9, excavations were carried out by the Rajasthan Archaeological Department at the important site of Noh in the Bharatpur District. According to Dr Satya Prakash, Director of the Department, the results indicate that the Aryans entered Rajasthan from the east. A cultural sequence from the Ochre colour Pottery through the painted grey ware, northern black polished ware, to Sunga and Kushan period was brought to light.

Another excavation by the same Department was at Bagoro, Bhilwara District, where a Late Stone Age settlement, claimed to be the first in Rajasthan, was partially exposed. Higher up, Sunga-Kushana pottery from the second century B.C. to the second century A.D. associated with iron objects came to light (*India News*, 18 October 1969).

In the summer of 1969, Dr B.P. Sinha, Director of Archaeology and Museums in Bihar, reported the discovery of Neolithic, Chalcolithic and early historical material from Chirand, an important site in North Bihar. Apart from Burzahom, Chirand is said to have produced the clearest sequence of stratified neolithic deposits in North India (*India News*, 18 October 1969).

In the same year, important excavations were carried out by J.P. Joshi of the Excavations Branch of the Archaeological Survey and Professor S.B. Deo of Nagpur University at Pauni, Maharashtra, situated on the ancient road from Madhyadesa to south India. This place must have been an important Buddhist centre from the fourth century B.C. till the second century A.D.; Phase I contained the remnants of a brick *stupa* dating from the pre-Maurya period, which remained in use for about four centuries. Originally, it was more than 38 m in diameter. Not long afterwards it was encased and enlarged to 41.40 m and a *pradaksinapatha*, 3 m wide was added. In the

Maurya-Sunga period a wooden railing was probably erected around this path which was later on replaced by one of stone. The figures carved on the railing pillars are standing in *anjalimudra* and their appearance is similar to that of the sculptures on the balustrades at Bharhut and Sanci. The inscriptions on the coping-stones of the railing are written in Brahmi characters of the Maurya-Sunga period. In the late Maurya Sunga time the *pradaksinapatha* was further widened to 7.50 m and paved with flat slabs. By then the stupa also had an elaborate *torana* at each of the four cardinal points and the whole monument must have been most impressive (*India News*, 7 May 1969; *India News*, 12 July 1969).

Further east a second century B.C. Brahmi inscription was discovered in 1969 in the Akkanna Madanna Cave at Vijayawada. It contains the word 'therasa' from which the discoverers infer that it was probably a Buddhist monument of the second century B.C. and not a Hindu cave temple of the fifth century A.D. as has hitherto been believed (*India News*, 2 August 1969).

Finally, I should mention in passing the excavations by the Banaras Hindu University of a Gupta period brick shrine at Bhitari, in the Ghazipur District of UP (*India News*, 29 March 1969; *India News*, 24 May 1969).

Coming to some of the discoveries of 1970, I should like to mention first of all an important find at Guntapalli. This site lying 28 miles from Eluru, was first explored by Rea at the end of the nineteenth century and later on by Longhurst. They both found, among other things, a rock-cut temple with a monolithic *stupa* and a *vihara*, dating from the second century B.C. In September 1970, a lime-stone pillar was discovered at this site with a Brahmi inscription which was repeated on each of the four sides. Dr Subrahmanyam of the Archaeological Department of the Government of Andhra Pradesh has read and published the inscription. It provides us with the interesting information that one of the court dignitaries of king Kharavela of Kalinga built a *mandapam* to which I suppose the pillar in question probably belonged. He presumably erected this building at Guntapalli when Kharavela's armies had marched victoriously through Godavari and Krishna Districts reaching the Krishna River. The town Musika, mentioned in the Hathigumpha inscription, the identification of which has hitherto caused great difficulties, is now suggested by Dr Subrahmanyam to be the same as the present Kondapur. Moreover, there are reasons to believe that the *mandapam* in question was probably erected for the Jaina community and so one is tempted to assume that the caves at Guntapalli were also perhaps meant for the Jainas and only later on taken over by the Buddhists (*The Hindu*, 19 July 1970).

An interesting excavation which took place in 1970 is that at Kaveripattinam in the Thanjavur District, at the mouth of the Kaveri River. It was carried out by the Southern Circle of the Archaeological Survey of India. Kaveripattinam is known to have been the ancient port of the Colas and one of the most important harbours on the east coast. It acted as a capital of the great Karikala Cola, who ruled in the first or second century A.D. and was mentioned by Ptolemy and in the Periplus, as well as in the Silappadikaram and the Manimekhalai. Among the discoveries of 1970 were an early wharf, an inlet channel of a reservoir and part of a Buddhist *vihara*. The excavation of the Sampapati Amman shrine on the banks of the Kaveri revealed an early medieval temple built of moulded brick. Its rammed earthen platform, 1 m in height, had three courses of bricks in the centre on top, and then the temple itself had nearly eight courses of bricks below the adhisthana. Among the finds were a votive tank and terracotta horses. I have no doubt that we are dealing here with an ancient shrine dedicated to Aiyanar (*The Hindu*, 6 October 1970; *The Hindu*, 28 February 1971).

Not far away from Kaveripattinam, Dr V. Mahalingham of Madras University carried out several excavations at Kancipuram in the same year. Among the various finds were sherds with Brahmi inscriptions of the third century and more than three dozen amphorae, dating from the beginning of the Christian era, similar to those found at Arikamedu (*India News*, 9 May, 1970). Since then a further announcement has been made in which the discovery of the first Buddhist *stupa* at Kancipuram was reported. The monument is about 30 feet in diameter and is surrounded by a *pradaksinapatha* made of bricks (*The Indian Express*, 21 June 1971).

However, let us return to 1970. In May of that year, scholars from Calicut University made several intriguing discoveries in Wynad Forest such as (1) rock-cut sculptures in a cave believed to be prehistoric, (2) a great number of megaliths and a temple in an allegedly Pallava style, which seems most unusual in that area. However, clarification of these finds seems necessary before one can accept these statements (*The Indian Express*, 29 May 1970).

Among the many prehistoric discoveries of the last few years, no less than four new Megalithic sites have been found in Kashmir, apart from the already well-known north-west Indian sites of Asota and Burzahom, the latter having recently been excavated once more by Shri T.N. Khazanchi. In view of these discoveries it is apparent that this Neolithic culture must have been more or less wide-spread in Kashmir (*The Hindu*, 7 November 1970).

Back to the historical period: Archaeology in Goa is at last getting into gear. Dr V.T. Gune of the Goa Archives Department reported in

March 1970 that at Mapusa pottery and terracotta objects had been discovered which he attributed to the third century A.D. A stone channel with a *simhamukha* spout dating perhaps from the thirteenth century A.D. and which might indicate the presence of temple ruins, was also brought to light (*The Indian Express*, 24 March 1970).

From among the numerous finds during 1970 belonging to the mediaeval period I shall only mention the discovery in September of no less than 24 temples near Udipi in South Kanara. This group which dates from the ninth-tenth centuries is obviously quite interesting and can probably be compared in importance with such groups as that at Pattadkal, though the recently discovered temples are later in date (*The Indian Express*, 26 September 1970).

Finally, I should mention two more excavations carried out in 1970, both referring to the Muslim period. The first is that at Purana Qila at Delhi, conducted by the Archaeological Survey of India under Shri B.K. Thapar. Here, the lowest layers so far reached revealed remains of the Mauryan period. Higher up the early Mughal strata produced Chinese porcelain and celadon wares indicating extensive trade relations between India and China in the fifteenth and sixteenth centuries A.D. (*The Hindu*, 17 May 1970).

The second is the work in the Qutb Shahi tombs of Golconda by Mr Abdul Waheed Khan, Director of Archaeology and Museums, Government of Andhra Pradesh. He found in the gardens of one of these tombs a square underground structure with inner galleries supported by arches and cisterns in each corner. The niches were painted in blue tempera. In another area the remains of a palace of the early Qutb Shahi period (middle of the sixteenth century) were uncovered, consisting of more than 36 rooms decorated with glazed tiles and fine stucco work and containing also washing rooms, toilets and kitchens. In front of the rooms and terraces were cisterns with fountains and water cascades. Apart from a lot of imported Chinese porcelain and various other small antiquities, a gold ring set with precious stones was discovered. Many of the objects found during the excavations threw an interesting light on life in the palace (*The Hindu*, October 1970).

So much for 1970, although one could easily add more to this random selection. In spite of the fact that 1971 has only run half of its course at the time of writing, many interesting discoveries have already been announced in the first six months.

In January, a newspaper reported the work done by the Archaeological Department of Andhra Pradesh, at the Satavahana site of Kondapur, 42 miles from Hyderabad. The excavation revealed a *stupa* and two *caitya* halls. No less than 1845 coins, including a gold coin of Augustus, were discovered. Other finds comprised coin moulds, terracotta, ivory, metal and glass bangles with embossed design, as well as a great variety of beads. Ivory carving seems to have been particularly important at Kondapur. Five unspecified varieties of pottery were found as well as figurines made of terracotta and kaolin, the latter with traces of green, red and yellow paint (*Poona Herald*, 31 January 1971).

In March the Andhra University excavated at Jami in the Visakhapatnam District. The occupational strata showed three distinct periods. An important find from the latest phase were some Satavahana coins discovered for the first time in this district. Kharavela boasts that he defeated the Satavahanas and that his horses drank the water of the Krishna River. The discovery of these coins therefore probably confirms that this part of the country was indeed at one time in the hands of the Satavahanas. The second phase showed rudiments of what could be called town planning, for the streets all ran from east to west (*The Indian Express*, 16 March 1971).

Also in March, excavations in Tilaurakot near Lumbini in the Nepalese Terai were in progress, but the report on the discoveries is confused and one does not quite understand what the newspaperman is trying to convey (*The Times of India*, 7 March 1971).

In April, Professor S.B. Deo of Nagpur University discovered some Buddhist caves near Pullar in Chandla Forest, 40 miles from Nagpur. The rock-cut votive inscriptions at this site are written in Prakrit and the Brahmi script can be assigned to the third century B.C. (*The Indian Express*, 3 April 1971).

In the same month Dr N. Venkataramanayya discovered a group of 11 temples in Mahbubnagar District. The temples date from the fifth to the seventh centuries and belong to the period of the Visnukundins of which we know very little. Consequently this group is a most welcome addition and, in fact, constitutes a highly important discovery. (*The Indian Express*, 1 April 1971).

In June 1971 Mr S.R. Rao of the South-Western Circle of the Archaeological Survey reported the excavation near Cave 32 at Ellora of a temple of Svami Chakradhar of the Mahanubhava sect, with an image in black stone of the saint himself. The Svami was born in Gujarat and later on came to Paithan, where he founded his sect in about A.D. 1200. Near the temple, which is constructed of black stone and measures 7.50 x 7.50 m square, many black bangles were found which the women of this sect used to wear (*The Indian Express*, 3 June 1971).

Also in June, a search was launched for the throne of Sivaji, the heroic Maratha leader who died in 1680. It is believed that it was thrown into the Gangasagar lake of Raigarh Fort in the Kolaba

District. However, Mr Vidwans of the South-Western Circle of the Survey reports that the labourers were unwilling to co-operate, out of respect for the great Sivaji and in addition – to use a cricketing expression – 'rain stopped play'. (*The Indian Express*, 1 June 1971).

In June a remarkable announcement was made in Kashmir by Mr Moh. Amin, Muslim archivist. He claims to have discovered the pillar under which, according to tradition, the stone boxes were deposited containing copper plates on which the records of the fourth Buddhist Council under Emperor Kanishka were engraved. If Mr Amin's claim turns out to be correct, an astonishing discovery will have been made (*International Herald Tribune*, 22 June 1971).

The South-Western Circle of the Archaeological Survey recently announced that the work at Aihole, which has been going on now for several years, has brought to light evidence indicating that building activities at Aihole did not start with the Calukyas as hitherto believed, but had begun under the Satavahanas (*The Indian Express*, 29 June 1971).

Many interesting finds discovered in 1971, dating from the prehistoric period could be mentioned, such as the Neolithic axes found in some places along the Periyar River in Kerala (*The Hindu*, 21 January 1971) or the queer copper prong unearthed during excavation of some megaliths at Mahurjhari, about 9 miles north-west of Nagpur by Professor S.B. Deo and Dr A.D. Jamkhedkar (*The Indian Express*, 11 March 1971). The latter is coming to work in Amsterdam, so we shall soon have more details. However, I have deliberately confined myself to the historical period, so I leave out all further mention of some of the exciting prehistoric finds of 1970 and 1971.

I shall conclude with a swift summary of the work at Sonkh by Dr Hartel. The German expedition has been excavating this mound at Mathura since 1966. The first two seasons were spent in getting down, through the Jat fortress, to the top of the mound. It soon became apparent from a trench at the side of the mound that the site had been occupied for about 3000 years, for there is plenty of Painted Grey Ware. Consequently, the third season began hopefully, but it turned out that the mediaeval layers were badly disturbed. The grey stone plaques belonging to this phase, usually showing Surya or Vishnu, deserve special mention. Approaching the late Kushana layers meant mounting excitement. Among the pottery belonging to this period, one piece with red-brown, yellow and black paint is entirely new. Apart from several houses, an apsidal hall was uncovered. These buildings are among the very few architectural remains ever excavated at Mathura. Some of the walls still stand up to 2 m high. Coin finds and a hoard have securely dated these late

Kushana layers to about A.D. 200. In the apsidal temple a stone image of a Mother Goddess with two figures on either side was discovered but whether this figure originally belonged to the Krishna period seems doubtful.

Special mention should be made of two bronzes, one representing Skanda and the other showing a remarkable group of a standing male deity flanked by a Mother Goddess whose head seems to be that of a lion. Dr Hartel is probably right in believing that these two images are the first Kushana bronzes which have come to our notice, but they are not the oldest bronzes from the historical period, as the small Mother Goddess which I discovered in the Peshawar Museum in 1956 is undoubtedly late Sunga in style. However, this in no way detracts from the importance of the two Kushana bronzes unearthed by Dr Hartel. Another interesting find is a terracotta plaque showing Durga Mahishasuramardini with four arms in an iconographical form hitherto unknown. In short, Sonkh may well produce exciting material in the years to come. Whether it will also help in determining the date of Kanishka at A.D. 78, as Dr Hartel hopes, is another matter, but it is surely a most interesting excavation which may well have great discoveries in store for us.

20

Styles of Bengal Temple Terracottas: a preliminary analysis

DAVID McCUTCHION

From the sixteenth to the nineteenth century there was a revival of Hindu art and architecture in Bengal largely inspired by the same cultural movement of neo-vaisnavism as lay behind the better-known West Indian miniature painting of Rajasthan and the hills. The cult of Radha-Krishna, which had been a constant inspiration to poets in Bengal from as early as Jayadeva's *Gita Govinda* of the twelfth century, reached its culmination in the ecstatic trances of Sri Chaitanya (1486-1533) of Nabadwip, whose followers and codifiers set off numerous conversions especially among the petty rajas, landowners, and their queens.

During the preceding period (thirteenth-fifteenth centuries) architecture had been predominantly Muslim in the provincial (Bengal) style, but from the late sixteenth century on an increasing number of temples have survived — many of them in styles for which there is no clear earlier record. Distinctive among these new styles are those based on the design of village huts (*bangla* and *chala* styles), and a pinnacled variety (*ratna* style), probably originating in central and upper India, inspired from Muslim design. A full descriptive classification of these temple styles may be found in my monograph in press at the time of writing with the Asiatic Society of Bengal.

The second remarkable feature of these temples of the Hindu revival in Bengal is their terracotta decoration. In the case of the Syama Raya (pl. 20.1) and Keshta Raya temples of Bishnupur, built by the Malla king Raghunath Singh in 1643 and 1655 respectively, or the temple of Kantaji at Kantanagar, built by the Raja of Dinajpur in the early eighteenth century, these not only completely cover all four exterior facades, but inner walls and upper stories as well — a mass of tiny pullulating figures inspired to very excess, one might feel, by the joyous abandon of the Chaitanya movement which swept the country with swaying dance and frenzied song. Generally

Plate 20.1 Seventeenth-century style. *Bishnupur* (Bankura district): base friezes on the central tower of the Syama Raya temple (1643).

speaking, however, even on the more ambitious temples, only one facade (or sometimes two) is richly carved, and interiors are left plain.

The sudden appearance of this art, in the last quarter of the sixteenth century, raises the question of its origins. The layout is in continuity with the terracotta-decorated facades of the Sultanate period, especially with the later Hosain Shahi period (1493-1538). Facades like those of the Jhanjhaniya Mosque (1535) or Qadam Rasul building (1531) of Gaur lead directly to those of the Radha-Ballabha temple at Krishnanagar in Hooghly district or Madana Mohana temple (1694) at Bishnupur: rectangular frame filled with twisting rose sprays (later: battle scenes cf. pls. 20.5, 6) above the pointed archways, the rest of the facade encircled by rows of small flat rectangular panels in which the Muslim hanging lamp motifs give way to *krishnalila* and *dasavatara*. There is little doubt that many of the families of artists working on the mosques during the Sultanate period shifted to temple-decoration in the second half of the sixteenth century, for the Mughals brought the imperial style of Muslim architecture with them from Delhi: colonnaded mosques gave way to three domes on arches, the Bengali curved cornice was replaced by the straight parapet, and terracotta was abandoned for smooth plaster panelling. At Bindol in West Dinajpur district a curious example has survived, probably from the sixteenth century, completely overgrown, of a mosque design adapted to temple use and decorated with large flat wall panels repeating the motifs of contemporary mosques.

One of the early schools of temple decoration, as on the Baidyapur Deul (1598) in Burdwan district, or the Chaitanya temple at Guptipara in Hooghly district, shows great affinity with con- temporary mosque decoration (e.g. Kusumba, 1558, in Rajshahi district, or Sura, somewhat earlier, in Dinajpur district), and tends to have very few figures. In Mymensingh district, where terracotta continued in use for mosques well into the seventeenth century, we find some feedback from temples to mosques, for the *mihrab* inside the Sadi Mosque (1652) at Egarasindur is framed exactly like a Hindu temple entrance, a development anticipated at Kusumba. The alternating horizontal ridges and recesses of the Kodla Math in Khulna district or the Mathurapur Deul in Faridpur district are as developed in the mosque tradition for the corner bastions, the recesses being filled with the same designs as at Sura, Bagha in Rajshahi district, or Adisaptagram in Hooghly district. Many temples of this early period, as at Raynagar (1588) in Jessore district, or Gokarna (1590) in Murshidabad district, take their vegetal and geometrical ornamentation from the mosque tradition; plaques in museums recall others no longer standing.

But figure decoration had to be taken from other sources, now largely lost. There is no continuity with the Mahasthan or Paharpur tradition, which is different in style, layout and scale, and died out long before the Muslims overran these centres. Apart from two large terracotta plaques in the north and east niches of the temple at Bahulara in Bankura district — plaques which probably date from a repair after the images which the niches were originally intended to hold had disappeared — the pre-Muslim temples of Bengal were decorated with stucco or incised brick. A parallel to the seventeeth century Bishnupur style may be found in the few surviving scroll paintings of the late eighteenth century or painted manuscript covers of the seventeeth, both of which represent a much older tradition: the emphasis is on linear rhythm, with faces in profile and strong indentation of limbs. The old Pala sculptures, with which the terracottas occasionally reveal a distant affiliation, showed faces frontally, naturalistic and idealized, but this is not found in early terracotta, suggesting that the stone-cutter's art was dead (the later Krishnas and Kalis are totally different). Not so in Orissa, however, where a degenerate style persisted up into the modern period. The terracotta figures of Durga, Krishna, and others incorporated round the facade of the renovated temple of Narasimha Deva at Gokarna

Plate 20.2 Eighteenth-century 'Hooghly' style. *Bihirgarh* (Hooghly district): base friezes on the Damodara temple (1743) of the Tat family. Upper (left to right): birth of Krishna while the guards sleep; fording the Jamuna preceded by a jackal. Lower: travel by Europeans in eighteenth-century Bengal.

are remarkably similar to the later stone and wood carving of Orissa, and may date back to the sixteenth century if they belong to the original temple, which a later stone inscription claims (plausibly) to have been built in 1590. But there is little other evidence of Orissan influence on terracotta; it is significant that when the Raja of Mayurbhanj had a temple in the Bengal style built at Haripurgarh for the worship of Krishna round about 1575, he brought in artists from Bengal to build it — and the style is the early 'Hooghly' style.

Surveying the temple decoration as a whole, from the sixteenth to the nineteenth century, the styles of terracottas may be differentiated according to three principles: (1) chronological, (2) regional, (3) local or individual. Chronologically, a steady devitalization may be discerned from the seventeenth to the nineteenth century (pls. 20.5, 6). This gives a certain affinity to styles from the same period in all areas, but certain schools dominated particular areas in particular periods. Thus the Bishnupur school is largely confined to the seventeenth century, the Hooghly school (pl. 20.2) dies out before the end of the eighteenth, and nineteenth century schools flourished mainly in the outlying western districts of Midnapore, Bankura, Burdwan and Birbhum (pl. 20.4). Terracotta

Plate 20.3 Eighteenth-century Baranagar style. *Baranagar* (Murshidabad district): base friezes on the northern temple (1760) of the *char-bangla* group. Upper (right to left): beginning of the Krishna story; lower: travel by the gentry.

Plate 20.4 Nineteenth-century style. *Itanda* (Birbhum district): base panels on the Kali temple.

was evidently old-fashioned to those who had contact with the stuccoed palaces of Calcutta.

The early style is rhythmical, often rather flat, with plenty of vigour and a certain caricatural (or at least highly stylized) force. Panoramic battle scenes above the archways tend to be conceived whole, whereas later they are generally arranged in horizontal rows (pls. 20.5, 6) — but not always: the Raghunatha temple (1772) at Bhalia or Radha-Govinda temple (1786) at Atpur, both in Hooghly district, have very dynamic battle scenes, whereas many earlier temples in the same district present a far more static arrangement. In these panoramic scenes the major figures stand out boldly from the mass of detail, just as on the facades as a whole the confusion of tiny figures is subordinated to a scheme of architectural projections. Pattern and texture dominate subject matter: every space where an ugly shadow might fall is filled with a lotus stud or hanging tassel, dogs invariably walk between horses' legs, limbs are disposed to fill space evenly and rhythmically. If the space to be filled required that an attendant be as tall as a dignitary on an elephant, then proportion is cast aside. But in the nineteenth century under the influence of imported British art (pl. 20.4) a kind of realism is increasingly pursued, and considerations of pattern or rhythm increasingly abandoned. Bodies become rounded, faces frontal, postures naturalistic. The Midnapore style is smooth and cursory, the Birbhum and Bankura styles fussy and detailed (but also sometimes smooth and cursory). Subject matter becomes more varied, innovation possibly being an attempt to meet the challenge of imported novelty and the demands of parvenu taste. At the same time the conviction went out of the work: preparation of clay, modelling, finishing, and firing were no longer carried through with the old care — much more work has survived from the nineteenth century, but it looks clumsy, crumbles and breaks away far more readily than that of the seventeenth and eighteenth centuries. Nevertheless, in Midnapore, Burdwan, and Birbhum districts, temples continued to be decorated with terracottas right up into the twentieth century, the latest that I know of being the *rasmancha* of 1910 at Kantabenia in Burdwan district and the Sridhar temple of 1931 at Dhamtor (P.S. Debra) in Midnapore district.

From the evidence of nineteenth century inscriptions, especially in Midnapore district, we know that temples were built by a master mason assisted by a team. Daspur in the Ghatal subdivision was a typical centre of such architects and artists (*sutradhar* caste), from where they spread out all over Chetua Parganas, adjoining Jahanabad, and beyond, for distances of thirty to forty miles or more. One Thakurdas Sil, for instance, built temples not only in Daspur itself

Plate 20.5 Seventeenth-century Battle of Lanka. *Jugsara* (Murshidabad district): archway panorama on one of the small Shiva temples.

Plate 20.6 Nineteenth-century Battle of Lanka. *Mamudpur* (P.S. Goghat of Hooghly): archway panorama on the Vishnu temple (1836) of the Sen family.

(e.g. the Chakravartys' temple in 1847) and nearby Surathpur (Sitala temple in 1849), but in Balarampur (Sitarama temple of the Malliks in 1860) and Chak Bajit (Ramesvara Siva temple in 1865) in adjoining Debra P.S., and his son — or grandson — Sasibhusan, was still at work in the area in the twentieth century (at Dhamtor, Chak Bajit, and Kharar for instance). Sasibhusan built a Shiva temple at Kharar (P.S. Ghatal) in 1905-6 in collaboration with another *mistri* (*sutradhar*) from Senhat in the Arambagh subdivision (former Jahanabad) of Hooghly district. We may easily suppose that throughout the three centuries of the revival, groups of artists from particular centres would carry their own particular style (essentially the style of their region) wherever they were called upon to work — which could be quite far afield: Haripurgarh in Mayurbhanj and Kantanagar near Dinajpur town are the extreme west and east limits of the 'Hooghly' style. Sri S.K. Ray in his study of the artisan castes of West Bengal for the 1951 Census confirms that the *sutradhars* were divided into groups according to area. He distinguishes four main *thaks* (family groups): (1) The *Bardhamana Thak* which includes Bankura, Burdwan, Birbhum and Murshidabad; (2) the *Astakula Thak* which includes Midnapore (south of the Kansai river), 24-Parganas, Howrah, Hooghly, and part of Nadia; (3) the *Brahmajajnia (Rajhansa) Thak* which includes Jessore, Khulna and part of Nadia; (4) the *Purbabangiya Thak* which includes North Bengal, Assam and East Bengal, etc. (see *The Tribes and Castes of West Bengal*, ed. A. Mitra, 1953: 325).

On the basis of style a number of the more important schools may be empirically distinguished: (Table 20.1, pps. 274-5).

Such a table, apart from being incomplete, is deceptively simple, no more than an initial framework from which to begin a more detailed breakdown. The extension of the Bishnupur style to Dignagar and Baragari and Jaugram, for instance, means no more than that the base friezes in particular show a significant similarity of style — it does not mean that artists from Bishnupur worked on these temples, which in the layout and style of the rest of their facades belong more to the seventeenth century 'Hooghly-Burdwan' school; but these three temples were evidently by artists with close affiliations. On the basis of the style of individual plaques alone it would be difficult to distinguish schools or even area — the small plaques encircling the facade, for instance, may change very little from the seventeenth to the eighteenth century, or from Midnapore to Faridpur. But different schools in the same century may be distinguished by motifs and layout. The characteristic 'Howrah-Hooghly' temple has a double frieze across the base, battle scenes (*lankajuddha* (pl. 20.5) and/or *devijuddha*) above the archways, double or triple row of encircling panels, and more figures in blocks of two or three up the edges of the facade. Alternatively, the archway panels may be filled with tightly stylized foliated scrollwork. Both these layouts continue from the seventeenth into the eighteenth century, the scrollwork more characteristic of Burdwan district, where it is later replaced by more realistic vegetal swathes; occasionally floral/vegetal motifs replace all the figures. In the Jessore-Khulna-Faridpur area of East Bengal, there is generally only one base frieze, in which both mythological and social scenes are depicted; nor do we find the panoramic battle scenes above the archways, but large springing lions, and scattered lotus studs. The temples of Baranagar (pl. 20.3) may be linked with East Bengal by the springing lions above the archways of the Gangesvara *jorbangla* temple, and with Puthia both by the arrangement of the clusters of figures at the edges of the facades, and the style of the terracottas on the western temple of the *char-bangla* group. The nineteenth-century 'Damodar Valley' school has antecedents in a less flattened style as at Bahadurpur (P.S. Ausgram) or Sankari (P.S. Khandghosh) in Burdwan district, or on the splendid Radha-Kanta temple of 1764 at Akui in the Indas P.S. of Bankura, where the terracotta layout recalls the Madana-Mohana temple of 1694 in Bishnupur town. The Pratapesvara temple (1849) at Kalna in Burdwan district was built by a *sutradhar* from Sonamukhi in Bankura district, providing a link between the 'Ajay Valley' style and the later Bankura style.

A full analysis of the material will distinguish more precisely the various sub-schools operating across nineteenth century Bankura-Midnapore-Burdwan-Birbhum. It will establish the affinities and differences between the styles of terracottas on the seventeenth century temples at Cheliama (1697, Purulia district), Ghurisa (1633, Birbhum district), Naldanga (Jessore) and Pabna, for instance, which clearly have more in common with each other than with those on the Kapilesvara temple of 1635 at Taras (Pabna district). The largest single area of significant conformity is the 'Hooghly' style (pl. 20.2) of the eighteenth century, extending into adjacent district and beyond, yet no two facades are exactly alike: subject matter and order vary, and even similar panels differ in detail; style too varies, as between different teams — in the case of the temple at Krishnapur (1762, P.S. Dadpur) to a surprising degree. Unfortunately we have almost no record of builders' names from the inscriptions on these eighteenth century temples.

In general, the seventeenth-century style merges into the eighteenth, and the eighteenth century into the nineteenth. In nineteenth-century Midnapore and Bankura the base friezes are dropped, and ornamentation much simplified; more varied subject

Table 20.1

period	main area (district)	examples (t. = temple)	extending to (district)	examples	characteristic features
16-17th c.	Burdwan	Baidyapur Deul (1598); Āmadpur: Gopāla t. Guptipārā: Chaitanya t.; Singārkon: Rādhā-Kānta t.	Hooghly	Krishnanagar: Rādhā-Ballabha t. Bainchigrām Deul (1582 or 1682), ruin at Rāvnagar (1588), Kodlā Math.	vegetal/geometrical motifs as on mosques; very few figures; tufts round archways.
			Jessore Khulna Faridpur	Mathurāpur Deul; also ruins at Bhusana, Nanikshir & Ujāni.	
17th c.	Bankura: Bishnupur town	temples of Syāma Rāya (1643) (Pl. 20.1), Keshta-Rāya (1655), Rādhā-Vinoda (1659), & Madan-Mohana (1694).	cf. Nadia Hooghly Burdwan Jessore Pabna	Dignagar: Rāghavesvara t. (1669) Borāgari: Gopāla t. Jaugrām; Rādhā-Kānta t. Naldāngā: Mahādeva t. Pābnā: former Kālachānd t.	rhythmical & vigorous; linear stylization, tending even to caricature.
17-18th c.	Birbhum Murshidabad	at Rāmnagar (P.S Mayureshwar), Jubutiā & Daskaigrām (P.S Nānur). at Jugsara (Pl. 20.5) & Sādpur (P.S Burwān).	Birbhum	Ghurishā: former Raghunātha t. (1633)	archway battle scenes, but no base friezes; rythmical patterning; much vegetal/geometrical 'filler'; small temples.
17th c.	Hooghly	Bānsberiā: Vāsudeva t. (1679); Guptipārā: Rāmachandra ruined temple at Bakharpur (P.S Pursurā)			
18th c.	Hooghly	Dasgharā (P.S Dhaniakhāli): Gopinātha t. (1729), Bahirgarh (P.S Jangipara): Dāmodar t. (1743) (Pl. 20.2) Khedāil (P.S Arambagh): Dāmodar t. (1767) Ārpur: Rādhā-Govinda t. (1786), etc. etc.	Howrah	Mahisāmuri (P.S. Āmtā) Bhuvanesvari t. (1679)	battle scenes above the archways; rythmical stylization.
17-18th c.	Howrah	at Rāutarā, Jhikirā & Amarāgari (all in P.S Āmtā)	Burdwan	Kālnā: Lālji t. (1739), Krishnachandra t. (1751), Ananta-Vāsudeva t. (1754); or at Rāyan, Basatpur & Suhāri (P.S. Burdwan)	battle scenes above the archways; figures tend to be stiffening up.
	Hooghly	Haripāl: Rādhā-Govinda t. (1654), Kankrākuli (P.S. Dhaniakhāli): Lakshmi-Janardana t. (1733), or at Dwārhatta & Gobindapur (P.S. Jangipārā)	Midnapore	Malancha (P.S. Kharagpur) Kāli t. (1712).	
	Burdwan	Dogāchhiā (P.S. Purbasthali): Gopinātha t. (1654), Hāt Gobindapur (P.S. Burdwan): Sridhara t., Kālnā: twin Siva temples (1753), or at Pānchkhrā, Āmadpur, Mulgrām, Sātgāchhiā (all in P.S. Memāri), etc.	Birbhum 24-Parganas Dinajpur	Kenduli: Rādhā-Vinoda t. Haishahar: Nandkishora t. (1743) Kāntanagar: Kāntaji t.	
			Mayurbhanj Howrah	Haripurgarh: Rāsika-Rāya t. Amarāgari: Gaja-Lakshmi t. (1729) Dhasha (P.S. Jagatballabhpur): Gopinātha t. (1708)	tight scrollwork above the archways; figures as previous.
18th c.	Burdwan	Putundi (P.S. Burdwan): Dāmodar t. (1749) Mandalay (P.S. Pānduā): Gopāla t. (1758), Bahabpur (P.S. Memāri): Syāma Sundara t. (1765), or at Suhāri & Hat Gobindapur (P.S. Burdwan), Gauripur, Andur, Sridharpur & Ajhāpur (P.S. Memāri), & Baidyapur (P.S. Kālnā)	Midnapore	Dāspur: Gopinātha (1716), Baikunthapur (P.S. Dāspur): Madana-Mohana. t. Birnagar (P.S. Rānāghāt): jor-bānglā (1694), Sāntipur: Jalesvara t.	
			Nadia		
			Hooghly	Gurap (P.S. Dhaniakhāli): Nandadulāla t. (1751)	leafy swathes above the arches, otherwise figures.
			Hooghly	at Krishnapur (P.S. Dadpur), Nityānandapur (P.S. Mograā), Uttarpārā, etc.	vegetal motifs over all or most of the facade.
			Murshidabad	Gobarhāti: (P.S. Kāndi): Vrindābana-Chandra t. (1772)	

variants and development of a single school

Period	Region / Style		Temple examples	District	Temple examples	Characteristics
18th c.	Khulna	close affinities	jorbāṅglā temples at Lohāgara, Śālnagar, Rāygrām, & Kotākol (1732).			and/or scattered lotus studs above the archways; single base frieze sometimes with animals; figures rythmical.
18th c.	Murshidabad		Dhulgrām: Raghunātha & jorbāṅglā temples at Khāliā or Kaichā in the area of Bhāṅga. Baranagar group. (Pl. 20.3)			soft realistic tendency.
18th c.	Rajshahi		Puthiā group.			
18th c.	Dacca		at Bāghiā (plaques in Dacca Museum), or Laskardighir Barh in Munshiganj sub-division.			
18-19th c.	Bankura		Hadal-Nārāyanpur (P.S. Pātrasāyer): Dāmodar t. (1806); or at Bālsi & Bāmirā in Pātrasāyer P.S., & Indas.			flattened figures, often frontal; simplified ornament, spreading, also flattened, often with criss-cross filling.
	Burdwan ('Dāmodar Valley' style)		Rāmesvara t. at Simāśimi (P.S. Galsi) and nearby villages, jorā Siva temples in the Sarvamangalā compound in Burdwan town, or at Belgrām & Bahādurpur (P.S. Ausgrām), Orgrām & Bara Belun (P.S. Bhātār), etc.			
19th c.	Midnapore ('Daspur style')	very strong affinities	numerous examples in Dāspur P.S. and adjacent Debrā, extending north into Ghātāl P.S., and south to the Raghunātha temple (begun 1810) at Ālangiri (P.S. Egrā), from the beginning of the century (e.g. Raghunātha temple of 1804 at Dāipur) to the end (Raghunātha temple of 1899 at Anandapur).	Bankura	Sonāmukhi: Srīdhara t. (1845) Bānkādaha (P.S. Bishnupur): Dāmodara t. (1845): Pārul (P.S. Ārambāgh): Bishālakshi t. (1859), Bāli (P.S. Ārambāgh): Dāmodara t. of Ghosh family (1822)	smooth rounded, frontal, cursory figures; not much 'filler' ornamentation.
				Hooghly	Jaypur (P.S. Āmtā): Sridhara t. (1782) Asanda (P.S. Āmtā): Sridhara t. (1789)	
				Howrah		similar to above with crudely scratched details.
19th c.	Goghat P.S. of Hooghly + adjoining Bankura and Midnapore		Māmudpur: Vishnu temple (1836) (Pl. 20.6) Badanganj: Dāmodara t. (1810), Kshirpai: Madana Mohana t. (1817), or at Jibtyā, Kotulpur, etc.	Burdwan	Kālnā: Pratāpesvara t. (1849)	fussy, with crudely incised or pinpointed detail.
19th c.	Bankura		Bishnupur: Srīdhara t. of Bose family, Pātrasāyer: Raghuvir t.			
19th c.	Burdwan		Mānkar (P.S. Galsi): Deulesvara & others, Sribāti (P.S. Kātwa): 3 Siva temples (1836), jorā Siva temples (1839) at Kālidāpur, or at Banpās (P.S. Bhātār), Bankāti (P.S. Kānksa), etc.	Murshidabad	Kāgrām (P.S. Bhāratpur): jorā Siva temples.	rounded, frontal, on a smaller scale than Midnapore; sometimes very elaborate detail & fussy ornamentation; the most realistic under European influence.
	Birbhum ('Ajay Valley' style)		Siva temples at Surul and Supur (P.S. Bolpur), jorbāṅglā and other temples at Itanda (Pl. 20.4) (P.S. Bolpur), Siva temple (1833) at Thupsara (P.S. Nānur), and at Illāmbāzār, Hetampur (P.S. Dubrājpur), Suri Kālibāri, etc. up to the end of the 19th century.			

matter is introduced above the archways. From the Simhavahini temple (1770) at Paikpari (P.S. Debra), the Lakshmi-Janardana temple (1791) of the Pal family at Daspur, the Janaki-Ballabha temple (1811) at Tilandapara (P.S. Sabang), the abandoned temple (1835) of the Chakravarti family at Daspur, to the Lakshmi-Varaha temple (1868) at Karkai (P.S. Pingla) one can follow the steady emergence of the rounded and increasingly cursory nineteenth-century 'Midnapore' style from the eighteenth-century 'Hooghly' style. In Howrah district we see this smooth roundedness developing already in the eighteenth century on the Sridhara temple (1782) of the Das family at Jaypur, or the Sridhara temple (1789) at Asanda, whereas on the *nava-ratna* Shiva temple (1802) at Baidyapur in Burdwan district the 'Hooghly' style persists into the nineteenth century. A sub-school of the Midnapore style placed very large terracotta figures across the top of the facade, as on the Satya-Narayan temple (1837) at Sarberia, Mahaprabhu temple at Brindabanpur – both in P.S. Daspur – or Sridhara temple (1856) at Lachhipur in P.S. Ghatal. This style is already degenerate by 1856, whereas at Anandapur in P.S. Keshpur the Midnapore style persists with competence and inventiveness almost into the twentieth century. Only in the case of the 'Ajay Valley' style is a sharp break apparent both in layout, subject matter, and style with the earlier tradition: a high frieze is introduced across the top of the facade, the base friezes are radically rearranged as non-continuous panels, the *dasamahavidya* are regularly introduced, and the Enthronement of Rama and Sita replaces the Battle of Lanka as the favourite archway panel. But the persistence of the earlier Burdwan tradition is apparent on the large temple of Lakshmi-Janardana (1844) at Debipur in P.S. Memari.

Finally we may take note of aberrant or local styles, seeming to depart from the norm of period and area, as on the ruined Siva temple (1775) at Gazipur in Howrah district, the chunky style above the archways at Uchkaron (1769) in Birbhum district, or the curiously flat style on the Lakshmi-Narayana temple (1718) at Metala in Bankura district. From the earlier periods they may represent established styles of which few examples have survived or been recorded. In the nineteenth century at Kshirpai in Midnapore district we have clear evidence of two distinct styles in the same area and period on the Madana Mohana temple of 1817 and the two slightly later Siva temples, one of which is dated 1839. Within the area of a general style, we may find a local layout, as round Baidyapur in Burdwan district, where large encircling lotuses combined with vegetal motifs and criss-cross panels repeated on small *at-chala* temples at Kumarpara, Singarkon, Patilpara and Ramnagar.

Other limited areas with local layouts and/or styles are at Perua
and nearby Gopalpur in the Khayarasol P.S. of Birbhum district, at
Dubrajpur in the adjacent P.S., or at Barisha and Tollyganj south of
Calcutta. The eighteenth-century Baranagar style as on the Gangesvara temple and northern temple (pl. 20.3) (1760) of the *char-bangla*
group is not found anywhere else — except in somewhat degenerate
form at Bhattamati in the same district — and may have been
inspired from the flourishing school of Murshidabad ivory carving:
terracotta is rare in the district. At Hetampur near Dubrajpur in
Birbhum district, the Chandranatha Siva temple of 1847 is unique in
having most of its plaques directly copied from European portraits
and genre scenes, coats of arms, and the like. Equally unique are the
large terracotta panels on the temple of Ananda-Bhairavi (1813) at
Sukhira (P.S. Balagarh) in Hooghly district: they probably date from
a later repair, when the art had died out in the district. Some plaques
in the museum of the Bangiya Sahitya Parishad in Calcutta, said to
come from Rajshahi district, but on a larger scale than those of
Puthia, show more affinity with those from Baghia (1705) in the
Dacca Museum or those on a ruined temple at Laskardighir Barh,
both in the Munshiganj subdivision of Dacca district: they may
represent a school from which only scattered examples have survived.
So, too, specimens in the Rangpur or Balurghat museums.

Terracotta schools were not confined to particular architectural
styles, though they (or their patrons) had evident preferences. Thus
the 'Hooghly' layout and style are most commonly found on the
at-chala design, the late Midnapore school preferred *pancha-ratna*,
and the 'Ajay Valley' school the small *rekha deul*. A group working
in the area round Lohagara (Jessore district) in the first half of the
eighteenth century built *jor-bangla* temples at Lohagara, Salnagar,
Raygram, Kotakal, and presumably other places as well; but they
also built *charchala* temples. The Bishnupur and Naldanga temples are
of both pinnacled and hut types, and the Hooghly style may be
found on *eka-ratna*, *pancha-ratna* and *nava-ratna* designs, *at-chala*
with single or triple entrance, *jor-bangla*, flat-roofed, and even the
small *rekha deul*.

The artists worked not only in terracotta, but also in wood and
stone. The style of the wood-carvings of the *chandi-mandapa* at
Atpur (18th century, Hooghly), or of temple doors in Nidnapore as
at Dubrajpur (nineteenth century) in Sabang P.S., corresponds to
that of the terracottas on the temple. Facades in Birbhum district
were frequently faced with a fine-grained crimson laterite
(*phulpathar*), carved to the same layout as terracotta. On a temple
such as the former Radha-Syama temple at Suri the carving is almost
indistinguishable in style from the seventeenth-eighteenth century

'Hooghly' type — very close to that of the Radha-Vinoda temple at Cheliama in Purulia district. Later, at Ganpur or Maĺuti near Rampurhat, these artists developed a style of their own, which, unable to imitate the rounded modelling of the European-influenced style, remained linear and flat into the nineteenth century. Sandstone carving in terracotta style is also found in Birbhum (e.g. Ghutgeria) districts. Temples built of coarse brown laterite in Midnapore and Bankura districts were decorated with an overcoating of plaster, often carved to the same layout and subject matter as of terracotta, but the effect was generally crude. Stucco — incised to vegetal/geometrical patterns, or moulded to crude figures — gradually replaced terracotta over the whole of Bengal in the nineteenth century. In the Midnapore school, which persisted later than any other, it became the practice to combine incised plaster panels above the archways with a series of doll-like terracotta figures (brightly painted) in the small niches encircling the facade. Finally cement took over, and the *sutradhars* fell back on carpentry.

21

The extent and limitations of Indian influences on the protohistoric civilizations of the Malay Peninsula.

JANICE STARGARDT

The title of this paper sets out a problem which, whether implicitly or explicitly, informs many studies of the South East Asian past. The most sustained consideration of this theme in relation to social forms, religion and the organization of the state in successive stages of South East Asian civilization is Georges Coedès' great work *Les états hindouisés d'Indochine et d'Indonésie*. More precisely focussed on my area of concern is Dr H.G. Quaritch Wales' *Archaeological Researches on Ancient Indian Colonization in Malaya*. These and other studies listed in the bibliography take widely different views of the 'indianization' process.

Stating the problem in the title serves in this case as a warning to both writer and reader of the concepts against which specific archaeological findings will finally be tested.

Early in 1971, I carried out a series of test excavations in Kedah, West Malaysia, on the middle reaches of the Bujang Valley, near the Pengkalan Bujang village. Unusual concentrations of ceramics in this area were found to exist by Wales in 1940 and by Lamb in 1959. The resumption of work by the Federated Malay States Museums' Department on the cluster of monumental remains in the Bujang Valley and on the headwaters of the nearby Sungei Batu Pahat revived the desire to know more about the economic and social background of the protohistoric communities which produced the temples. My main task, then, was to acquire material evidence to show the type and level of domestic technology, the range of economic and social contacts and to consider this evidence in the light of the monumental remains which have already been described by Evans, Wales and Lamb in some detail (see bibliography). This was part of my comparative study of protohistoric monumental and industrial/habitation sites of isthmian Thailand and Malaysia.

Certain general topographical features should be emphasized at the outset. It is very difficult to obtain detailed scale maps for the whole area for two reasons:

Firstly, the area is divided politically between Thailand and Malaysia; secondly, both the Southern Thai provinces and the North West states of Malaysia are insurgency areas and the maps are subject to security controls. In general maps of the region, the relations of archaeological sites to coast, river and mountains appear to be different from their actual situation; this has often led historians of the early period of South East Asian civilization, who have worked wholly or largely from literary sources, to make serious errors in their assumptions. It is only too easy to assume that a site which appears to be close to the coast will have been accessible to all the influences, benefits and dangers of maritime trade. In fact, even a few miles of land travel under conditions of tropical jungle and saturated soil can constitute a handicap, if not a barrier, to contacts of various sorts.

All of the provinces on the east coast of the isthmus – i.e. the Thai side – share in heavy and prolonged rains. They are affected by them and communities have responded to them in different ways. One general statement is valid despite these differences in local geography: the heavy rains and flash floods make land transport extremely difficult. Even today, when considerable efforts have been made to extend the ancillary road system of Southern Thailand, it is common to find them impassable for long periods because floods have caused bridge damage.

Waterways – whether natural or man-made – were certainly a key factor in the development of early urbanized, manufacturing and trading communities.

Again, a word of caution is necessary. The physical environment of the tropical zones of Asia is more volatile than its dry zones: coastlines extend more rapidly into the sea from the great river deltas, flood plains are established, the contours of beach, inlet, lagoon and swampland alter radically and rivers change their course. Williams-Hunt makes these points very plainly for Songkhla and the Satingpra peninsula in his study of archaeological evidence in aerial photographs of peninsular Thailand (Williams-Hunt, 1949, 108 and pl. 9). Such factors make the task of site reconnaissance difficult and pose special problems in the reconstruction of the ecology of a particular period. It is probably also the reason why, at the time of writing, few if any sites in the wet zone of Asia provide firm evidence of continuous occupation through the Neolithic, Bronze and Iron Ages.

The west coast of the isthmus – the Malaysian side – has a lighter rainfall but is still subject to the strong influences of water running off the central ranges where much rain falls. The general conditions of relative volatility continue to hold good for Kedah, though to a lesser degree than the east coast. The state is dominated by two extensive river systems, by their flood plains and alternate channels and their action on the coastline, on tidal estuaries and swamplands. Some of the photographic evidence may easily be consulted in Williams-Hunt's companion study, *Notes on Archeology from the Air in Malaya*, pls. 6 and 8, and p.155.

The two river systems are the Merbok and Muda which may once have been linked by the Sungei Sempor but at present debouch separately into the sea opposite Penang Island (fig. 21.1). Today the area is being developed as Malaysia's rice bowl. A substantial investment has been made in an irrigation system which, for the first time, permits two annual crops of rice to be harvested. The other important feature of the terrain is an isolated spur of hills running almost east-west and dominating the coastal plains and estuaries. The highest peak is Gunong Jerai (English name Kedah Peak). The greatest concentration of monumental sites occurs along the Bujang River, itself a tributary of the Merbok, and rises up the slopes of Gunong Jerai, to traces of a monumental structure on its summit — preserved from final decay by Evans in 1917 (Evans, 1922).

The first inscription in northern Malaysia — the Buddhagupta inscription — was found last century by Colonel Low. Altogether four inscriptions have been found: the Buddhagupta, Bukit Meriam, Bukit Choras inscriptions and the inscribed stone tablet from Wales' site No. 2. It is on the basis of these that the Kedah civilization is termed historic, yet the problem of the relation of these inscriptions to their find context remains unresolved.

Limited studies of the Kedah monuments began in the nineteenth century. More systematic and extensive archaeological investigations were done during the twenties and thirties by my benefactor, I.H.N. Evans, then Ethnographer of the Federated Malay States and Officer in Charge of the Perak Museum at Taiping. At the end of the decade, Dr and Mrs Quaritch Wales undertook their exhaustive survey of ancient Indian colonization in Malaya, as Field Director and Associate Field Director respectively of the Greater-India Research Committee. Altogether they identified thirty sites at that time and subsequently reported on three more (JMBRAS XX, 1947, 1-11). Research was resumed during the fifties and sixties by Alistair Lamb and other historians at the University of Malaya and by the Museums' Department. It has been chiefly concerned with identifying and re-appraising the sites written up by Wales. The largest site, Chandi Bukit Batu Pahat has been restored up to the level of surviving material evidence which means the temple platform, pillar

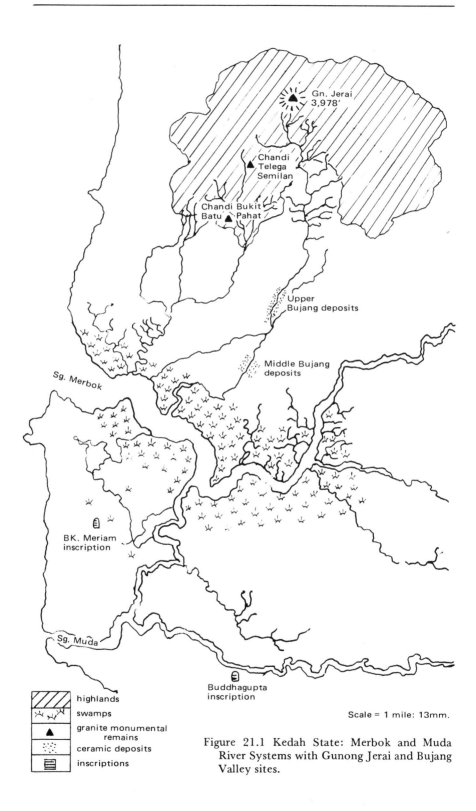

Figure 21.1 Kedah State: Merbok and Muda River Systems with Gunong Jerai and Bujang Valley sites.

Plate 21.1 The Chandi Bukit Batu Pahat temple, Kedah.

bases and lower courses of the sanctuary wall (see pl. 21.1). Other sites
are scheduled for restoration. Lamb's work on individual sites has
added much archaeological detail to Wales' report and challenged his
conclusions in many spheres. On the other hand, some of Wales' sites
have all but disappeared owing to the corrosive action of the climate
upon sites once exposed. This means that the Wales' excavation
report will remain the only comprehensive account of all their sites
in Kedah and Perak. Subsequent research has, to date, only produced
one tentative addition to their list — Chandi Telega Semilan.

Although much remains to be done on the Kedah temple sites, it is
true to say that they have already received a great deal more
attention than the sites of habitation, industry and trade in the
vicinity of the temples.

I made several test excavations on the bank of the Bujang River in
the area of Pengkalan Bujang village and Table 21.1 shows the details
of the most productive of these test pits. The shaft was dug on the
east bank of the river, 8 m from the present bank. It measured 1 m x
1 m and was aligned by cardinal points.

There was a striking predominance of unglazed red earthenwares
at this site, of which I have found no comprehensive record
elsewhere. In Lamb's work on the area one finds little beyond the

Table 21.1 Pengkalen Bujang Valley Site (1). P.B. (1)			
Layer No.	Depth	Soil	Comments
I	0-10 cm	brown humus	No finds.
II	10-16 cm 18 cm 20 cm	brown humus brown humus brown humus	2 fragments grey stoneware 1 frag. green celadon 1 frag. red lateritic earthenware
III	20 cm 22 cm	brown humus and grey sand brown humus increasing grey sand content	236 frag. red earthenware; 1 frag. green celadons; 1 fine earthenware spout. 32 large frag. grey stoneware.
IV	28 cm	brown humus West side of shaft grey clay; east side grey sand.	W̲ 8 fragments Arab-type glass 15 fragments green celadon, 2 pieces of carbon E̲ 16 semi-glazed frags. grey stoneware.
V	30-36 cm	Grey clay	scanty deposits chiefly grey stoneware (10) and red lateritic fragments (38); 3 frags. green celadon; no glass.
VI	36 cm 38 cm	grey sand grey sand	deposits more frequent but less than III; 192 red lateritic fragments; 4 frags. celadons; 11 frags. grey stoneware; 1 piece Arab glass; 1 lateritic spout. 2 pieces Arab glass; few lateritic fragments; carbon traces on the floor at this level; 41 frags. of buff clay. 1 large frag. of pale buff stoneware.
VII	39-50 cm	grey sand spotted with orange — root or plant fibres ?̲	1 large piece grey stoneware; 13 frags. celadons; 15 frags. grey stoneware; 116 frags. of red lateritic ware (light and heavy texture) some with black burnishing; carbon lumps; 1 bead-shaped pebble white with coral veins; 2 pieces green glass, 1 piece brown glass.
VIII	50-52 cm 54 cm 55-60 cm	grey sand + orange flecks N-W corner grey sand grey sand + dark streaks	carbon traces on floor; 3 pieces heavy red lateritic ware; carbon lumps sterile
IX	60-100 cm	grey sand + dark streaks	sterile

Statistical tables of finds are presented in Figs. 21.2-8.

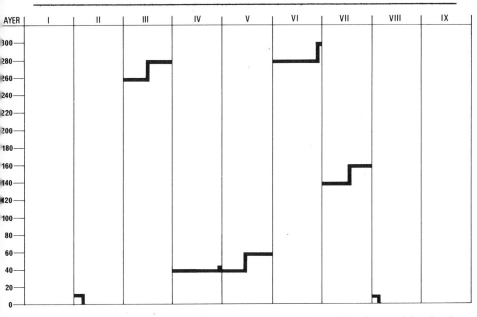

Figure 21.2 Pengkalan Bujang I: Total finds per layer, showing activity level variation.

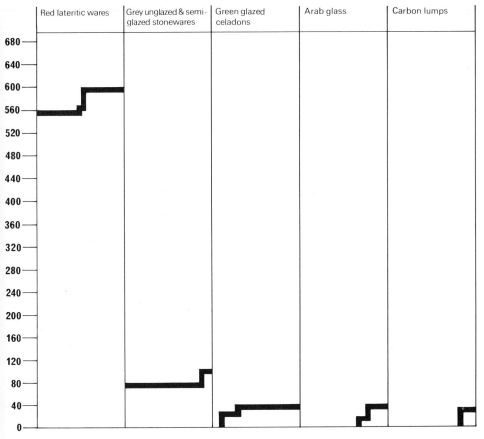

Figure 21.3 Pengkalan Bujang I: Typological totals for all levels.

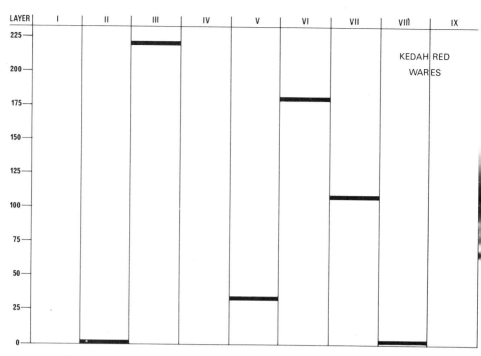

Figure 21.4 Pengkalan Bujang I: Typological distribution of layers.

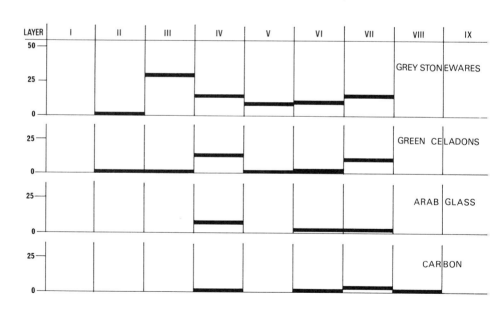

Figure 21.5-8 Pengkalan Bujang I: Typological distribution by layers.

brief statement that they were numerically preponderant, his interest being almost exclusively in the imported wares.

It remains, then, for me to give a detailed account of the Kedah Red Wares, which I believe to be local wares for common domestic use. The clay types are locally available and their large number suggests this. I carried out thermometric and other physical tests on a limited number of representative specimens in Cambridge with the advice and expert assistance of Mr Alan Spencer Green, the potter. On physical and aesthetic grounds, it has been possible to establish a typology of these wares. We have acquired as well a body of information from which one can deduce a good deal about the technology involved in their manufacture.

Thermometric tests on Kedah Red Wares

Specimens were heated in a kiln on a rising scale of controlled temperature readings and tested for signs of increased oxydization and shrinkage. The objects of this method of testing were: (1) to find the level at which the wares were originally fired; (2) to differentiate superficially similar wares by their heat reaction; (3) to find out whether the original firing levels were the result of limitations in the type of clay used and, if not, what temperature levels these earths could reach before disintegration of the vessel took place.

The first type of red ware to be tested had a dark grey to black core and red exterior and interior surfaces. This type shall be called T.i.

Red Ware Test Firings: T.i

$100°C$ — no change
$200°C$ — no change
$300°C$ — no change
$400°C$ — change begins with shrinkage
$500°C$ — shrinkage continues
$700°C$ — marked shrinkage and complete oxydization

When tests were suspended the dark core had turned to terracotta colour as a result of oxydization but in shade and texture it remained distinct from the external earth, which retained its original colour throughout. From this it may be deduced that the T.i pots were made from two earths originally and in fabrication were fired to a temperature just under $400°C$.

Sawn cross sections of T.i showed, in the striation profile, clear evidence that they were wheel formed and that the outer earth was applied to the core vessel in liquid form, probably by dipping not pouring as the surface of the outer earth preserves the striation profile of the core body.

T.i sherds were of two weights consistently maintained at 4 mm body thickness (fine) and 7 mm (medium) respectively, but presented a variety of rim profiles (see figs. 21.9 and 10).

Figures 21.9-10 Kedah Red Wares — ceramic profiles.

Red Ware Test Firings: T.ii

The second type tested was of medium texture, i.e. 8 mm cross-section and red throughout (T.ii).

$60° -   90°C$ — change of colour to buff
$100° - 300°C$ — change to terracotta
$400°C$ — oxydization complete and shrinkage

This result indicates that T.ii wares were fired to a similar temperature as T.i but the earth used was quite different. This point was worth establishing as the wares possessed a superficial resemblance in their find condition.

Sawn cross-sections of T.ii showed evidence of wheel forming. A variety of rim profiles were present (figs. 21.11 and 12).

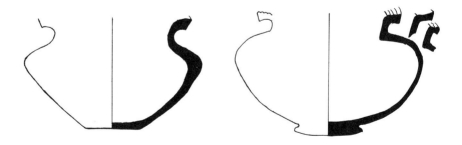

Figures 21.11-12 Kedah Red Wares — ceramic profiles.

Red Ware Test Firings: T.iii

A numerically small type of sherd found at the site was of a dark grey, almost black colour. When fragments of these were placed in the kiln, it was found that they behaved in identical fashion to T.ii.

$$60° - \ \ 90°C - \text{change of colour to buff}$$
$$100° - 300°C - \text{change to terracotta}$$
$$400°C - \text{oxydization complete and shrinkage}$$

T.iii wares were also of medium weight (8 mm cross section) and wheel formed. Only one lip profile could be identified.

The results of T.ii and T.iii kiln tests indicated that the dark grey, buff and uniformly red wares were in fact the same ware at different stages of oxydization and firing. In the open-hearth kiln, which was almost certainly used in Kedah, great variations in temperature and atmosphere do occur in the heap of pots at any one firing. Those near the centre of the heap reach a higher temperature and are subject to more acute oxydization than those on its outer edges.

Red Ware Test Firings: T.iv

In the lower levels of this site, a number of heavy red potsherds occurred with cross sections of 1.5-2 cm. The texture of the clay was noticeably gritty. In hardness, these wares re-acted similarly to T.i, ii and iii. Firing tests produced the following results:

$$60° - \ \ 90°C - \text{no change}$$
$$100° - 300°C - \text{no change}$$
$$400°C - \text{shrinkage begins}$$
$$500°C - \text{marked shrinkage and oxydization}$$

These would suggest that the heavy red wares reached a somewhat higher temperature than T.i, ii and iii in their original firing.

Red Ware Test Firings: T.v

This category was created largely on aesthetic grounds to include wares of similar physical properties to T.ii, but having a paddled or burnished exterior. I shall not repeat the temperature scale and reaction as it is to be found in T.ii.

Specimens of all types of Kedah Red Wares were then subjected to regulated tests in the kiln to ascertain the potential of the clay in ceramic manufacture. It was found that all specimens stood temperatures up to 1100°C. By 1250°C, the earth began to break down. In other words, the ceramic potential of these earths was such that a temperature of 900°C — the commonly accepted threshold of irreversibility in ceramic firing — could easily have been achieved. The earths were not capable of withstanding the 1250°C + temperatures which are involved in the manufacture of stonewares and porcelains.

From other specimens of open-hearth fired earthenwares, we know that temperatures of 900°C can be reached at the centre of the heap of pots. In the case of the Kedah Red Wares, no wares seem to have been fired at more than 500°C and most at less than 400°C. This is relatively low on the scale of earthenware firing temperatures, and leads us to consider the ceramic technology of the Kedah Red Wares in a wider context.

Discussions with Dr B.K. Thapar, Director of the Indian Archaeological Survey, led to the conclusion that these wares did not relate directly to any Indian prototypes. On the other hand, the same general problem does present itself in India that in the material context of great monumental building, artistic invention and architectural ingenuity the domestic ceramic industry continued to function at a relatively low technological level.

As the excavation tables show, there was an abundance of imported wares at this site:

(a) grey stonewares which have subsequently been identified as Khmer pots;

(b) lugged stoneware amphorae of Annamite type;

(c) semi-glazed early Sukhodaya wares, with a characteristic stippling of the glaze due to under-firing;

(d) nineteen different patterns of celadons of various shades of green. These may be Sung;

(e) four different shades of Arab glass. Interestingly enough, there were no blue and white wares.

In answer to the question, why did the Kedah ceramic industry not develop further, it would seem that lack of technical skill was probably not the limiting factor. Consideration must be given to the following:

1. *Motivation:* the Red Wares were probably for common domestic use. The material evidence shows that local potters formed their clay well. Our firing tests have shown that the earths of the Red Wares can stand much higher temperatures — as high as 1100°C — without disintegrating. Quick and low temperature, open-hearth firing was probably deemed sufficient for vessels in daily use. The association of higher and top quality imported wares in the site shows that such wares were available for special uses. The presence of the superior imported wares on the local market probably imposed a plateau on the evolution of the domestic ceramics of the Middle Bujang Period.

2. *The presence of a high lateritic content* in the clay made high firing not so necessary as these earths attain a surprising hardness when free of the saturated soil.

3. *Selectivity of material remains:* a common archaeological problem but perhaps more pronounced in this environment with its annual flooding and saturated soil. The finest craftsmanship of this culture has traditionally been expressed in textiles and wood but

only exceptional specimens have survived the action of the climate. What has survived is not necessarily this culture's greatest area of competence.

There is one curious feature of this site which should be considered when we come to the end of the examination of it. All the sherds were fragments and, in the case of the imported wares — the grey stonewares and green celadons — these fragments could not be matched to make a whole vessel.

In searching for an explanation of this phenomenon, there are several factors which are relevant.

1. This section of river bank in the Bujang village area is seriously disturbed by water buffalos which are brought to bathe and drink there. The animals gouge out the surface soil in a characteristic circular pit about 20 cm deep, to make a cool resting place. These 'buffalo excavations' have, in fact, brought many surface finds to light but may have fragmented both these and other ceramics lying beneath the surface.

2. The frequent flooding of the site which takes place at least once a year may have swirled deposits and the matching pieces of the valuable celadons may come to light when the entire river bank is excavated.

3. Perhaps the ceramics reached this spot in a fragmentary state at the end of a trans-isthmian porterage route which came up the Sungei Pattani by boat, crossed the watershed on foot and came down the Muda by boat again, to be reloaded into bigger boats at this point. Certainly, there is an unusual concentration and variety of wares at this spot. Also, the tables show quite clearly, variations in the type and intensity of activity on this site. Perhaps in the process of reloading, sherds were dropped or discarded at this point.

4. Today, the Bujang River is not navigable at this point. It is very narrow and shallow (pl. 21.2). Yet this process of silting up must be quite recent as I was reliably informed that 'before the war, there were crocodiles in the river', and that presupposes a much bigger watercourse.

Yet it is improbable that the watercourse was wider during the time that the Pengkalan Bujang deposits were laid since the concentration is heaviest upon the present river banks. One is led to suppose, then, that it must have been deeper and carrying a bigger volume of water during the period when trade wares from Western Asia, mainland South East Asia and Southern China arrived at its shores.

It is notable that there were no identifiable Indian wares at this site. On the other hand, large numbers of beads came to light in the Pengkalan Bujang area which are either of Indian provenance or

Plate 21.2 The Bujang River near Peng Kalan Bujang village.

closely associated with trade at Indian ports (Lamb, 1966). It is probable that Indian textiles were also imported and traded at this site but in this environment have left no trace.

What of the chronology of the site and its relation to the monumental complex of the Bujang Valley? Typological arguments, including my own, inevitably possess circular elements. If the semi-glazed stonewares are indeed Sukhodaya wares, then they cannot be earlier than the end of the thirteenth century. If the green celadons are indeed Sung, then they cannot be earlier than the eleventh century. Dr T.K. Cheng has kindly looked at a glazed fragment and offered the tentative opinion that it could be Annamite of the late fourteenth century.

The heavy specimens of Kedah Red Ware occur in the lowest level of the site, below stonewares and celadons. Can one assume that they date from an older level of activity? I think some allowance must be made for downward gravitation during the seasonal flooding of the site, but the possibility of an early, entirely domestic use of the site cannot be excluded. Carbon dating of the carbon specimens extracted from levels VIII, VII, VI and IV should throw a great deal of light on this problem.

The problems raised in trying to relate the Pengkalan Bujang ceramic sites to the cluster of monuments in the Bujang Valley are no less complex.

The first point to note, it seems, is that of all Wales' monumental sites only No. 18 and to a lesser extent No. 19, yielded quantities of potsherds. These two sites are both close to the Pengkalan Bujang ceramic site. Of Site 18, Wales noted:

> Comparatively little rough earthenware, but on the other hand large quantities of excellent Sung porcelain, mostly fragmentary, were excavated both outside and inside the building. The Sung porcelain included a high percentage of good Lung-ch'üan celadons but perhaps almost as common was a ware with olive-green glaze that has been excavated in Tonkin and was in 1935 excavated by me at C'aiya, Peninsular Siam.

Partly on the basis of his ceramics, Wales assigned the site to the eleventh or twelfth century A.D. Yet is is equally possible, on the basis of the same evidence, to assign the site to the late Sung or early Yüan period.

The ceramic site at Pengkalan Bujang produced similar Chinese wares but, in addition, a variety of South East Asian wares which cannot be earlier than the latter half of the thirteenth century. This might easily be converted to an argument for a later date for the temple sites and, if I understand it correctly, the current opinion among colleagues in the Museums' Department is tending in this direction. On the other hand, we cannot presume exact contemporaneity of the two sites. The ceramic site reflects activity over a considerable period to judge from successive layers with marked variations in the type and density of deposits (pl. 21.3). The temple site 18 was presumably built during a relatively short section of the total period covered by PB I. The lack, so far, of datable material from any of the monumental sites means that one is forced back on typological arguments with the difficulties that they involve. Fresh light could be thrown on the problem if a habitation or industry site were found directly adjacent to a temple site and identifiable with it by means of the distribution of the deposits.

Wales apparently had such a site in his temple No. 11 — also not far from Pengkalan Bujang on the Sungei Batu Estate, where he recorded:

> Ceramics — fragments of rough unornamented earthenware were common on the contemporary habitation level 2' to 2' 6" below present ground level. Below this to about 4' rough sherds continued to be found which suggested an occupation antedating the building.

With today's methods, even the approximate dates which thermo-luminescence tests could provide for those two different ceramic levels would have provided a good deal of help in the monumental dating problem.

Plate 21.3 The test excavation at Pengkalan Bujang village.

This is an appropriate place at which to pause and make some comments on other puzzling features of the Kedah monuments. Since readers will find a brief description of every site and a list of finds in Wales' report, as well as detailed studies of Site No. 8 in Lamb's work, the following comments do not attempt to recapitulate that work so much as to draw attention to certain curious features of the Kedah civilization viewed within the wider context of other 'indianized' civilizations of South East Asia.

The first thing one notices is their small size. Wales does not consistently give the sizes of monumental remains in his report. Adding personal observations to those he does give, plus Lamb's details, the following picture emerges:

The medium-sized temples comprise the most numerous type such as site 16, which had two chambers, the larger being 6.25 x 4.80 m and the smaller 3.20 x 4.25 m (my notes). Chandi Bukit Batu Pahat (No. 8) is the largest site so far uncovered and Lamb gives its dimensions in the following manner:

2. the sanctuary basement, a structure about 35 feet square and five feet high on which the remains of the sanctuary stand.

3. the *mandapa,* the remains of a rectangular pillared hall extending some 44 feet to the South East . . . (Lamb, 1960, 17).

The smallest type of temple ranges around nine-twelve feet square (Wales, 1940).

The second notable feature of Wales' sites was the simplicity of platform patterns. Built on a simple rectangular plan, these structures lack the elaborations of the rectangle, through projections and recesses, which give stylistic character of one kind or another to the temples of India and most parts of South East Asia.

Variations in the ground plans of the Kedah temples were restricted to questions of size, and the space left between the entrance chamber (*mandapa*) and the sanctuary chamber (*vimana*). In some cases, there was a small gap of about 30 cm between the foundation rubble of each chamber; in others these were contiguous. In two other cases (sites 1 and 2), there were remains of one chamber only and Wales, rightly I believe, considered the possibility of these being in reality Buddhist *stupa* bases rather than hindu temples as the rest have been classified.

Building materials are of mixed type. Figs. 21.13 and 14 give a typical ground plan and sequence of building materials from foundation to platform. The temples along the middle reaches of the Bujang River are built largely of laterite blocks or sun-dried clay bricks with a high lateritic content and therefore attain a considerable hardness without kiln-firing. Clearly the materials and skills used in the preparation of these laterite blocks and bricks were similar to those used in the manufacture of the Kedah Red Wares. One may speak, provisionally, of a 'lateritic culture' in the Bujang Valley.

Chandi Bukit Batu Pahat is built of granite. This temple is built on the slopes of Gunong Jerai and downsteam from its site is the quarry from which its stones were presumably taken and two half-dressed slabs still lie in the bed of the river. The temple above this one, Chandi Telega Semilan, is also a granite temple. The ruined structure just below Kedah Peak, visited by Noone was also granite, while the monumental traces on the summit itself were of laterite, clay bricks, river boulders and granite fragments. While one may say then that the temples of the upper reaches of the valley and mountain slopes are preponderantly granite, the division by building materials is by no means simple nor one dictated only by local availability. Conversely, granite slabs have been found in the laterite temples as lintels, socket stones, somasutra channels, pillar and image bases. There is nothing, therefore, to suggest that the lowlands temples were built by people greatly estranged by time or enmity from the culture of those who built the uplands temples.

The granite slabs of Chandi Bukit Batu Pahat are strikingly small (pl. 21.4) – well below the optimum size of this rock in terms of quarrying, dressing and structural strength. Lamb inferred from this

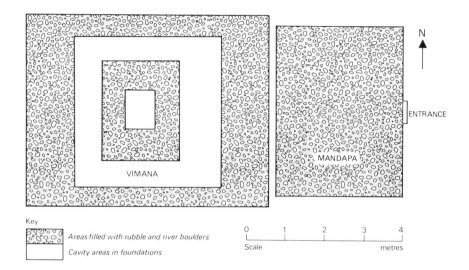

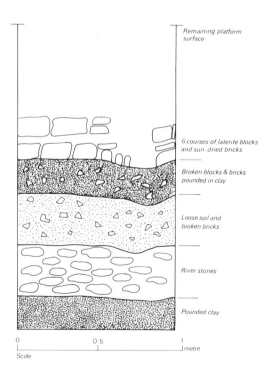

Figure 21.13 Foundation plan, Kedah Laterite Temple, site No. 16.

Figure 21.14
Sequence of
foundation
material,
Kedah
Laterite
Temple.

Plate 21.4 Part of the Chandi Bukit Batu Pahat temple, Kedah.

that the temple was built by people more familiar with the use of laterite blocks or bricks, who therefore made unnecessary labour for themselves by hewing stone to that size. It would follow from this that the mountain temple is later than the lowland temples.

On the other hand, Chandi Telega Semilan, yet higher up the mountain slope, displays a quite different technique of stone-working and building. At the time he wrote, Lamb was unaware of this temple so it is worthwhile giving a little space here to its more remarkable features. As the name suggests, it lies beside the ninth waterfall of the Sungei Batu Pahat well up the slope of Gunong Jerai and can be reached only by a narrow mountain trail which winds through the jungle along that water course. The temple site was originally enclosed by a stone wall of an approximate N. – S. length of 240 m (downslope) and an approximate width of 140 m. Other courses of interrupted stonework suggest that the enclave may have been terraced to reduce the natural landfall and the force of seepage.

The temple itself was built upon an outcrop of living granite which, today, slopes on a 30° plane. The dressed stone slabs of the temple platform lie asymmetrically upon each other within a confined area. The site was cleared of jungle by workers of the Museums' Department early in 1970, but when I visited the site in January 1971, it was crowded with secondary growth and defied adequate photography. Nonetheless, it was possible to obtain some useful information: the massive granite slabs were sections of the temple platform measuring approximately 2 m x 1 m and varied in thickness between 10 and 15 cm. The living granite outcrop appears to me to have been used as the foundation of the structure. There are no rubble materials or river boulders, which normally form the foundations for the Kedah temples, at this site. I discovered shallow grooving in the rock outcrop which may correspond to a tenion in the slabs about it. The Kedah granite has been shown to be relatively susceptible to weathering and in this case the wearing away of the grooves by seepage may explain the way the platform slabs have collapsed without being dispersed. This interpretation must remain tentative at present.

At the south-west corner of the site, the snadroni or yoni stone is lying in the undergrowth. It was split diagonally but the larger section still showed quite clearly that it had had two central cavities placed diagonally in relation to the squared perimeter of the stone. This would seem to suggest that the object of sacred lustrations which originally surmounted this stone was something other than a Shiva-linga. From the same site, came a low granite pedestal of circular shape, carved in low relief with an open lotus design. It is the only site, moreover, at which I have seen a cylindrical pillar-shaped stone of the same granite. Otherwise, one commonly finds granite pillar bases but no trace of the pillars which, presumably, were timber.

It can be seen, therefore, that the stone masonry of Chandi Telega Semilan does not support the inferences drawn by Lamb on the basis of Chandi Bukit Batu Pahat. Nor are we yet in a position to say what is the chronological sequence of the temples of the Bujang Valley. It can be stated with reasonable certainty that the communities which built these two temples chose their sites with great regard to the nearby pools and falls of the Sungei Batu Pahat and the natural rises on the mountain's slopes which give both temples a commanding view to the south-east and south, respectively.

Moving from the exterior to the interior features of the Kedah monumental complex, a number of general observations can usefully be made. Again viewing this complex against the background of the monumental complexes of Burma, Cambodia, and Indonesia with which it seems to have been roughly contemporary, certain differences emerge. There is no evidence in the Kedah temples of the decorative detail of friezes, bas-reliefs or mural paintings with which the religious buildings of the latter countries are embellished. Indeed we have only very limited fragments of the Kedah structures above the level of the sanctuary walls. One must assume, from this general absence, that the superstructures and pillars were of wood and thatch or wood and tiles in some cases. Wood-carvings as architectural decoration would disappear completely.

A small number of bronzes has been recovered over the past fifty years. Seven of these have been recovered in the course of tin-mining operations, some from great depths. These came from the neighbouring state, Perak, not from Kedah itself. Wales records also (p. 47) the finding of a number of bronze fragments at the Kedah sites. What is one to infer from this? The accepted view has been that the islamic conversion led to systematic iconoclasm for Buddhist and Hindu temples and their ornaments. This speculation may well be correct but it may be worthwhile to bear in mind that there is little to suggest that the body of statuary was very large in the first place. Among the surviving specimens, there are two of considerable beauty and several have interesting features to which we shall return shortly. On the other hand, they do not suggest in the way that the sculpture of Java, Burma, Thailand or Cambodia does suggest, the successive stages of an indigenous school of iconography.

Detailed examinations of the Avalokiteśvara from Bidor, Perak, are to be found in van Stein Callenfels' study, JFMSM 1939 pl. LII and in Lamb's note XII, FMJ 1961, pp. 101-4. The statue possesses elements of the tantric tradition. There is considerable variation in hand positions, attributes and ornamental detail among Javanese and South Indian specimens of this type. While its general aesthetic affinities are clear, van Stein Callenfels rightly calls attention to the surprising results of the metal analysis he carried out: the statue is nearly pure copper — 94.9% copper with some insoluble silicious material and traces of iron, aluminium and bismuth. It is coated with bronze, again the copper content is high — 77.2% copper, remainder tin with trace impurities.

Lamb concentrates attention on the presence of a tiger's head on the right thigh of the statue, an unusual feature which again may take its origins in Indian tantric traditions. Finally, I should add that this statue, which is less than 1 m high, is the largest of the bronzes found in Malaysia. They all, therefore, fall within the range of easily transportable figures. Neither their find site nor the discussions of their stylistic affinities have so far brought us much closer to their actual provenance.

An interesting sidelight on this problem is cast by a short note concerning the chemical analysis of metal objects contained in six stone reliquaries from Chandi Bukit Batu Pahat (Treloar, 1968: 193-8). The author comments on the purity of the copper both in the copper pot and the copper lotus flower and speculates further on the possible origin of the metal in the Bau district of Sarawak. He was apparently unaware that the Avalokitesvara is also almost pure copper. A.B. Griswold has written a valuable note on the Jalong Bronze (1962: 64-6).

Detailed lists and plates of the contents of reliquaries are to be found in Wales' and Lamb's reports. For our purposes, it will be sufficient to point out that the nine chambered granite reliquaries of Chandi Bukit Batu Pahat have no known prototype in Indian architecture although the nine concept relates clearly to Indian cosmology. Granite reliquaries of a general similarity have been found in Java. The contents of the Kedah reliquaries in many cases had a high intrinsic value as precious metals and precious stones were employed. A close investigation of the stamped and incised designs on small metal leaves and discs reveals general Brahmanic affinities — the bull, the goddess, the sun, without being truly identifiable with any particular Indian iconographic tradition. In addition, there are disks with Buddhist motifs such as the open lotus blossom as well as seeds and vegetable matter which probably derive from much older rites of agrarian and social regeneration. At my request, Lamb's photographs of the seeds from these reliquaries have kindly been examined by Professor Sir Joseph Hutchinson and provisionally identified as rice. These objects may well be regarded as funereal talismans of royal cremation burials, having their origins in local traditions but partly modified by Indian symbolic forms of both Brahmanic and Buddhist affinities.

While almost all the Kedah monumental sites have been regarded as Hindu temples, it is noteworthy that the majority of surviving statuary and inscriptions are Buddhist. The evidence does not support notions of thriving Hindu communities along the Bujang Valley nor does it support a theory of Hindu colonization of the area. In either of these two cases — both of which have been advanced — one would expect to find by the ninth to thirteenth centuries, completely stone temples, an abundance of decorative materials in stone, and a larger body of stone and bronze statuary with the iconographic features of a recognizable Indian school.

Even allowing for possible destruction of Hindu material, it seems to me that one should recognize:

(*a*) the importance of Buddhist elements in this culture, and

(*b*) the possibility that both Buddhist and Hindu traditions were employed selectively for a limited rather than a popular purpose.

What, in fact, was the purpose of the Kedah monuments? Current thinking among some members of the Museums' Department is inclined to view them as village temples. While it is possible that they served a purpose in village religious rituals, it seems unlikely that clusters of temples adjacent to one another would have their origin in this way. The tendency towards groups or clusters of temple sites does, however, conform with patterns of 'tomb-temples' belonging to one house or one period. The presence of reliquaries and precious foundation deposits further strengthens the view that these temples represent a series of royal funereal temples such as we know, on somewhat grander scale, in Cambodia, Java, Burma and Thailand.

What material evidence remains suggests that these temples incorporated local materials and architectural practices elaborated by, and thus heightened in ritual significance by, an eclectic mixture of Hindu and Buddhist elements. The temples on the mountainside are placed where they would have had sacred and auspicious associations in the pre-Indian, animist traditions of the region.

The evidence does indicate that the Kedah communities enjoyed a measure of prosperity bringing them commercial contacts from a wide geographic area. They produced a series of monumental structures in which, it may be supposed, the power of their rulers was consecrated and preserved. We have noted Indian influences in this community. They were not, however, exclusive. In commercial life both Chinese and Arab influences were at least as important. In religious practice, while one may agree that the general character of the Kedah monuments places them in the traditions of 'indianized' South East Asia, their Indian affinities are not clearly defined and may reflect an only partial assimilation of both Hindu and Buddhist religious and aesthetic standards.

Although smaller than the monumental civilizations of Cambodia and Burma, the Kedah temple complex has its own contribution to make to our understanding of the problem with which we set out and now conclude. It reveals to what extent a South East Asian kingdom of moderate size and prosperity absorbed Indian influences and to what extent it remained unaffected by them.

REFERENCES

de Casparis, J.G. (1956) *Prasasti Indonesia II*. Bandung.
Coedés, G. (1964) *Les Etats hindouisés d'Indochine et d'Indonésie*. Paris.
Cheng Siok Hwa (1969) The rice industry of Malaya – a historical survey. *Journal of the Malaysian Branch, Royal Asiatic Society*, 42, 2.
Colless, B. (1969) Persian merchants and missionaries in medieval Malaya. *Journal of the Malaysian Branch, Royal Asiatic Society*, 42, 2.
Evans, I.H.N. (1922) On the ancient structures on Kedah Peak. *Journal of the Federated Malay States Museums*, 19, 5.
Evans, I.H.N. (1926) Results of an expedition to Kedah. *Journal of the Federated Malay States Museums*, 12, 3.
Evans, I.H.N. (1928) On ancient remains from Kuala Selinsing Perak and further notes on remains from Kuala Selising. *Journal of the Federated Malay States Museums*, 12, 5.

Evans, I.H.N. (1929) Notes on the relationship between Philippine Iron Age antiquities and some from Perak. *Journal of the Federated Malay States Museums*, 12, 7.

Evans, I.H.N. (1932) Buddhist Bronzes from Kinta, Perak. *Journal of the Federated Malay States Museums*, 15, 3.

Griswold, A.B. (1962) The Jalong Bronze. *Federation Museums' Journal*, 7, NS.

Hirth, F. (1896) Chau Ju-kua's ethnography; a table of contents and extracts regarding Ceylon, India and some articles of trade. *Journal of the North China Branch, Royal Asiatic Society*.

Hirth, F. and Rockhill, W.W. (1911) Chau Ju-kua. His work on the Chinese and Arab trade in the twelfth and thirteenth centuries, entitled Chu-fan-chi. St. Petersburg.

Ishibashi, Goro (n.d.) Concerning coastal trade and commercial ports during the T'ang and Sung periods. *Shigaku Zasshi*, 12, 8, 9, 10.

Kedah Annals, *trans. from the Malay by Col. James Low, repr. Bangkok 1908.*

Lamb, A. (1960) Report on the excavation and reconstruction of Chandi Bukit Batu Pahat, Central Kedah. *Federation Museums' Journal*, NS.

Lamb, A. (1964a) Beads from Johor Lama and Kota Tinggi. *Journal of the Malaysian Branch, Royal Asiatic Society*, 37, 1.

Lamb, A. (1964b) Miscellaneous archaeological discoveries. *Journal of the Malaysian Branch, Royal Asiatic Society*, 37, 1.

Lamb, A. (1964c) A copper casket from Pondicherry, South India: a possible parallel for the stone caskets of Chandi Bukit Batu Pahat, Kedah. *Federation Museums' Journal*, 9, NS.

Lamb, A. (1966) Some observations on stone and glass beads in early South-East Asia. *Journal of the Malaysian Branch, Royal Asiatic Society*, 38, 2.

Solheim, W.G. II (1963) Southeast Asia. *Asian Perspectives*, 6, 21-23.

Solheim, W.G. II (1964) The archaeology of the Central Philippines: a study chiefly of the Iron Age and its relationships. *Monographs of the National Institute of Science and Technology*, Manila, 10.

Stargardt, J. (1970) Social and Religious Aspects of Royal Power in Medieval Burma, from inscriptions in Kyansittha's reign, 1084-1112. *Journal of the Economic and Social History of the Orient*, 13, 3.

Stargardt, J. (1971) Burma's Economic and Diplomatic Relations with India and China from Early Medieval Sources. *Journal of the Economic and Social History of the Orient*, 14, 1.

Stargardt, J. (1973) Southern Thai Waterways: archaeological evidence on agriculture, shipping and trade in the early Srivijayan period. *Man, March.*

van Stein Callenfels, P.V. (1939) An interesting Buddhistic bronze statue from Bidor, Perak. *Journal of the Federated Malay States Museums*, 15, 4.

Treloar, F.E. (1968) Chemical analysis of some metal objects from Chandi Bukit Batu Pahat, Kedah: suggested origin and date. *Journal of the Malayan Branch, Royal Asiatic Society*, 41, 1.

Quaritch Wales, H.G. (1940) Archaeological researches on ancient Indian colonization in Malaya. *Journal of the Malaysian Branch, Royal Asiatic Society*, 18, 1.

Quaritch Wales, Dorothy C. and H.G. (1947) Further work on Indian sites in Malaya. *Journal of the Malayan Branch of the Royal Asiatic Society*, 20, 1.

Quaritch Wales, H.G. (n.d.) Malayan archaeology of the 'Hindu' period: some reconsiderations. Kindly loaned to me in manuscript form by Dr Quaritch Wales; forthcoming in the *Journal of the Malayan Branch, Royal Asiatic Society*.

Wang Gung-wu (1958) The Nanhai trade — a study of the early history of Chinese trade in the South China Sea. *Journal of the Malaysian Branch, Royal Asiatic Society*, 31, 2.

Wheatley, P. (1959) Geographical notes on some commodities involved in Sung maritime trade. *Journal of the Malayan Branch, Royal Asiatic Society*, 32, 2.
Williams-Hunt, P.D.R. (1949) An introduction to the study of archaeology from the air. *Journal of the Siam Society*, 37, 2.
Williams-Hunt, P.D.R. (1948) Notes on archaeology from the air in Malaya. *Journal of the Malayan Branch, Royal Asiatic Society*, 21, 1.

Index

Authors The page numbers of papers in this volume are given in bold.

Places Archaeological sites are given in roman, other place names in italics. Page numbers in bold indicate a complete chapter on one site or area.

Adamgarh, 6, 10*n*, 40
Adams, R.McC., 69, 70, 80
Aden, 254
Adisaptagram, 267
Afghanistan, 1, 5, 131, 137, 140, 160, 163, 166, 168, 203, 207, 208, 212, 213, 218
Afrasiab, 250
Agrawal, D.P., 6, 157, 168
Agrawala, R.C., 208, 212, 233, 240
Agrawala, V.S., 207, 213
Ahichchhatra, 213
Aihole, 263
Aitken, E.H., 70, 71, 73, 84
Ajay valley, 273, 276, 277
Akui, 273
Alcock, L., 92, 104, 252
Alexandria, 243
Aliabad, 140, 144
al-Isfahani, 253
al-Jahiz, 253
Allahabad, 45, 47
Allchin, B., 5, 6, 10, 31, 33, 35, 36, **39-50**, 52, 63, 157, 168
Allchin, F.R., **1-11**, 40, 40, 157, 168
Altun-tepe, 118
Ambrona, 23
Amirkhan, 140
Amkheri, 9
Amri, 7, 10, 86, 89, 90-1, 104, 162, 164, 168
Amu Darya (Oxus) river, 137, 198
Anandapur, 276
Anau, 107, 108
Andhra Pradesh, 257, 261
Arabia, 2
Aravallis, 32, 81, 83
Ardebil, 251
Arghandab, river, 105, 106
Arikamedu, 260
Asanda, 276
Asken-Am, lake, 137, 140, 142
Asota, 260
Assam, 51, 52, 272
Aswin, river, 34
Atpur, 270, 277
Aubin, J., 242, 254
Auboyer, J., 207, 213
Australia, 56, 61, 63

Babylon, 228
Bachhofer, L., 224, 230
Bactria, 230

Baden, 200
Baerreis, D.A., 70, 84
Bagha, 267
Baghia, 277
Bagor, 6, 258
Bahadurpur, 273
Bahirgarh, 268
Bahulara, 267
Baidyapur, 276
Baihaqi, 252
Balarampur, 272
Balkh, 131
Baluchistan, 67, 68, 84, 87, 118, 160, 162, 163, 166, 167, 168, 169, 171, 193, 194, 195, 196
Balurghat, 277
Bamiyan, 131
Bampur, 165, 166, 167, 168, 169, 191, 195
Banbhore, 245, 249, 252
Bandi, H-G, 61, 63
Bandung, 61, 63
Banerjee, P., 212, 213
Bankura, district, 266, 267, 268, 270, 272, 273, 278
Baragari 272
Baranagar, 269, 273
Barganga, river, 49
Bargaon, 9
Barisha, 277
Barrett, D., 207, 208, 213
Beas, river, 49
Begram, 222, 230
Belan, river, 46
Belenickij, A.M., 212, 213
Bengal, 39, 51, 52, 61, 257, **265-78**
Beyer, H.O., 62, 63
Bhalia, 270
Bhandarkar, D.R., 232, 236, 240
Bharatpur, district, 258
Bharhut, 259
Bhattamati, 277
Bhilwara, district, 258
Bhitari, 259
Bibby, G., 85, 104, 167, 168
Bibi Khatun, 245, 250, 252
Bibi Nani, 181, 193
Bidor, 299, 302
Bierling, J., 62, 63
Bihar, 51, 258
Bindol, 266
Birbhum, district 268, 269, 270, 272, 273, 276, 277, 278
Biscione, R., 7, **105-18**
Bishnupur, 265, 266, 267, 268, 272, 273, 277

Bivar, A.D.H., 229, 230
Boger, 61
Bolan, pass and plateau, **181-96**
Bombay, 29, 50
Boriskovsky, P.L., 53, 54, 48, 63
Borneo, 62, 246
Bostam, 136
Bostaneh, 250
Bosworth, C.E., 135, 151
Bowler, J.M., 32, 36
Brahmagiri, 9
Brahminabad, 250, 254
Brindabanpur, 276
Brink, A.B.A., 29, 36
Bryson, R.A., 70, 84
Buckley, R.B., 72, 73, 74, 84
Bujang, valley, 279, 281, 284, 291-2, 295, 300
Buner, 201
Burdwan, district, 267, 268, 270, 272, 273, 276
Burj-i Samad (Chehel Burj), 145
Burkitt, M.C., 39, 49
Burma, 1, 51, 52, 56, 58, 59, 62, 64, 298, 299, 301, 302
Burubadur, 246
Burzaham, 258, 260
Butzer, K.W., 29, 36

Calcutta, 1, 270, 277
Cambay, Gulf of, 125
Cambodia, 64, 298, 299, 301
Cammiade, L.A., 39, 49
Casal, J-M, 7, 10, 86, 104, 106, 107, 111, 118, 157, 162, 168, 171-9, 191, 195
Castaldi E., 197, 201
Cegini, 142, 145
Central Asia, 1, 136, 142, 168, 201
Ceylon (Sri Lanka), 1, 3, 51, 61, 245, 249, 252, 302
Chak Bajit, 272
Chakhansur, 137, 138, 139, 141, 145, 151
Chakhansurak, 145
Chandi Bukit Batu Pahat, 281, 284, 294, 295, 298, 299, 300, 302
Chandi Telega Semilan, 284, 295, 297-8
Chandla, forest, 262
Chanhu-daro, 119, 123, 124, 129
Chang, K-C., 59, 62, 63
Charsada, 215
Chautang, river, 92
Cheliama, 273, 278
Cheng Siok Hwa, 301
Chetna Parganas, 270
Chigha Sarai, 131
China, 2, 51, 52, 53, 55, 62, 63, 83, 201, 242, 247, 248, 249, 253, 291, 302, 303
Chirand, 258
Chirki, 13-28
Chitral, valley, 201
Chittick, N., 245, 250, 254
Christie, A., 62, 63
Chukhsa, 219
Chorasmia, 142
Coedès, G., 279, 300
Colani, M., 62, 63
Conolly, E., 135, 151, 153
Corvinus, G., 6, **13-28**
Cunningham, Alexander, 2, 222
Curiel, R., 218, 222, 230
Curzon, Lord, 3-4, 131
Cust, 117

Darbar Kot, 187
Dacca 277
Dadhar, 181, 190
Daffinà, P.D., 135, 151
Dales, G.F., 7, 10, 100, 104, 134, 151, **156-69**
Dam, 145
Damb Sadaat, 106, 111, 112, 181
Damghan, 136
Damin, 169
Dani, A.H., 40, 49, 215, 230
Daniel, G.E., 91, 104
Danube basin, 200
Daodar, valley, 273
Daspur, 270, 276
Debipur, 276
De Cardi, B., 157, 166, 168, 187, 191, 194, 195
De Casparis, J.G., 301
Deccan plateau, 29, 35, 36, 68, 81, 258
Deh Morasi Ghundai, 163, 164
Delhi, 85, 137, 261, 266
De Terra, H., 5, 13, 29, 36, 39, 49
Devnimori, 233, 240
Dewale Gunde, 142
Dewale Lawur, 145

Dewal-i Khodayad, 140, 141, 154
Dhahran, 250
Dhamtor, 270
Dholbaha, 257
Dignagar, 272
Dilaram, 137, 145
Dilmun, 104
Dinajpur, district, 265, 266, 267, 272
Dir, region, 200
Djeitun, 118
Drower, M.S., 72, 84
Dubrajpur, 277
Dupree, A., 207, 213
Dury, G.H., 32, 36
Dyson, R.H., 29, 36, 70, 72, 84, 166, 168

Egarasindur, 267
Ellora, 262
Eluru, 259
Enault, J.F., **181-96**
Evans, I.H.N., 279, 281, 301-2

Faccenna, D., 197, 201, 218, 230
Fagan, P.F., 70, 74, 84
Fairservis, W.A., Jr., 8, 70, 72, 73, 76, 80, 82, 84, 91, 104, 106, 118, 134, 151, 167, 168, 183, 189, 190, 193, 195
Farah, 137, 139, 151
Farah-rud, river, 135
Faridpur, district, 267, 272, 273
Fars, 242
Ferghana, 117
Fergusson, James, 2
Field, H., 70, 84
Firuzkoh, 136
Fischer, K., 131-55, 207, 213
Flam, L., 167, 168
Flint, R.F., 33, 36
Flores, 55, 56, 60, 64
Fondukistan, 131, 203, 213
Foote, Bruce, 3, 13
Forbes, R.J., 72, 84
Fox, R., 54, 56, 60, 63
Frankfort, H., 85, 104, 115, 118
Fried, M., 83, 84
Frumkin, G., 166, 168, 198, 201
Frye, J.C., 33, 36
Fustat, 250

Gai, G.S., 234, 240
Gandhara 8, 131, 218, 227, 228
Gangapur, 14
Gangasagar, lake, 262
Ganges, river, 6, 45
Ganpur, 278
Gardan reg, 167
Gardez, 131, 207, 209, 222
Gardin, J-C., 155
Gardner, P., 221, 224-5, 230
Gaur, 266
Gazipur, 276
Gedrosia, 196
Geoksjur, 108, 109, 110, 111, 114, 116
Ghaggar, river, 85, 92
Ghaligai, 197, 201
Ghazipur, district, 259
Ghazni, 131, 151, 203
Ghirshman, R., 155, 219, 229, 230
Ghose, B., 32, 36
Ghosh, A., 29, 36, 39, 50, 91, 104
Ghurisa, 273
Ghutgeria, 278
Glover, I.C., **51-65**
Goa, 160-261
Göbl, R., 229, 230
Godavari river, 14
Goetz, H., 207, 213
Gokarna, 267
Golconda, 261
Gole Safedka, 138
Golson, J., 56, 61, 63
Gomal valley, 7, 86, 160
Gopalpur, 277
Gorband, valley, 201
Gorman, C., 58, 59, 62, 63
Goudie, A., 6, 10, **29-37**, 47
Gray, B., 252, 254
Griswold, A.B., 300, 302
Grove, A.T., 32, 36
Gudri, 193-4, 195
Gujarat, 6, 10, **29-37**, 30, 49, 50, 60, 84, 233, 262
Gullini, G., 218, 222, 230
Gumla, 159, 160, 168
Gunong Jerai (Kedah Peak), 281, 295, 297, 301

Guntapalli, 259
Guptipara, 267

Hackin, J., 155, 203, 204, 213
Hadda, 131
Haig, M.R., 70, 84
Hallade, M., 207, 213
Hammond, N., 20, 134, 155, 437-59
Hamun-i Seistan, lake, 140, 142
Hansen, C.L., 29, 36
Hansman, J.F., 250, 252, 253, 254
Harappa, 7, 71, 79, 82, 83, 86, 89, 90-1, 92, 100, 101, 104, 162, 169
Haripurgarh 268, 272
Hari-rud, river 105, 106
Harle, J.C., **231-40**
Haro, river, 90-91
Harrison, T., 56, 63, 245, 246, 251, 254
Harvan, 200
Haryana Pradesh, 257
Hasanlu, 198
Hathala, 7
Haudricourt, A.G., 71, 84
Heekeren, H.R. van, 54, 55, 59, 60, 61, 62, 63
Hegde, K.T.M., 6, 10, 29 33, 35, 36
Heine Geldern, R., 62, 63
Helmand, river, 105, 106, 116, 134, 135, 151, 166, 194
Herat, 131, 137
Herzfeld, E., 155
Hetampur, 277
Higham, C.F.W., 62, 64
Himachal Pradesh, 257
Hindu Kush, mountains, 106
Hirth, F., 302
Hissair, District, 92
Hissar, 109, 200
Hlopin, I.N., 105, 118
Hobson, R.L., 250, 254
Hooghly, district, 266, 267, 268, 270-7
Hooijer, D.A., 53, 54, 64
Hoop, A.N.J. Th. á Th. van der, 59, 64
Hoshiarpur, 257
Howrah, 272, 276
Hunan, 249
Hungarian plain, 200
Hyderabad, 261

Ibn Hauqual, 149, 151
Inamgaon, 8
India, 1, 2, 4, 5, 609, 10, 11, 13, 29, 30, 36, 39, 50, 51, 52, 53, 58, 61, 64, 67, 68, 70, 72, 81, 83, 84, 85, 129, 136, 140, 142, 213, 230, 242, 254, 257-64, 265, 279, 291-2, 501, 302
Indochina, 5, 56, 58, 59, 62, 63
Indonesia 57-66, 298, 301
Indus, river/valley, 5, 10, 36, 37, 40, 67, 68, 69, 70, 72, 76, 82, 83, 84, 92, 131, 157, 160, 162, 163, 166, 167, 168, 169, 181, 218, 222
Iraq, 254
Iran (Persia), 2, 83, 115, 118, 119, 136, 140, 142, 156, 163, 164, 166, 167, 168, 169, 196, 198, 213, 241-255
Ishibashi, G., 302
Istanbul (Constantinople), 243, 251, 254
Itanda, 269
Iyer, K.Bh., 209, 213

Jacobabad, 171
Jahanabad, 270
Jalilpur, 159, 160, 166, 168
Jalong, 300, 302
Jam, 136
Jami, 262
Jamuna, river, 45, 46
Jarrige, J.F., **181-96**
Jaugram, 272
Java, 53, 54, 55, 56, 59, 61, 62, 64, 246, 249, 299, 301
Jaypur, 276
Jenkins, G.K., 217, 223, 226, 230
Jennings, J., 59, 64
Jessore, district, 267, 272, 273, 277
Jhirk, 79
Johnson, B.L.C., 72, 84
Johnson, D., 33, 36
Johor Lama, 302
Jones, Sir William, 2
Joshi, N.P., 232, 240
Joshi, R.V., 6, 14, 35, 36, 39, 40, 49
Joye Kuhna, 141, 142
Joye Zarkano-zurkan, 141
Jugsara, 271

Kabanov, S.K., 212, 213
Kabul, 203, 208, 212, 213, 229
Kacchi lowland, 181, 189, 194

Kafirnigan, valley, 198
Kahle, P., 252, 254
Kalam, 201
Kalat, 168, 194, 195
Kalibangan, 7, 20, 71, **85-104**, 162, 164
Kalna, 273
Kalyana, 258
Kanara, South, 261
Kancipuram, 260
Kandahar, 131, 151, 213
Kanheri, 258
Kantabenia, 270
Kantanagar, 265, 272
Kansar, 209
Kara-tepe, 107, 108, 111, 118
Karkai, 201
Karnal, District, 92
Kashmir, 5, 29, 68, 260, 263
Katelai, 198-9
Kathiawar, 35, 82, 83
Kausambi, 234
Kaveri, river, 260
Kaveripattinam, 260
Kechi Beg, 117, 195
Kedah, 254, **279-303**
Kendeng hills, 54
Kerala, 243
Kerinchi, Lake, 64
Khan, F.A., 7, 86, 90, 104, 162, 168
Khandivli, 39
Kharar, 272
Khash-rud, river, 135, 137, 139, 141
Khérai, 201
Khorassan, 116, 142
Khulna, district, 267, 272, 273
Khuspas, river, 135, 139
Khuzistan, 250, 252, 254
Khwaya Siah Posh, 135-7
Kinta, 302
Kirta, 190-2, 193, 194, 195
Kisapostag, 200
Koechlin, R., 250, 252, 254
Koenigswald, G.H.R. von, 54, 64
Kohzad, A.A., 155
Kolaba, district, 262
Kondapur, 259, 261-2
Kondapuram, 257
Kopetdagh, mountains, 105, 106, 108, 117
Kophen, river, 219, 228
Kordu, 140, 147, 148
Kot, 189-90
Kotakal, 277
Kota Tinggi, 301
Kot Diji, 7, 11, 86, 90-1, 104, 162, 168
Kotri, 79
Krishna valley, 13, 259, 262
Krishnanagar, 266
Krishnapur, 273
Kshirpai, 276
Kuala Selinsing, 301
Kulli, 191, 193, 194
Kumarpara, 276
Kusumba, 267
Kutch, Rann of, 35, 82
Kwangtung, 59

Laang Spean, 58, 64
Lachhipur, 276
Lal, B.B., 39, 49, 85, 100, 104
Lalitpur, 14
Lamb, A., 249, 254, 279, 281, 284, 294, 299, 302
Lal Qila, 9
Lamu, archipelago, 254
Langhnaj, 6, 11, 31
Lane, A., 252, 254
Lashkari Bazar, 131
Laskardighir Barh, 277
Latamne, 21
Leonard, A.B., 33, 36
Leshnik, L.S., 8, **67-84**
Lisicyna, G.N., 111, 118
Loebanr, 197-9
Lohagara, 277
Loralai, district, 181, 195
Lothal, 82, 84, 125, 129
Lugdunum, 228
Lumbini, 262
Luni, river, 33, 36

Mac Dowall, D., 215-30, 231, 240
Mackay, E.J.H., 92, 104, 119, 120, 123, 124, 125, 129
Madhyadesa, 258
Madhya Pradesh, 6, 14, 232

Mahadeo Piparia, 14
Mahajanapada capitals, 9
Maharashtra, 8, 49, 258
Mahbubnagar, district, 262
Mahi, river, 33, 34
Mahurjhari, 263
Makran, 168
Malaya, 52, 58, 59, 64, 249, 279-303
Malik, S.C., 8
Mallmann, M-Th. de, 209, 213
Maluti, 278
Malwa plateau; also district, 68, 81, 232, 234, 237
Mamudpur, 271
Manchhar, Lake, 76
Manda, 246, 250
Mansuy, H., 56, 64
Mapusa, 261
Mardan, 40
Maringer, I., 55, 64
Markoff, A.K., 224, 230
Maros (Lamontjong), 59, 60, 61, 64
Marsak, B.I., 212, 213
Marshall, Sir John, 4, 73, 84, 217, 218, 225, 230
Mason, R.J., 29, 36
Masson, James, 5, 222
Masson, V.M., 105, 106, 108, 109, 111, 112, 116, 117, 118, 166, 168
Mathews, I., 59, 64
Mathura, 131, 231, 232, 233, 234, 236, 237, 240, 263
Maunde Thompson, E., 225, 230
Mayurbhanj, district, 268, 272
McCutchion, D., 265-78
McGuire, J.D., 125, 129
Mehta, R.N., 233, 240
Melanesia, 63
Mellaart, J., 166, 169
Merbok, river, 281
Mengeruda (Boaleza), 55, 64
Merghar, 181-9, 191, 193, 194, 195
Mesopotamia, 69-70, 80, 83, 85, 91, 117, 157, 165, 166, 167, 168, 171
Metala, 276
Michael, H.N., 164, 169
Midnapore, district, 268, 270, 272, 273, 276, 278
Mikami, T., 252, 254
Mil-i Kasimabad, 135
Minab, 250
Mingora, 218, 230
Mirali, 145
Mir Zakah, 218, 222
Mithatala, 92
Mirti, river, 32
Mohapatra, G.C., 39, 49
Mohenjo-daro, 4, 69, 84, 92, 100, 101, 104, 162, 257
Moore, D.R., 61, 64
Mourer, T and C., 58, 64
Movius, H.L., Jr., 63, 54, 56, 64
Muda, river, 281, 300
Mughal, M.R., 162, 164, 166, 169
Mula, pass, 194
Mulla Musa, 140
Mulvaney, D.J., 60, 61, 64
Mundigak, 105, 106, 107, 108, 111, 116, 118, 131, 163, 165, 166, 167, 168, 191, 195
Murshidabad, district, 267, 269, 271, 272
Murty, M.L.K., 45, 47, 49, 58, 64
Musika, 259
Mymensingh, district, 267

Nadia, district, 272
Nad-i Ali, 137, 151
Nagar, 209
Nagpur, 262, 263
Nahre Kalane Kuhna, river, 145
Nal, 188, 194, 195
Naldanga, 273, 277
Nalrajar Garh, 258
Namazga, 105, 106, 107, 108, 111, 112, 113, 116, 117, 165, 166
Narain, A.K., 223, 224, 221, 230
Narmada, river, 13, 33, 34, 36, 37, 40, 50
Navda Toli, 81
Nepal, 1, 5, 262
Nevasa, 14
New Guinea, 56, 60, 63, 65
Niah Cave, 54, 55, 56, 58, 59, 63
Nidnapore, district, 277
Nimruz, 137, 145
Nindowari, 171, 188, 191, 195
Nishapur, 252
Noh, 258

Ol'denburg, S.Th., 209, 213
Ongba Cave, 59

Oppenheim, A.L., 167, 169
Ordos, river, 201
Orissa, 49, 51, 267, 268
Orsang river, 31
Orsoy de Flines, 249, 252, 254

Pabna district, 273
Pacha, 201
Paikpari, 276
Paithan, 262
Pakistan, 1, 4, 7, 8, 11, 29, 39, 50, 84, 86, 118, 160, 163, 171, 181, 197, 198, 249
Palawan, 54, 56, 60, 62, 63
Panganreang Tudea, 60
Parthia, 230
Partridge, T.C., 29, 36
Patandak, 148
Paterson, T.T., 5, 13, 29, 36, 39, 49
Pathani, Damb, 187, 194
Patilpara, 276
Pattadkal, 261
Pauni, 258
Pečel, 200
Penang Island, 281
Pengkalan Bujang, 284-7, 291, 294
Perak, 281, 284, 299, 301, 302
Periano Ghundai, 187
Periyar, river, 263
Perua, 277
Peshawar, 222, 264
Philippines 54, 55, 60, 63, 302
Phillips, F.C., 71, 74, 75, 79, 84
Philostratus, 228, 230
Piggott, S., 7, 105, 106, 118, 119, 129
Piperno, M., 119-29
Pirak, 171-9, 181,
Pjandzikent, 212, 213
Pondicherry, 302
Pope, J.A., 251, 254
Possehl, G.L., 72, 84
Poste Gaw, 139, 140
Pravara river, 14, 16, 17, 20, 21
Prinsep, James, 2
Pullar, 262
Punjab, 9, 29, 70, 71, 73-9, 82, 84, 217, 219, 222, 257
Purana Qila, 261
Purulia, district, 272, 278
Puthia, 273, 277

Qais, 242
Qalca-i Cegini, 142
Qala Chakhansur Ebrahimkhan, 137, 140
Qala-i Naw, 148
Qala-i Nisk, 140
Qala-i Surkh, 148
Qalca Amir Muhammad, 207
Quaritch Wales, H.G., 279, 302
Quetta Valley; also sites/style, 87, 105, 106, 107, 109, 110, 111, 113, 116, 117, 118, 171, 177, 187, 189, 190, 194, 195
Qunduz, 131
Quth Shahi, 261

Raghavan, D., 79, 81, 84
Raigarh fort, 262
Raikes, R.L., 29, 36, 70, 72, 84, 171, 179
Rajaguru, S.N., 29, 36
Rajasthan, 6, 30, 31, 32, 33, 35, 36, 67, 81, 83, 84, 209, 212, 258, 265
Rajshahi, district, 267, 277
Ralph, E.K., 164, 169
Ramnagar, 276
Rampurhat, 278
Rangpur, 83, 277
Rao, S.R., 125, 129
Rao, T.A.G., 209, 213
Ravi, river, 79
Rawalpindi, 222
Rawlinson, H., 134, 155
Raygram, 277
Raynagar 267
Renfrew, C., 157, 164, 169
Renigunta, 45, 46, 47, 49, 64
Rishahr, 245
Rockhill, W.W., 302
Rohtak, District, 92
Rosenfield, J.M., 231, 240
Rowland, B., 204, 213

Sabah, 246, 254
Sabarmati, river, 33
Safai Lichchhwai, 9
Salnagar 277
Samarkand, 137

Samarra, 250, 252, 253, 254
Sambhar Lake, 31
Sanchi, 4, 259
Sangar, 134, 148
Sanghao, 40-5, 47, 49
Sangiran dome, 54
Sankalia, H.D., 5, 8, 14, 29, 36, 81, 84
Sankari, 273
Sannothi, 257
Sarai Khola, 7, 90-91
Sarai Nahr Rai, 6, 10*n*
Sarasin, P and F, 59, 64
Sarawak, 54, 63
Sarberia, 276
Sarianidi, V.I., 105, 106, 108, 109, 110, 111, 118, 129
Sarjeant, R.B., 252, 254
Sarre, F., 250, 254
Satingpra, peninsula, 280
Saurashtra, 160
Sawal, 142, 143
Scerrato, U., 134, 155
Schlumberger, D., 207, 213, 218, 222, 230
Schumm, S.A., 33, 37
Seistan, 131-55, 160, 163, 164, 166, 167, 168, 169, 196
Sen, D., 39, 50
Senhat, 272
Shah 'Abdullah, 250
Shahr-i Sokhta, 105-18, 119-29, 166, 168, 169, 196
Shaikhan-Dheri, 215-30
Sharma, G.R., 6, 45, 46, 50
Shilau, 243, 254
Sialk, 109
Sibi, 171
Siksin, 209
Silvi Antonini, C., 197, 201
Sind, 71, 73, 74, 75, 76, 79, 80, 82, 84, 129
Singarkon, 276
Singh, G., 29, 31, 36
Siraf, **241-55**
Sirjan, 250
Sirkap, 218, 219
Siwaliks, 5
Smith, J.W., 70, 76, 84
Socotra, 245
Soojon, R.P., 60, 64
Sogdia, 212
Solheim, W.G., 62, 64
Solo, river, 54
Son, river, 46
Sonamukhi, 273
Songkhla, 280
Sonkh, 263-4
Sopara, 258
Sorburt, 148
South-East Asia, 1, 51-65, 241, 242, 246, 249, 279, 291, 293, 294, 301, 302
Spate, O.H.K., 72, 84
Spirit Cave, 58-9
Stacul, G., 8, **197-201**
Stargardt, J., **279-303**
Stein, Sir Aurel, 187, 191, 195-6, 250, 254
Stein Callenfels, P.V. van, 60, 62, 64, 299, 302
Sukh, 79
Sukhira, 277
Sulaiman, 253
Sulawesi (Celebes) 55, 56, 59, 60, 61, 64
Sumatra, 52, 59, 62, 64
Sungei Batu, estate, 293
Sungei Batu Pahat, river, 279, 297, 298
Sungei Pattani, river, 290
Sungei Sempar, river, 281
Sura, 267
Surathpur, 272
Suri, 277
Sur Jangal, 181, 189
Surkh Kotal, 131, 230
Susa, 165, 250, 254
Sutlej, river, 79
Swat, 11, 40, **197-201**, 209, 213, 218
Szechwan, 59, 250

Tabon Cave, 54, 55, 56, 58, 59, 63
Taddei, M., **203-13**
Tadjikistan, 198
Tagao valley, 207
Taiping, 281
Takuapa, 249, 254
Tal-i Sabz, 245, 250

Tanukhi, 253
Tapa Iskandar, 212
Tapa Sardar, **203-13**
Tapti valley, 13
Taras, 273
Tarn, W.W., 229, 230
Tartary, 2
Tate, G.P., 135, 155
Taxila, 4, 90, 217, 218, 219, 222, 227, 228, 229, 230
Tedžen, river, 105, 106, 110, 111, 114, 116
Tel Moragh, 250
Tel Zibid, 252
Tepe Yahya, 164, 166, 168
Thailand, 51, 58, 59, 62, 279-80, 299, 301
Thanjavur, district, 260
Thapar, B.K., 7, 9, 71, **85-104**
Thar Desert, 29, 37
Tilandapara, 276
Tilaurakot, 262
Timor, 59; 60, 61, 63
Tjabenge, 55
Todd, K.R.U., 39, 50
Tollyganj, 277
Tonkin, 63
Torralba, 23
Tosi, M., 106, 108, 113, 114, 117, 118, 119, 129, 134, 163, 166, 168, 187, 196
Tregear, M., 252, 254
Treloar, F.E., 299, 302
Tucci, G., 197, 201, 208, 209, 212, 213
Tungabhadra valley, 13
Turkmenia, 105, 106, 108, 114, 116, 117, 118, 160, 163, 166, 167, 168
Tweedie, M.W.F., 56, 58, 64

Uchkaron, 276
Udayagiri Hill, 232, 234, 240
Udegram, 218, 222, 230
Udipi, 261
Ulu Leang, 60
Ur, 165
Uttar Pradesh, 9, 213, 237, 259

Vanden Berghe, L., 116, 118
Van Lohuizen de Leeuw, J.,219, 224, 229, 230, 231, 234, 236, 237, 240, 257-64
Vatya, 200
Verhoeven, Th., 55, 64
Verstappen, H.Th., 31, 37
Vidiśa, 232, 233, 234, 236, 237, 240
Viennot, O., 209, 213
Vietnam, 63, 246
Vijayawada, 259
Visadi, 31, 47-9
Visakhapatnam, district, 262

Wace, F.B., 71, 74, 75, 79, 84
Wa Ch'a Ping, 249, 254
Wainganga, river, 49
Wainwright, G.J., 29, 37
Wang Gung-wu, 302
Watson, W., 253, 254
Wayland, E.J., 29, 37
Waziristan, 195
Western Ghats, 20, 23
Wheatley, P., 303
Wheeler, Sir Mortimer, 4, 9, 29, 37, 69, 84, 86, 91, 104, 157, 162, 169, 179
White, C., 56, 65
White, J.P., 56, 60, 65
Whitehead, R.B., 219, 221, 222, 224, 225, 226, 230
Whitehouse, D., **241-55**
Wilhelmy, H., 32, 37
Williams-Hunt, P.D.R., 280, 281, 303
Wilson, H.H., 222, 230
Wilson, N.G., 231, 240
Woolley, Sir Leonard, 4
Wroth, W., 226
Wynad, forest, 260

Yunnan, 59

Zaranj, 137, 151
Zeuner, F.E., 29, 37, 39, 50
Zeymal, E.V., 229, 230, 231, 236, 240
Ziyarate Amiran Saheb, 145, 146
Zhob, district, 195